William Roulston is a native of Bready, County Tyrone, and was raised on a farm that has been in his family's possession for nearly two centuries. He joined the Ulster Historical Foundation as a researcher in 1997, becoming Research Officer in 2002 and Research Director in 2006. He was awarded a PhD in Archaeology by Queen's University Belfast in 2004. He is the author of a number of books looking at different aspects of the history of Ireland and its families, including *Abercorn: the Hamiltons of Barons Court* (2014), *Researching Scots-Irish Ancestors: the Essential Genealogical Guide to Early Modern Ulster, 1600–1800* (2nd edition, 2018) and *Researching Presbyterian Ancestors in Ireland* (2020).

A farming family during the harvest in the Clogher Valley, County Tyrone, early 1900s (PRONI, T2411/1). Courtesy of the Deputy Keeper of Records, Public Record Office of Northern Ireland

# Researching
# Farming Ancestors
# in Ireland

William J. Roulston

ULSTER HISTORICAL FOUNDATION

COVER IMAGE
Harvest time in the Clogher Valley, County Tyrone, early 1900s (PRONI, T2411/1).
Courtesy of the Deputy Keeper of Records, Public Record Office of Northern Ireland

INSIDE FRONT COVER
Printed Primary (Griffith's) Valuation for the townland of Fort-town, parish
of Ballymoney, Poor Law Union of Ballymoney, County Antrim, (1861)

INSIDE BACK COVER
Revised edition of OS map (1859), with valuation boundaries for Fort-town
in the Tenement Valuation (1859). Reproduced from W.H. Crawford and
R.H. Foy (eds), *Townlands in Ulster: Local History Studies* (1998), p. 47

Published 2021
by Ulster Historical Foundation
www.ancestryireland.com
www.booksireland.org.uk

© William J. Roulston and Ulster Historical Foundation
ISBN 978-1-909556-91-1

DESIGN AND FORMATTING
FPM Publishing

COVER DESIGN
J.P. Morrison

PRINTED BY
Bell & Bain Limited

# Contents

# Acknowledgements

This book was begun during the 'lockdown' of spring and early summer 2020, and completed over the following months. It draws on my experiences of numerous visits to archives and libraries over the past quarter of a century, and to all of those who have assisted me in these institutions, whether staff or fellow researchers, I express my sincere thanks – without their help this book could never have been written. In particular, I wish to acknowledge the assistance given to me by the staff of the Public Record Office of Northern Ireland, especially Dr Des McCabe, who kindly read and commented on my chapter on farmers and land reform, and Ian Montgomery, whose knowledge of the records there is unrivalled.

No book of mine can be written without acknowledging the enormous debt I owe to the late Dr Brian Trainor whose enthusiasm for making archives accessible to all was second to none. Many years ago Dr Bill Macafee opened my eyes to the potential of Valuation records and I have enjoyed numerous conversations with him on this subject. I remain grateful to my colleagues at the Ulster Historical Foundation for their interest and encouragement. Finally, my greatest debt is to my own family: to my wife Heather, son Harry and daughter Sarah for putting up with my research excursions, and to my parents and brothers.

I grew up on a farm situated on the border between Tyrone and Donegal and virtually all of my forebears over the last four centuries have been farmers in these counties. Some of them appear in this book and I trust the reader will not think me too self-indulgent in using their experiences as examples from which we can learn broader lessons about our farming ancestors.

# Abbreviations

| | |
|---|---|
| *DIFHR* | *Directory of Irish Family History Research* |
| GO | Genealogical Office |
| IMC | Irish Manuscripts Commission |
| *JCHAS* | *Journal of the Cork Historical and Archaeological Society* |
| *JGAHS* | *Journal of the Galway Archaeological and Historical Society* |
| *JRSAI* | *Journal of the Royal Society of Antiquaries of Ireland* |
| NAI | National Archives of Ireland |
| NLI | National Library of Ireland |
| NRS | National Records of Scotland |
| *PRIA* | *Proceedings of the Royal Irish Academy* |
| PRONI | Public Record Office of Northern Ireland |
| RIA | Royal Irish Academy |
| TCD | Trinity College, Dublin |
| UHF | Ulster Historical Foundation |

# Note on sources

The record collections in some of the repositories mentioned in this book include material that is held off-site and needs to be ordered in advance. Occasionally items go missing – which usually means misplaced – and at times records are closed on preservation grounds. If wishing to clarify if a particular document is available for inspection, it is best to contact the relevant archive or library in advance of a visit. It may be helpful to note here that counties Laois and Offaly were known formerly as Queen's County and King's County, respectively. Researchers should also be aware that until 1752 the new year in Ireland did not begin until 25 March.

# 1

# Introduction

Agriculture has been central to Irish life for millennia and though in recent decades there have been significant social, economic and demographic changes, the people of Ireland are still generally thought of in terms of their historic relationship with the land. The aim of this book is to help those with roots in the farming communities of Ireland find out more about their ancestors. Throughout this volume, attention is drawn to the richness of the documentation held in archives and libraries on the island of Ireland, as well as highlighting a selection of material found beyond these shores. Prior to the late nineteenth century, very few farmers owned their farms outright, but rather were tenants on an estate. Considerable attention is given in Chapters 3 and 4 to the records generated by the management of landed estates in Ireland and how these can help uncover much about the lives of farming families.

As the result of legislation passed in the late 1800s and early 1900s, the estate system came to an end and an owner-occupier class of farmers was created. The records relating to this major period of change, generated by the Land Commission and other bodies, are highlighted and discussed in Chapter 9. Other archives and sources discussed include the Registry of Deeds, Valuation records, and the Encumbered Estates Court and its successors. There are also chapters on records produced by farmers themselves, such as diaries and account books; the records of farming organisations, including agricultural improvement societies and the co-operative movement; and farmers and the electoral system. A further chapter considers documentation relating to agricultural labourers, cottiers and farm workers.

## 1.1 Farmers and farming families in Ireland

The backbone of rural society in Ireland has long been the farming community. Strong families and strong family networks created stability and a sense of order. There were, however, wide variations in the farming community in terms of wealth, status, connections, etc, and it was certainly not one homogeneous grouping. Although the definition of a farmer might appear straightforward, it has been one that has vexed census enumerators and social scientists for centuries. One of the main areas of debate has been in deciding how much land an individual needed to possess before being considered a farmer. Acknowledging that the 'line of distinction is not easily drawn', the statistician William Shaw Mason commented in 1823 that 'most persons who earn the chief part of their subsistence as hired labourers, hold also a small portion of land, and therefore, in the common language of the country, are entitled to the name of Farmers'.[1] The directions issued to the 1821 census enumerators included the following instruction, 'Every person holding two acres or more of land is to be deemed a farmer'.

Difficulties with terminology can also be found in official papers in the late nineteenth century. Testifying before a Royal Commission in October 1886, Dr Grimshaw, the Registrar General of Ireland, provided the following responses to questions put to him on figures contained in the 1881 census:

> Q. In fact, there are a great number of agricultural labourers in Ireland who call themselves farmers?
> *Yes, a great many of these people work themselves — these are farmers' sons and members of the family — they would not call themselves labourers even if they worked as labourers.*
> Q. Because we know that small holders do work and would gladly accept labour?
> *Yes, but they would not return themselves as labourers. There is a very common return in the Census – "land holder"; a great number of the labourers return themselves as land holders – they won't demean themselves by calling themselves labourers and they are not dignified enough to call themselves farmers.*[2]

David Fitzpatrick cited the example of Thomas Gaughan of Srah, Glencastle, County Mayo, who had a share of 300 acres of land along with 19 others, and who also worked as a tradesman. In the 1911 census his occupation was given as 'Landowner, mason and carpenter also'.[3] In the 1901 census, however, he gave his occupation simply as farmer.

Variations in stated occupations can also be found in church registers. Taking the example of the Chambers family, the register of Aghaderg Church of Ireland, County Down, records the baptisms of four children of William and Ann Chambers of Ballynaskeagh in the mid-1800s. The baptismal entries for 1846 and 1852 record William's occupation as farmer, while those for 1849 and 1861 (the latter for a child born seven years earlier in 1854) state that he was a shoemaker. In another example from the Aghaderg register, the occupation of John Thompson of Ballygowan was recorded in the baptismal register as weaver in 1840, 1844 and 1854, and farmer in 1846 and 1851. The baptismal register of Ballinderry Church of Ireland, County Antrim, has entries for nine children of Richard and Sarah Ellis. When his children were baptised in 1853 and 1854 Richard's occupation was recorded as weaver. In 1856 he was a shopkeeper, while in 1857, 1861 and 1871 he was more specifically described as a grocer. However, in 1863, 1867 and 1868 his occupation was given as farmer.

The question of just how much land was needed to ensure a comfortable lifestyle also interested contemporaries. When asked this very question before a parliamentary commission in 1880, Walter Connison of Dunnamanagh, County Tyrone, replied, 'Well, some people can live respectably upon twenty or twenty-five acres of a farm, with prudence and attention to business.' On the other hand, Connison felt that a tenant in possession of a farm of less than 25 acres needed additional means of support:

A man may have a small bit of ground and members of his family may be engaged in other kinds of business, and thus enable him to live; he may have a son a tradesman – a shoemaker or a mason or something of that kind, and their earnings contribute to the support of the family.[4]

The following table, based on the Poor Law returns of 1845, sets out farm sizes in Ireland on the eve of the Great Famine.[5]

## Farm size in Ireland, 1845

| | |
|---|---|
| Not exceeding 1 statute acre | 135,314 |
| Above 1 to 5 acres | 181,950 |
| Above 5 to 10 acres | 187,909 |
| Above 10 to 20 acres | 187,582 |
| Above 20 to 50 acres | 141,819 |
| Above 50 acres to 100 acres | 45,394 |
| Above 100 acres to 200 acres | 17,121 |
| Above 200 acres to 500 acres | 6,393 |
| Above 500 acres | 1,533 |
| Unclassified, mainly due to joint tenancy | 30,433 |
| **Total** | **935,448** |

Note: the figure for not exceeding 1 acre includes 42,705 'gardens'.

As the table makes clear, of holdings of one acre and above, some 70% were no more than 20 acres in extent. After the Famine there was a significant decline in the number of very small farms. At the same time, the acreage of a farm did not necessarily reflect its agricultural value. Lowland farms on good arable land were obviously worth more than upland farms of rough grazing, even if the latter were considerably larger.

In addition to the size of the farm, there were other factors that distinguished between farmers. One of the most important of these was the tenure on which land was held. This could range from outright ownership to tenancy at will. Security of tenure was prized by tenant farmers. This was acknowledged by the Earl of Abercorn's agent, John McClintock, who observed to his employer in 1749: 'nothing gives such encouragement to tenants or causes them improve with such spirits as a good tenure'. This issue is discussed in greater depth in Chapter 4, but it may be noted here that there was a correlation between the size of the farm, the terms on which it was held and the status of the farmer. Marriage registers demonstrate that farmers' sons tended to marry farmers' daughters. More than that, the more substantial farmers' sons usually married the more substantial farmers' daughters.

Another feature that highlighted the differences within the farming community was the fact that the more prosperous farmers were generally able to provide better job opportunities for younger sons. Some younger sons trained for the ministry or priesthood which in itself required the expense of a good education, usually to university level. Others became merchants or pursued careers in medicine. Developments in local government over the course of the nineteenth century allowed farmers to have greater access to positions of responsibility and authority for those who aspired to them. For example, farmers served on Board of Guardians, and on the medical committees of dispensary districts. In many cases those who served in such positions were already active in their local churches or other organisations. However, involvement in the top tier of local government remained beyond any farmer as the grand jury, which controlled county affairs, was the preserve of the landed elite. This changed with the passing of the Local Government Act of 1898 which replaced grand juries with elected county councils and urban and rural district councils, with many farmers serving on the latter.

Many families lived on the same farm – or at least in the same district – for centuries, and successive generations could play a major role in their localities. Farmers could emphasise their lineage in their dealings with landlords. For example, in 1792, in a dispute over tithes, Andrew Cooper of Milecross, County Down wrote: 'My forefathers and myself have lived in Craigogantlet and parish of Newtownards for more than one hundred years' (PRONI, D607/B/377A). In 1796, in a lease proposal to Lady Antrim from the tenants of the lands of Cloghs, the following appeal was made: 'My lady there are 33 families of us on the above said lands which will be put to great distress if any petty landlord will get these lands, there are some of us whose ancestors have lived for upwards of 500 years on said land' (PRONI, D2977/3A/4/36/5A). Nonetheless, the farming community as a whole was replenished regularly by newcomers to an area. It was also the case that changing fortunes within the farming community could see certain families increase in importance and thus be in a position to play a leading role in local affairs. Contrariwise, other families declined in status and influence and died out.

## 1.2 Archives and libraries

This book draws attention to research materials from a wide range of archives and libraries. Guides to these institutions include: Seamus

Helferty and Raymond Refaussé, *Directory of Irish Archives* (2003), and Robert K. O'Neill, *Guide to Irish Libraries, Archives, Museums & Genealogical Centres* (2013). It is worth checking the Irish Archives Resource (https://iar.ie) which provides access to a selection of descriptions of various collections from contributing institutions (not the records themselves). Mention can also be made here of the Archives and Records Association, Ireland (www.araireland.ie), which maintains an Archives Directory providing links to repositories across the island. What follows is a brief summary of the main archives and libraries on the island of Ireland.

## National Archives of Ireland, Dublin

Established in 1988 through the amalgamation of the Public Record Office of Ireland and the State Paper Office in Dublin Castle, the National Archives of Ireland (NAI) is the official repository of governmental records relating to the Republic of Ireland. The National Archives also holds a large collection of privately-deposited records. At present there is no single comprehensive listing of the records held by NAI, though a catalogue relating to some collections is available on the institution's website (www.nationalarchives.ie). A number of important sets of records, several of which are of particular interest to those researching farming families can be searched on its website (www.genealogy.nationalarchives.ie).

## National Library of Ireland, Dublin

In addition to a huge collection of books and printed materials, the National Library of Ireland (NLI) holds an extensive collection of manuscripts. These include many papers relating to the management of landed estates in Ireland. The National Library's website hosts two important catalogues: the Online Catalogue (http://catalogue.nli.ie) and the Sources Catalogue (http://sources.nli.ie). The latter includes information derived from the multi-volume guide compiled under the editorship of a former director of the institution, Richard Hayes: *Manuscript Sources for the History of Irish Civilisation* (plus subsequent volumes). Detailed catalogues for many individual sets of manuscripts can also be downloaded from the NLI website. Note that the catalogue references beginning with the letters 'n' and 'p' followed by a number indicate that the item is available on microfilm. The National Library has digitised a number of collections and these can be accessed through its Online Catalogue.

## Public Record Office of Northern Ireland, Belfast

The documentary collections in the Public Record Office of Northern Ireland (PRONI) cover both public (i.e. official) and private records. Furthermore, PRONI's holdings of private records include documentation for not just Northern Ireland, but for the entire province of Ulster and further afield. With regard to the referencing system used by PRONI, a record prefixed D is an original document from a private (i.e. not governmental) collection, while T is the prefix for transcriptions or copies of private documents. MIC refers to microfilms, while CR is the prefix for original church records. Many PRONI collections have been listed in some detail and the information in its once voluminous paper catalogues is now available electronically via the institution's eCatalogue (www.nidirect.gov.uk/services/search-ecatalogue). The PRONI website includes a number of databases, some of which are of particular relevance for those researching farming ancestors. These include the database of Freeholders' Records, listing those who registered to vote (see Chapter 8).

## Registry of Deeds, Dublin

The Registry of Deeds opened in 1708 as a repository for registering all kinds of documents relating to the transfer of title to land. Unlike other archives in Ireland, its records are intact. It is of particular value for those searching for farming ancestors and is the subject of Chapter 5 of this book.

## Libraries and local archives

In the Republic of Ireland the local library network is maintained by each county council. Many county councils in the Republic of Ireland provide a separate archives service.[6] As will be highlighted throughout this book, much information of value for those seeking farming ancestors can be found in these institutions. The network of public libraries across Northern Ireland is managed by LibrariesNI.

# 1.3 Publications and printed sources

## *Online guides and resources*

Hosted and managed by the Royal Irish Academy, Irish History Online (www.ria.ie/irish-history-online) is a database listing publications on the history of Ireland, primarily focused on material that has appeared since the 1930s. It includes books, pamphlets, chapters in books, and articles in journals published both in Ireland and internationally. It is a very helpful resource for identifying publications on a specific locality, individual or family, and subject area, or works by a particular author. Online access to journals and a selection of other publications is provided by JSTOR (www.jstor.org). Irish academic journals available include *Analecta Hibernica*, *Archivium Hibernicum* and *Irish Historical Studies*, while local historical journals on JSTOR include *Clogher Record*, *Journal of the Galway Archaeological and Historical Society* and *Seanchas Ardmhacha*. Valuable discussions of the nature of Irish farming society can also be found in journals published outside Ireland.[7]

## *Genealogy guides*

Many books have been written on tracing ancestors in Ireland. The best general guide is John Grenham's *Tracing Your Irish Ancestors* (5th edition, 2019). A volume that provides much practical guidance is Claire Santry's *The Family Tree Irish Genealogy Guide: How to Trace Your Ancestors in Ireland* (2017). Other genealogical guides deal more closely with a specific area, period or theme, such as William Roulston's *Researching Scots-Irish Ancestors: the Essential Genealogical Guide to Early Modern Ulster, 1600–1800* (2nd edition, 2018). Flyleaf Press has published many county guides, while the North of Ireland Family History Society has issued booklets for several counties in the province of Ulster. There are some excellent volumes in the Maynooth Research Guides for Irish Local History series, including Terence Dooley, *The Big Houses and Landed Estates of Ireland: a Research Guide* (2007) and Frances McGee, *The Archives of the Valuation of Ireland, 1830–1865* (2018). Other thematic volumes include Chris Paton's *Discover Irish Land Records* (2015). With so much genealogical material now available online, Chris Paton's

*Tracing Your Irish Family History on the Internet: a Guide for Family Historians* (2nd edition, 2019) is indispensable.

## Books on farming and rural society

As a browse of the online databases Irish History Online and JSTOR reveals, numerous publications consider Irish farming over the centuries and no attempt will be made here to provide an exhaustive listing of these. For explorations of agricultural practices, livestock, tools and implements and technological advances since the mid-eighteenth century onwards, see the works by Jonathan Bell and Mervyn Watson: *Irish Farming, 1750–1900* (1986) and *A History of Irish Farming, 1750–1950* (2009). Both authors have written extensively on Irish farming in other publications, including the journal *Ulster Folklife*. Bell was the author of *Ulster Farming Families* (2005), which drew on recordings of interviews with farmers across the province.

A selection of books on landed estates is discussed in Chapter 3.1.5 and works by Vaughan and Dooley are especially recommended. James S. Donnelly has written several important books including: *Landlord and Tenant in Nineteenth-century Ireland* (1973); *The Land and the People of Nineteenth-Century Cork* (1975) and *Captain Rock: the Irish Agrarian Rebellion of 1821–1824* (2009). David Dickson has contributed much to this subject area and his major work is *Old World Colony: Cork and South Munster, 1630–1830* (2005). Other studies include: John Feehan, *Farming in Ireland: History, Heritage and Environment* (2003), Liam Kennedy and Peter M. Solar, *Irish Agriculture: a Price History from the Mid-Eighteenth Century to the End of the First World War* (Royal Irish Academy, 2007); and Margaret Murphy and Matthew Stout (eds), *Agriculture and Settlement in Ireland* (2015).

Some excellent books on Irish farmers have been written from a transatlantic perspective. Bruce S. Elliott, *Irish Migrants in the Canadas* (1988) is an exceptional study of 775 families who left County Tipperary mainly between 1815 and 1855. Catharine Anne Wilson's book, *A New Lease on Life: Landlords, Tenants, and Immigrants in Ireland and Canada* (1994), considers the experiences of over 100 tenant families from the Ards peninsula in County Down who emigrated to Amherst Island, Lake Ontario, between 1820 and

1860. Jim Rees has explored the removal of families from the Fitzwilliam estate in County Wicklow in several works including *Surplus People: From Wicklow to Canada* (2014).

A range of local investigations have also been published, among them Brian M. Walker, *Sentry Hill: an Ulster Farm and Family* (1981); Kevin O'Neill, *Family and Farm in pre-Famine Ireland: the Parish of Killashandra* (1984); Jim Gilligan, *Graziers and Grasslands: Portrait of a Rural Meath Community, 1854–1914* (1998); and Michael Cox, *Overlooking the River Mourne: Four Centuries of Family Farms in Edymore and Cavanalee in County Tyrone* (2006). Brian Casey's book *Class and Community in Provincial Ireland, 1851–1914* (2018), analyses the experiences of small farmers, labourers and graziers in east Galway. Local histories of rural districts usually devote space, sometimes quite considerable, to farmers and agricultural practices. These can often include material of interest that may otherwise be hard to track down.[8]

### Older works

Arthur Young (1741–1820) was an English writer on agriculture who toured Ireland twice, in 1776 and 1777, and who spent a short period as an estate agent in County Cork. In 1780 an account of his travels was published in two volumes as *A Tour in Ireland with General Observations on the Present State of that Kingdom*. This work is a major source on the state of agriculture in Ireland at that time and includes much about farming practices.[9] Usually, the individuals named by Young were landowners or their agents. Occasionally, however, the name of the occupier might be recorded as the following example from County Tipperary demonstrates:

> To Sir William Osborne's three miles the other side [of] Clonmell. From a character so remarkable for intelligence and precision, I could not fail of meeting information of the most valuable kind. This gentleman has made a mountain improvement which demands particular attention, being upon a principle very different from common ones.
>
> Twelve years ago he met with a hearty looking fellow of forty, followed by a wife and six children in rags, who begged. Sir William questioned him upon the scandal of a man in full health and vigour

supporting himself in such a manner: the man said he could get no work. *Come along with me, I will shew you a spot of land upon which I will build a cabbin for you, and if you like it you shall fix there.* The fellow followed Sir William, who was as good as his word: he built him a cabbin, gave him five acres of a heathy mountain, lent him four pounds to stock with, and gave him, when he had prepared his ground, as much lime as he would come for. The fellow flourished; he went on gradually; repaid the four pounds and presently became a happy little cottar: he has at present twelve acres under cultivation, and a stock in trade worth at least [£]80. [H]is name is John Conory. (Vol. 1, pp 508–09.)

With greater access to out of copyright books through such online providers as Google Books, Hathi Trust and the Internet Archive, it is possible to identify potentially relevant material. The following paragraph appears in Thomas Campbell Foster, *Letters on the Condition of the People of Ireland* (1846):

A man named Hooley, the tenant of half an acre of land at Ashmere, near this town [Roscrea], wanted to emigrate to America, and sold his "good-will," as they call it, or the right to the peaceable possession of the land, for about £20, to a small farmer named Jackson, the tenant of a few acres of adjoining land, Jackson having also to pay a smart rent for it to the landlord. A younger brother of this Hooley took it into his head that he was entitled to the land, and that the elder brother had no right to sell the possession of it, and that Jackson ought to give it up. Without any offer to repay him the money he had paid for it, Jackson was threatened with murder if he did not give the land up, and this man now goes about his labour protected by two armed policemen. Hooley has since been sent to gaol for going about with a loaded pistol in his pocket, which was not registered. (p. 348)

## Statistical surveys of counties and parishes

Inspired by the model of the Statistical Account of Scotland, published in 27 volumes in the 1790s, the Dublin Society initiated a county survey of Ireland and received a parliamentary grant of £15,000 towards the work. The surveys focused in particular on agriculture (including farming practices, livestock, farm buildings and tree plantations), with an analysis of defects and suggestions for improvements. In the early decades of the nineteenth century a volume was published for every county in Ireland with the exception of Fermanagh, Kerry, Limerick, Longford, Louth, Waterford and Westmeath.[10] The website Askaboutireland.ie has downloadable PDFs of the published surveys for the following counties: Antrim, Cavan, Clare, Cork, Derry, Donegal, Down, Dublin, Galway, Kildare, Kilkenny, Laois (Queen's County), Leitrim, Mayo, Meath, Roscommon, Sligo, Tyrone, Wexford, Wicklow. These volumes can also be accessed online on the websites of Google Books and Hathi Trust.

William Shaw Mason (*c.* 1774–1853) played an important – though not especially successful – role in records management in Ireland in the early nineteenth century. In 1810 he was appointed secretary of the Irish Records Commission. Mason was also in charge of the earliest censuses undertaken in Ireland – in 1813–15 and 1821. Possibly as an accompaniment to the censuses, Mason published three volumes of statistical accounts of parishes across Ireland in 1814, 1816, and 1819, which devote considerable attention to farming practices. Along similar lines are Samuel Lewis, *Topographical Dictionary of Ireland* (2 vols, 1837), and the *Parliamentary Gazetteer of Ireland* (3 vols, 1846). These volumes can be read online on Google Books.

The Ordnance Survey Memoirs of the 1830s were written accounts intended to accompany the original Ordnance Survey maps. The project was abandoned around 1840 with only the northern part of Ireland covered – principally the province of Ulster – and the memoir of only one parish, Templemore in County Londonderry, published. However, in the 1990s the Institute of Irish Studies at Queen's University Belfast published the remaining memoirs in 40 volumes with an additional index volume covering the entire QUB series. The memoirs are most detailed for counties Antrim and Londonderry with 14 volumes each. By contrast, there is only one volume for County Armagh, while volume 40 of the series covers the material created for counties Cavan, Leitrim, Louth, Monaghan and Sligo. The Ordnance Survey Memoirs provide fascinating information on the character and habits of the people of the north of Ireland. Much attention is given to agricultural practices, including land improvement schemes, as well as the diet, accommodation and lifestyle of rural society.

## Newspapers and periodicals

It has long been recognised that newspapers have the potential to be excellent sources of information on family history. In recent years digitisation is providing ever greater access to old newspapers, dramatically improving the ease with which they can be searched. Two major online providers are the British Newspaper Archive (www.britishnewspaperarchive.co.uk) and the Irish Newspaper Archives (www.irishnewsarchive.com). A comprehensive record of the availability of Irish newspapers in archives and libraries in Britain and Ireland is contained in the NEWSPLAN database, which can be accessed via the website of the National Library of Ireland.[11]

Not surprisingly, farmers feature prominently in newspapers. In addition to notices concerning aspects of their lives, e.g. marriages and deaths, there are numerous items relating to the letting of land, which can sometimes name the sitting tenants. To give one example here, on 1 May 1770 an advertisement appeared in the *Belfast Newsletter* announcing that Lord Dungannon's estate in the parish of Island Magee in County Antrim was 'out of lease, and to be let for terms of years'. The advertisement included the names of the sitting tenants by townland along with the size of their farms. The value of an advertisement like this is that it is the only known eighteenth-century document relating to Island Magee that names farmers by townland.[12]

Beginning in the early nineteenth century, a number of newspapers and periodicals aimed specifically at Irish farmers were published. These included: *Irish Farmers' Journal and Weekly Intelligencer* (Dublin, 1812–26);[13] *Ulster Farmer and Mechanic* (Belfast, 1824–5); *North West Farmer and General Advertiser* (Londonderry, 1825–6); *Belfast Standard and Ulster Farmers' Journal* (Belfast, 1837); *Irish Sporting Chronicle and Farmers' Journal* (Dublin, 1840); *Lisburn, Hillsborough and Dromore and Farmer's Guide* (Belfast, 1850–51). *The Irish Farmer's and Gardener's Magazine and Register of Rural Affairs* began in 1833 and vol. 1 (November 1833 to December 1834) and vol. 2 (covering 1835) are available on Google Books. The *Farmers' Gazette and Journal of Practical Horticulture* was first published in Dublin in 1842. Around 1850 the word *Irish* was added to the start of the title and in 1882 it became the *Farmers' Gazette*, continuing until 1963.

## Directories

The earliest Irish directories appeared in the 1700s and were concerned primarily with towns and cities. Later directories often included farmers living in the vicinity of provincial towns and villages, though these tended to be the more prominent figures in their community. The Public Record Office of Northern Ireland has digitised a large number of directories in its custody and made these available through its website. In the 1880s George Henry Bassett published a number of county directories: Antrim (1888), Armagh (1888), Down (1886), Kilkenny (1884), Limerick (1880), Louth (1886), Tipperary (1889) and Wexford (1885). Similar publications include Lowe's *Fermanagh Directory* (1880). For a detailed listing of directories available online, see www.swilson.info/dirdb.php.

## Parliamentary papers

Throughout this book there will be references to the printed papers generated by the Houses of Parliament at Westminster from 1801 (when the Act of Union came into effect) onwards. More specifically, these are the papers produced to guide the formulation, development and execution of government policy. They comprise printed reports of select committees and royal commissions as well as accounts and returns. This collection of papers has come to be known as the 'Blue Books' because of the blue paper with which most of the volumes were covered. Cumulatively, they provide an enormous amount of information on Irish society in the nineteenth and early twentieth centuries, including much detail on farmers. Nonetheless they are a relatively untapped source of information.[14] Many parliamentary papers for Ireland can be accessed through the Internet Archive (www.archive.org) and the Enhanced British Parliamentary Papers on Ireland database (www.dippam.ac.uk/eppi).

In 1843 the government commissioned a major inquiry into the state of agriculture in Ireland. Known as the Devon Commission after its chairman, the Earl of Devon, this commission heard evidence from over 1,100 witnesses, many of whom were farmers, and visited nearly one hundred places during the course of its investigations. The results of the commission were published in several volumes in 1845 as the *Report of Her Majesty's Commissioners of Inquiry into the state of the law and practice in respect of the occupation of land in Ireland; Minutes of*

*Evidence*; and *Appendix to Minutes of Evidence*. Subsequently, a *Digest of Evidence Taken before Her Majesty's Commissioners of Inquiry into the State of the Law and Practice in Respect to the Occupation of Land in Ireland* was published in two volumes (1847–8). As Lord Devon wrote in the preface to the *Digest*: 'Although the report is not in itself very long, yet, when the appendix and evidence are added, the whole together, occupying four or five large blue books, present a very formidable appearance'.

Other examples of parliamentary papers that may be mentioned here include *Reports and Returns Relating to Evictions in the Kilrush Union* (1849). The Poor Law Union of Kilrush was in County Clare and the reports, written by Captain Arthur Edward Kennedy, a Poor Law Inspector, go into great detail on the many families removed from their holdings (2,700 families were evicted between 1847 and 1850). The details of the evicted families are set out in tables, with the following headings: Heads of families; No. in Family; Males; Fem[ales]; How dispossessed; Cause [of dispossession]; Title [tenure]; Quantity of holding; Yearly rent; Arrears; and Observations. The latter include such comments as: 'House thrown down, though built by her husband'; 'House thrown down; two of this family in poorhouse'; 'House thrown down: head of family in gaol'; and 'House thrown down; wife and child dead'.

For anyone researching families in north-west County Donegal, the *Report from the Select Committee on Destitution (Gweedore and Cloughaneely)* (1858) has the potential to offer superb material. Appendix 9 comprises papers delivered by Daniel John Cruice, Esq., among them a listing of the homes visited in Gweedore, giving the name of the householder and comments on living conditions and other matters. For example one of the householders in the townland of Meenacung was named as 'Pat Galagher (or James)' and the comment was, 'A large wooden dish of stirabout; but when I went into the house they commenced eating sea-weed.' The home of James Doherty in Upper Doore included '3 beds, bedsteads and bed-clothes; a quantity of potatoes; spinning-wheel; a sheep-house; a place for tying 5 cows.'

## 1.4 Irish land divisions

Visitors to this island often remark on – and are frequently mystified by – the number and great variety of place-names that they encounter.

There is no doubt that our heritage of place-names is one of the most enriching legacies that have been passed down to us by earlier generations. Ireland is divided into multiple categories of land divisions, some overlapping, but others sub-divisions of larger areas. The origins of place-names derive from many sources – predominantly Gaelic Irish, but also English and Scottish, among others – and their meanings can tell us much about the character and history of a locality. Ireland is divided into four provinces and 32 counties. Counties remain the basis of local government in the Republic of Ireland, but no longer have any administrative role in Northern Ireland. Each county was divided into a number of baronies, which were based to a large extent on earlier Gaelic land divisions.

The development of the territorial division of the parish is associated with the twelfth-century reforms of the Irish church (though often with deeper roots). Following the Reformation, the Protestant Church of Ireland took over and largely retained the existing network of parishes. Some alterations to the parish network were made, however, and a number of new parishes were created out of one or more existing parishes. The parish also had a civil function as an arm of local government, hence the term civil parish. The parish vestry was tasked with ensuring that particular areas of responsibility, such as road maintenance, were carried out effectively. When the Catholic Church began its institutional re-emergence in the late eighteenth and nineteenth centuries, it did not always build its parochial structures on earlier foundations. Therefore, researchers should be aware that Catholic parishes do not necessarily equate with civil/Church of Ireland parishes.

In earlier times, there were many names for smaller land divisions in Ireland. In his famous book published in 1672, *The Political Anatomy of Ireland*, Sir William Petty commented, 'As to their Town-lands, Plough-lands, Colps, Gneeres, Bullibos, Ballibelaghs, Two's, Horsmens, Beds, &c. they are all at this day become unequal both in Quantity and Value, having been made upon grounds which are now Obsolete and Antiquated.' The following selection of extracts from original records indicate the broad range of terms used for Irish place-names in documents relating to the ownership and occupation of land:

Surrender by Calvacius or Calloughe m'Tyilaugh M'Donel Hugh boy m'Echallowe m'Tirlaghe, and Godfrey M'Donell, gentlemen; of the town of Castellno called Newecastell in the lordship of Slewemarge, Queen's co. [Laois], and so much land called a **horseman's bed** adjoining the castle, 16 July 1585 (*Irish Fiants of the Tudor Sovereigns*).

Pardon of alienation for Owen O'Swylivane of Beerhaven, Cork co., who, being seised in his domain in fee of half the castle, town, and lands of Downebuoy otherwise Beerhaven, 3 **carucates** ... Killincowan, 9 **gneeves** ..., 20 December 1624 (*Calendar of the Patent Rolls, James I*).

Articles entered into by Shane boy mc Mahon of Lisneleigh, County Monaghan, and Sir Robert Forth; for the sale, for £20, of the **tate** of Lisneleigh in the **ballibetagh** of Ballylattacrossan and barony of Dartry, 17 May 1630 (PRONI, D3465/A/1/22).

Lease of the half **town** of Dromodownye purchased of Peter Hill and half **town** of Collydonye, County Down, purchased of Arthur Magenis, 24 September 1636 (PRONI, D671/D/8/1/41).

Feoffment by Mathew Oge O Loghlen to Murrough O'Brien, Terlagh O Connor and others of the **cartron** of land in Cahirpolla, County Clare, in consideration of £25 and livestock (including six milch cows), the marriage portion of his wife Slany ny Brien in trust for himself and his wife Slany, 20 September 1650 (NLI, MS 45,031/1).

Deed poll involving Thomas Welstead, Donnanstowne, County Cork, and John Nettles, Towrine, County Waterford, concerning part of the **ploughland** of Ballynemeagh, County Cork, 19 October 1659 (PRONI, D314/8).

Marriage settlement involving James Grattan and Mary Marlay, concerning various lands, including Three **Poles** of Barcony, County Cavan, 24 May 1740 (PRONI, T2007/8).

Counterpart lease from the Earl of Donegall to George Lynch for two **Ballyboes** of the **Quarter Land** of Carnamoyle, County Donegal, 14 November 1770 (PRONI, D2338/1).

In the nature of things, it is not surprising that there are numerous variations in the spellings of individual place-names, sometimes markedly so. In addition, some locations have acquired an entirely new name, perhaps an English name in place of the Gaelic Irish one. In the early nineteenth century, with the introduction of decennial censuses, the new Valuation of Ireland, and the mapping carried out by the Ordnance Survey, it became ever more important to record, define and standardise the spelling of the smaller land divisions across Ireland, and to keep a proper record of these. In reporting on the work of the 1821 census, William Shaw Mason wrote in 1823:

> The smallest subdivision of the country is that of Townlands. This name, however, is not universal throughout Ireland: some Counties have adopted the term of Ploughlands in lieu of it, each Ploughland being supposed to contain 120 acres; but as the quantity was taken by estimation, not by measurement, their extent varies considerably, even in the same county. Townlands in many instances have been subdivided, and in many cases the name has been changed. Much embarrassment in the progress of the Census has been occasioned by both these circumstances.[15]

In fact an alteration to the term used for a particular place-name was permitted in the 1821 census returns: 'N.B. In Counties where Plowlands or other denominations or sub-denominations are in use the word "Townlands" is to be struck out and the word Plowland (or other denomination, as the case may be) written in its stead.' Much valuable work was carried out through the Ordnance Survey and in particular through the efforts of the great Gaelic scholar John O'Donovan. The term 'townland' came to be accepted across Ireland as the name for the smallest land division for administrative purposes.[16]

Across Ireland as a whole there are over 60,000 townlands, and their meanings reflect many different things, including local geography, family names, animals, plants and folklore. Townlands are entities in their own right and are not subdivisions of counties, baronies or parishes. Therefore, while most townlands will be found in their entirety within these larger land divisions, a proportion will be divided between two or more of them. Generally speaking, the acreage of a townland depends on the quality of the land, so that in upland areas townlands will be much larger, occasionally extending to several thousand acres. Conversely, in low-lying areas townlands may be less than 100 acres. The smallest townland in Ireland is Old Church Yard in the parish of Termonmaguirk, County Tyrone, which extends to just over half of one acre.[17] As its name suggests, it is an old graveyard, in fact the site of the medieval parish church. The largest townland is Finnaun in the parish of Killanin, County Galway, at 7,555 acres.

Townlands are important for genealogists for a number of reasons. They were crucial location identifiers for individuals and families across the island for centuries (and still are in many rural areas, especially in the Republic of Ireland). In church registers, newspaper advertisements, and gravestone inscriptions, to name a few, the address given for a particular individual or family will usually be the townland of residence. Landed estates were composed of blocks of townlands and farms were the subdivisions of those townlands (unless the townland comprised a single farm). It is clear, therefore, that a study of the place-name evidence for a locality can be potentially of great genealogical value.

It is also important to acknowledge that numerous 'unofficial' place-names are found within townlands.[18] Often these sub-denominational names apply to a farm or a feature in the landscape and may have been acquired in recent centuries, though others have a medieval origin. They often include a personal name element. The practice of giving specific names to fields is widespread across Ireland. Each of the fields on the farm on which I grew up has a name, ranging from the topographical (e.g. the Hill Field) to a name signifying a particular agricultural activity (e.g. the Dam Field, so called because of the flax dams located at one end of it). Some excellent work has been carried out on field names, notably through the Louth Field Names Project (https://louthfieldnames.wordpress.com) and the Meath Field Names Project (www.meathfieldnames.com). In both cases, an interactive map has been created and a book published.[19]

Irish place-names have been a popular area of study. The Name Books produced through the work of the Ordnance Survey contain the names of townlands, including their Irish forms, as well as their meanings; these can be accessed on the Ask About Ireland website.[20] Published works include P.W. Joyce's volumes, *The Origin and History of Irish Names of Places* (1869–1913), and more recently Deirdre and Laurence Flanagan, *Irish Place Names* (1994) and Patrick McKay, *A Dictionary of Ulster Place-Names* (2nd edition, 2007).[21] Other books and essays can be found via the Irish History Online database referred to above. Given their importance as markers of local identity, many local histories devote at least some space to a discussion of the townlands found in their district. Important online resources include the Placenames Database of Ireland (https://www.logainm.ie) and the Northern Ireland Place-name Project (www.placenamesni.org).

## Notes

1  *Abstract of the Answers and Returns made pursuant to an Act ... for taking Account of Population of Ireland ...* [relating to the 1821 census] (1824), pp xii, 384.

2  *Report of the Royal Commission on the Land Law Ireland Act, 1881, and the Purchase of Land (Ireland) Act, 1885, Vol. II, Minutes of Evidence and Appendices* (1887), p. 5.

3  David Fitzpatrick, 'The disappearance of the Irish agricultural labourer, 1841–1912', *Irish Economic and Social History*, 7 (1980), p. 68.

4  *Irish Land Act Commission, 1880*, p. 372.

5  Appendix to the article by P.M.A Bourke, 'The extent of the potato crop in Ireland at the time of the Famine', *Journal of the Statistical and Social Inquiry Society of Ireland*, 20:3 (1959–60), p. 21. The Appendix includes a discussion of the reliability of these figures and those contained in the 1841 census. See also Bourke's article, 'The agricultural statistics of the 1841 census of Ireland: a critical review', *Economic History Review*, new series, 18:2 (1965), pp 376–91.

6  For more on archives in the Republic of Ireland, see www.askaboutireland.ie/reading-room/culturenet/archives.

7  For example, April 1983 issue of *Comparative Studies in Society and History* (vol. 25, no. 2) includes essays by David Fitzpatrick on 'Irish farming families before the First World War' and P. Gibbon and C. Curtin on 'Irish farm families: facts and fantasies'.

8  For example, J.B. Leslie, *History of Kilsaran Union of Parishes* (1908), includes a list of landholders in parish of Dromiskin in 1791.

9  PRONI has copies of some of his correspondence (T3469).

10  In the case of Louth, see D.A. Beaufort, 'Materials for the Dublin Society agricultural survey of County Louth', ed. by C.C. Ellison, *Journal of the County Louth Archaeological and Historical Society*, 18:2 (1974) and 18:3 (1975).

11 Accessible at: www.nli.ie/en/catalogues-and-databases-printed-newspapers.aspx.

12 A comprehensive index to the surviving issues of the *Belfast Newsletter* from 1738 to 1800 (there are many gaps in its early years) is available on the web: www.ucs.louisiana.edu/bnl.

13 PRONI has copies for 1825–6 (N/38).

14 See also William Roulston, 'British parliamentary papers and the local historian and genealogist', *Familia: Ulster Genealogical Review*, 18 (2002), pp 63–82, which provides an overview of material of Irish interest in the early nineteenth century.

15 *Abstract of the Answers and Returns made pursuant to an Act ... for taking Account of Population of Ireland ...* [relating to the 1821 census] (1824), p. x. The following footnote accompanied this paragraph: 'Many names, now antiquated, were formerly used to designate the smaller sub-divisions of land in Ireland. The following are the most remarkable: Gort – containing 6 acres; Pottle – 12; Ballyboe – 16 acres but in some parts 60 or 100 acres; Ballybeatach – 960 acres being 16 Ballyboes of 60 acres each; Cartron – 60 acres called also a Plowland; Poll or pole – 50 acres; Tagh or Tate 60 acres English; Gneon, or Gneeve – 5 acres being ½th of a Plowland. The Plowland and the Gneeve are the only names noticed by the Enumerators, as still in use in some parts of Ireland.'

16 'Like Irish *baile* (Bally – in place-names) the Old English word tun originally meant 'farmstead settlement', rather than 'town' or 'village'. The term townland was created to translate the Irish concept and does not occur in spell-checkers' (Kay Muhr, *Celebrating Ulster's Townlands* (1999), p. 5). See also William Reeves, 'On the townland distribution of Ireland', *PRIA*, 7 (1857–61), pp 473–90.

17 A tiny portion of Clonskeagh, County Dublin – less than one third of an acre – is in a different barony from the rest of the townland and therefore in townland schedules it is listed separately.

18 A database of unofficial/subdenominational place-names in the six counties of Northern Ireland is available on the website of the Ulster Historical Foundation (members-only).

19 Eve Campbell, *The Field Names of County Louth* (2014), and Joan Mullen (compiler), Frances Tallon (editor), *The Field Names of County Meath* (2013).

20 The Name Books are available on the same portal that provides access to Griffith's Valuation (www.askaboutireland.ie/griffith-valuation).

21 See also Jonathan Bardon, *Place names in Ulster* (2020).

# 2

# The three Cs: civil, church and census records

The basic building blocks for reconstructing families and family networks in Ireland are civil records of birth, marriages and deaths, church records and census returns. Although these are major source categories, they have been considered in some detail in many other genealogical publications[1] and so will be looked at more concisely in the following paragraphs.

## 2.1 Civil registration

Civil registration – that is, registration with the state – of non-Catholic marriages in Ireland began on 1 April 1845. The official registration of births and deaths as well as Catholic marriages began on 1 January 1864. The infrastructure of civil registration was based on the Poor Law system introduced to Ireland in 1838, with a Superintendent Registrar's District corresponding with a Poor Law Union and a Registrar's District with a Dispensary District within a Poor Law Union. Records were generated locally before copies of them were sent to the General Register Office in Dublin where a master set of registers and indexes was created. A research facility for the public is located in Werburgh Street, Dublin. Following Partition, a separate General Register Office of Northern Ireland (GRONI) was established in Belfast.

In summary, birth certificates record the name of the child (though in a proportion of registered births the child was not named), the date and place of birth, the names of the parents, as well as the father's residence and occupation and the mother's maiden name, and the name, address and qualification of the person registering the birth. Marriage certificates provide the date and place of the wedding ceremony, the names of the bride and groom, their status (e.g.

22

bachelor, spinster), age (often simply given as 'full', i.e. over 21), places of residence and occupation, and the names and occupations of the fathers of bride and groom, as well as the signatures of the witnesses. Death certificates include the name of the deceased, together with the date, place and cause of death, marital status, age at death, and occupation. Also provided is the name, address and qualification of the person registering the death.

The General Register Office of Ireland has copies of births, deaths and marriages for all of Ireland from 1845 to 1921 and for the Republic of Ireland from 1922 onwards. The great majority of records up to certain cut-off dates are available online for free on the Irish Genealogy website (www.irishgenealogy.ie).[2] GRONI holds the locally produced birth and death (from 1864) and marriage (from 1845) registers for the six counties of Northern Ireland. GRONI has made historic records available online on a pay-per-view basis (https://geni.nidirect.gov.uk) and a public search room is located in Colby House, Stranmillis Court, Belfast. Civil birth, marriage and death records for the majority of Irish counties can be accessed by subscribing to the Roots Ireland website (www.rootsireland.ie), though the coverage varies from partial to comprehensive.[3]

## 2.2 Church records

Prior to civil registration, vital information on family history can be found in church registers of baptisms, marriages and burials. The single largest religious denomination in Ireland is the Roman Catholic Church. Following the Reformation in Ireland, the Catholic Church went through a lengthy period when its activities were severely curtailed through the 'Penal Laws' and other legislation. During the eighteenth century the Catholic Church was able to re-establish diocesan and parochial structures, though rather than attempt to replicate the medieval parish network, its parishes were created to meet local needs. With its institutional re-emergence, the Church's record-keeping improved significantly. Nonetheless, comparatively few Catholic registers pre-date 1800 (and those that do generally relate to parishes in the south and east of the island). For the most part Catholic registers concern only baptisms and marriages. Forenames are often in Latin, though generally the English equivalents of these are recognisable. Occupations are usually not recorded.

Between them, the centres affiliated to the Irish Family History Foundation have transcribed around 80% of all pre-1900 Catholic records in Ireland (notable exceptions include the cities of Dublin and Cork) and these can be accessed via the Roots Ireland website (www.rootsireland.ie). The National Library of Ireland has microfilms of pre-1880 Catholic registers for the vast majority of parishes in Ireland (PRONI has copies of the microfilms for northern counties) and digital scans of these are available online (https://registers.nli.ie). The information in these registers forms the basis of the transcriptions available through Ancestry and Findmypast. The Irish Genealogy website (www.irishgenealogy.ie) has transcribed and digitised Catholic records for counties Cork and Kerry as well as the city of Dublin.

The Church of Ireland is the largest Protestant denomination on the island of Ireland. Until 1 January 1871 it was the established or state church and enjoyed various privileges as a consequence of this (even though only a minority of the population adhered to it). The parish system used by the Church of Ireland was based to a large extent on the pre-Reformation network, though in many instances smaller parishes were brought together in a single ecclesiastical union. In general, the records of the Church of Ireland start much earlier than those of other churches and comprise baptisms, marriages and burials. From the early 1820s onwards occupations are recorded routinely in baptism and burial registers. In 1922 over 1,000 sets of parish registers were lost in Dublin in the destruction of the Public Record Office of Ireland. However, over 600 sets of registers do survive, including a number that pre-date 1700.

The official archive of the Church of Ireland is the Representative Church Body Library in Dublin, which holds original registers from many parishes, mainly in the Republic of Ireland, and maintains a catalogue of what is available across the island as a whole.[4] PRONI in Belfast also has a significant collection of original records as well as microfilm copies; see the *Guide to Church Records*, which can be downloaded from the PRONI website, and which provides a comprehensive listing of the registers of all denominations held there.[5] Other Protestant denominations include the Presbyterian Church, the Methodist Church, and the Religious Society of Friends (Quakers), each of which has a historical society and/or an archive/library. Online access to Protestant registers is less comprehensive compared to Catholic registers, but material of interest may be found, among other places, on the Roots Ireland and Irish Genealogy websites noted above.

## 2.2.1 Other records generated by churches

While most of the focus on church registers has been on baptisms, marriages and burials, it must be borne in mind that within the broader category of church records there are many other items of interest for family historians. These include the minutes of meetings of a range of church bodies, accounts, lists of members, etc. A few parishes have what is, in effect, a census of the congregation. The 'census' of Clondevaddock Church of Ireland in County Donegal of 1796 is arranged by townland and names the head of each household, indicating the relationship of others in the household to him/her (e.g. spouse, children, servants); the census concerns the Anglican population in the parish, but indicates if a member of a household was affiliated to another denomination.

In particular, researchers should be aware of the value of vestry minute books. The vestry was a gathering of parishioners who met together to discuss and deliberate on various matters relating to the business of the parish. It acquired its name from the room in which the meetings were held originally – the vestry where the minister's vestments were kept. Where they survive, vestry minutes will be found with the Church of Ireland records for a particular parish. However, people from all denominational backgrounds can be found in a vestry book. Until these responsibilities were assumed by various government bodies in the nineteenth century, the role of the vestry included such matters as the care of the destitute and of abandoned children. The required funds were raised through a cess or tax on the land in the parish and occasionally there will be a list of the names of landholders arranged by townland drawn up for taxation purposes.

Further information on the records created by the major religious denominations in Ireland can be found in the following publications: James G. Ryan (ed.), *Irish Church Records: their History, Availability, and Use in Family and Local History Research* (2001); Patrick Corish and David Sheehy, *Records of the Irish Catholic Church* (2001), Raymond Refaussé, *Church of Ireland Records* (2006), William Roulston, *Researching Presbyterian Ancestors in Ireland* (2020); Steven

C. Ffeary-Smyrl, *Irish Methodists – Where do I start?* (No. 1 in the Exploring Irish Genealogy series published by the Council of Irish Genealogical Organisations); and *Guide to Irish Quaker Records, 1654–1860* by Olive C. Goodbody, with a contribution on Northern Ireland records by B.G. Hutton (IMC, 1967).

## 2.3 Census returns

The first census was held in Ireland in 1821. Unfortunately, the earliest census that survives in its entirety for the whole of Ireland is the 1901 census. Census returns 1821–51 were almost entirely lost in 1922 in the destruction of the Public Record Office in Dublin. Census returns 1861–91 were completely destroyed by government order and a minuscule number of transcripts survive.[6] The original returns of the 1901 and 1911 censuses are on deposit in the National Archives in Dublin and are now available online (www.census.nationalarchives.ie), along with surviving fragments from the nineteenth-century census returns.

### 2.3.1 Census returns 1821–51

The surviving original returns of the 1821 census in NAI cover parts of counties Cavan, Fermanagh, Galway, King's County (now Offaly) and Meath. In addition to names and ages, this census also recorded occupations and the number of acres that the householder possessed. There is also a column for observations which may, for example, include a comment on the absence of a family member (and the reason for it). An abstract of the returns for County Londonderry is virtually all that is available for 1831. This enumerates the number of persons in each household, distinguishing between family members and servants. This abstract also provides a breakdown of the religious affiliation within each household – this information was gathered subsequent to the taking of the census.[7]

For 1841, the only original returns to survive are those for the parish of Killeshandra, County Cavan. Portions of the 1851 census survive for a number of parishes in County Antrim.[8] When one browses through the information recorded in this census (and that of 1841), the scale of the loss is soon realised, with information recorded in these census returns not found in the early twentieth-century censuses. For example, there are additional forms recording details on individuals who had died since the previous census and also those who were normally resident, but not present in the family home on the night the census was taken. In some instances, the recorded absentees were overseas or serving in the army. As discussed below, information from the 1841 and 1851 censuses can also be found within early twentieth-century old age pension forms.

## 2.3.2 Census returns 1901–11

The census returns of 1901 and 1911 were organised by townland (or street in urban areas) within district electoral division and county. The information in the 1901 census – taken on 31 March – is listed under the following headings in Form A: Name and Surname; Relation to Head of Family; Religious Profession; Education; Age; Sex; Rank, Profession or Occupation; Marriage; Where Born; and Irish Language. A final column was used to record if any member of the household had a physical or mental impairment. The 1911 census, taken on 2 April, additionally includes columns for the number of years a married woman was married, the number of children born to that marriage and the number still living. While researchers focus most of their attention on the details recorded on Form A, additional census forms can help to illuminate the lives of our farming ancestors.

### Household Return (Form A)

Taking my own farming ancestors in the townland of Gortavea, County Tyrone, as an example, the 1901 census return shows that my great-great-grandfather Charles Roulston was the head of the household. He was an unmarried 30-year-old farmer who could read and write and was a member of the Church of Ireland. Living with him were a younger brother, Thomas, and his only sister, Mary. There were two other individuals in the household, one a general domestic servant (Agnes Dunn) and the other a farm servant (Samuel Wilson). The latter was a native of County Donegal, whereas everyone else in the household had been born in County Tyrone. Ages are always to be treated with some caution in census returns, especially 'round' figures. In fact, on the night of the census Charles was aged 35, having been born on 2 July 1865.

Moving forward to the 1911 census, we find that significant changes had occurred in the intervening period. Charles was still head of the household, though his age on the return was given as 50 (it should have been 45). He was married and the father of three children. His religious affiliation had changed for he was now listed as a Presbyterian. According to the census return, his wife Martha was aged 30 – in actual fact she was 33, meaning that what appeared to be a 20-year age gap between them was in reality less than 13 years. Charles's sister Mary was no longer in the household (we know she had married and moved to South Africa), but his brother Thomas was still there. There were still two servants in the household, though they were not the same as the individuals listed in 1901. One of them, Ellen Duffy, was a Catholic from County Donegal who could speak both Irish and English.

## House and Building Return (Form B1)

Form B1 was completed by the census enumerator and provided in summary form details about the houses in each townland. The use of the building – 'whether Private Dwelling, Public Building, School, Manufactory, Hotel, Public-house, Lodging-house, Shop, etc' – was recorded as well as the number of associated outbuildings (as returned on Form B2 discussed below). With regard to inhabited houses, the following details were recorded: whether the walls and roof were constructed using permanent or perishable material; the number of rooms in the house (categorised 1 (= 1 room), 2 (2–4), 3 (5–6), 4 (7–9), 5 (10–12), 6 (13+)); the number of windows in the front of the house; and the class of house.

If the figures in the columns headed Walls, Roof, Rooms and Windows totalled 1–2 the house was 4th class; if 3–5 then 3rd class, if 6–11 then 2nd class, and only if the figures totalled 12 or more was the house considered 1st class. Form B1 then goes on to record the number of distinct families in the house, the name of the head of the family, the number of rooms occupied by each family, and the name of the landholder on whose property the house was situated.

In 1911 Charles Roulston's dwelling in Gortavea was considered to be of the 2nd class. Under the heading 'Walls' the figure 1 was entered indicating that they were of 'stone, brick or concrete' (they were of stone). Under the heading 'Roof' the figure 0 was written meaning that the roof was of 'thatch, wood or other perishable material' (it was thatched). The figure under the heading 'Rooms' was 3. As noted above, this was not the actual number of rooms, but signified that there were 5–6 rooms in the house (in the column recording the actual number of rooms occupied the figure 5 was entered). The number of windows in the front of the house was 5. This return also noted that Charles Roulston possessed a second house in this townland, though it was unoccupied.

### Return of Out-offices and Farm-Steadings (Form B2)

Form B2 provides details on the outbuildings associated with each dwelling. The enumerator was directed to include buildings used for domestic or agricultural purposes, but not structures used for sanitation or horticulture, or for pleasure. No personal names are given on this form, but the number previously assigned to the house (found on Form A and Form B1) appears in the first column of Form B2. The rest of the columns are headed: Stable, Coach House, Harness Room, Cow House, Calf House, Dairy, Piggery, Fowl House, Boiling House, Barn, Turf House, Potato House, Workshop, Shed, Store, Forge, Laundry, Other Out-Offices (a series of five columns for any buildings not listed previously – spaces were left for the enumerator to write the building types), and finally the total number of outbuildings. In 1911 the outbuildings belonging to Charles Roulston in Gortavea comprised a stable, two cow houses, a calf house, a fowl house, a boiling house and two sheds – a total of nine outbuildings. It is obvious that this form can provide an insight into the farming activities of one's ancestors.

## 2.3.3 Old age pension forms

The old age pension was introduced on 1 January 1909 for those over 70 years of age and below a certain income level. All old age pension applicants at this time, and for many years afterwards, had been born before 1864, when the state registration of births began in Ireland. Prior to 1922, many people, if they could not obtain a copy of their baptismal record,[9] resorted to the 1841 and 1851 censuses held in the Public Record Office in Dublin in order to demonstrate their age and so claim their pension. Two distinct sets of records were produced as part of this process: the 'Green Forms' and the 'Form 37s'.[10]

The 'Green Forms' derive from applications for census searches made by or on behalf of private individuals hoping to claim the pension. The forms included the name and current address of the applicant as well as parents' names and place of residence in 1841 or 1851. A member of the PRO staff then conducted a search of the census returns and added relevant details to the form. The 'Form 37s' were submitted by local pension officials seeking details from the 1841 and/or 1851 census returns on particular individuals. These forms included the name and age of the applicant, the names of his or her parents, and the family's abode in either 1841 or 1851. The same form could contain multiple requests for information on different pension applicants.

On both forms the results of the search of the census returns by the PRO staff are often given in very summary format, perhaps simply an indication that the applicant had been found and confirmation of their age as recorded on either the 1841 or 1851 census return. There may be notes by the PRO searcher asking for clarification of certain details. Sometimes, however, fuller information was extracted from the census and added to the form, including on occasion a fairly complete abstract of the original census return listing everyone in the household along with ages and family relationships. It must be acknowledged that a high proportion of the searches produced negative results with the family not found at the specified location or, if the family was identified, the applicant was missing (usually for the simple reason that the individual had not yet been born). Nonetheless, even if the search was unsuccessful the information submitted initially can provide new details about a family.

Most of the surviving 'Form 37s' are in PRONI (T550), where they are available in bound volumes organised for the most part by barony, and concern pension applicants in what is now Northern Ireland as well as the 'border counties' (Cavan, Donegal and Monaghan). In the 1990s Josephine Masterson published two volumes based on these forms: *Ireland 1841/1851 Census Abstracts (Northern Ireland)* and *Ireland 1841/1851 Census Abstracts (Republic of Ireland)*.[11] Smaller numbers of 'Form 37s' (mostly relating to Cavan and adjoining counties) are in the National Archives of Ireland and these, together with the surviving 'Green Forms', are accessible as digital scans via the NAI website (www.censussearchforms.nationalarchives.ie).

# Notes

1   See, for example, John Grenham's *Tracing Your Irish Ancestors* (5th edition, 2019), which devotes considerable attention to civil, census and church records in chapters 1–3 and offers advice on how to make the most of them for genealogical purposes. For a detailed exploration of pre-1800 church records in Ulster, see William J. Roulston, *Researching Scots-Irish Ancestors ... 1600–1800* (2nd edition, 2018).

2   The cut-off date for online access to the records via www.irishgenealogy.ie is 100 years for births, 75 years for marriages and 50 years for deaths.

3   Access to the indexes and a portion of the registers is also available through FamilySearch, Ancestry and Findmypast.

4   Accessible at www.ireland.anglican.org/about/rcb-library/list-of-parish-registers.

5   Accessible at www.nidirect.gov.uk/publications/proni-guide-church-records.

6   Transcripts exist for the parishes of Enniscorthy, County Wexford (1861) and Drumconda & Loughbracken, County Meath (1871). The Drumcondra & Loughbracken transcript is available on www.irishancestors.ie.

7   Transcripts from the 1821 census can be found in various archives, e.g. the Thrift Abstracts in NAI. A locally discovered copy of the 1821 census for Forkill parish, County Armagh, has been published in *Kick Any Stone: Townlands, People and Stories of Forkill Parish* (2003). See the article by Bill Macafee on the 1831 'census' in *Familia*, 34 (2018), pp 73–87.

8   The parishes for which at least some returns survive are Aghagallon, Aghalee, Ballinderry, Ballymoney, Carncastle, Craigs, Dunaghy, Grange of Killyglen, Killead, Kilwaughter, Larne, Newtowncrommelin, Rasharkin and Tickmacrevan.

9   The forms used to verify ages of applicants through searches of the Church of Ireland registers in the old Public Record Office are in NAI; these are available online through Findmypast and Ancestry.

10   Helpful discussions of these records are provided by Claire Santry (www.irish-genealogy-toolkit.com/irish-pension-records.html), and Chris Paton (http://britishgenes.blogspot.com/2014/11/irish-pension-applications-and-census.html).

11   These volumes are available on Ancestry. The *Republic of Ireland* volume concerns people who were born or living in another part of Ireland at the time of the 1841 and 1851 censuses, but were making a pension claim while living in the counties that now make up Northern Ireland. Both volumes contain much additional 1841/1851 census material.

# 3

# Finding farmers in landed estate collections

Until the beginning of the twentieth century the most important unit of land organisation in Ireland was the estate. Anglo-Norman feudalism, the redistribution of monastic lands following the Reformation, the various schemes of plantation in the sixteenth and early seventeenth centuries, followed by the Cromwellian, Restoration and Williamite land settlements of the 1650s through to the beginning of the eighteenth century all contributed to the evolution of the landed estate system. Landownership was concentrated in a comparatively small number of hands and the overwhelming majority of farmers were tenants on these estates. It was not until the passing of a series of acts of parliament in the late nineteenth and early twentieth centuries that the estate system began to be dismantled and an owner-occupier class of farmers was created, a process that will be examined in Chapter 9.

## 3.1 Landowners in Ireland

The owners of estates in Ireland included private individuals and families, as well as institutions, such as the Church of Ireland and Trinity College Dublin, not to mention trading companies and the Crown. The term 'owner' is problematic, however, because while a proportion of estates were owned in fee simple by virtue of a patent from the Crown, others, even some extensive properties, were possessed through a lease of one form or another. Furthermore, while many farmers held directly from the ultimate owner of the estate, in numerous other instances there were several layers of 'ownership' between the absolute owner and the person who actually farmed the land. Such issues obviously have implications when trying to find farming ancestors in landed estate records and these will be addressed in due course.

The intermediary between the owner of the estate and the farmer was often termed a middleman and the fact that so much land was in the possession of such individuals was regarded by some as one of the major problems with landholding in Ireland. In 1782, one observer wrote 'there is no difficulty in believing that there are numbers of proprietors of estates who are ignorant of the severities practised on their tenants by that swarm of locusts, those middlemen or land-jobbers, as they are called, whose depredations are more destructive than all the plagues of Egypt' (PRONI, T3649/2). The term, however, embraced a number of different categories of landholder and even a substantial tenant farmer who sub-let part of his holding to others could be considered a middleman.[1]

In 1876 a return of landowners in Ireland was printed by Parliament.[2] Arranged by province and county, the return gives the name and address of the landowner and the acreage that he or she was in possession of. The return also provides numerical totals by county of landowners in possession of less than one acre. In addition to the absolute owners of land, the return includes 'lessees for terms exceeding 99 years, or with a right of perpetual renewal', a type of contract that will be discussed in more detail in the next chapter. Taking Tyrone as an example, in this county 1,717 people were in possession of more than one acre. However, only 137 of them owned more than 1,000 acres. Many of those classified in this return as 'landowners' were the descendants of farmers who had been issued with a renewable lease for lives in the eighteenth century. Although there is a need to take a cautious approach to the subject of the 'ownership' of land, several distinct categories of landowners can be identified and these are discussed briefly below.

### 3.1.1 Landowning families

The great majority of landed estates were privately owned by individual families and ranged in size from over 100,000 acres to under 1,000. There were thus considerable variations in the wealth and lifestyles of landowners, and to regard them as forming a single homogeneous group would be erroneous. The owners of the largest estates were often titled aristocrats who possessed properties in several parts of Ireland and in Britain. Their homes – the 'big houses' – were generally built on a grand scale and were set within extensive demesnes.

They exerted considerable control over representative politics in their respective counties. The smaller landowners, on the other hand, lived more modestly and for some of them their circumstances were little different from the more substantial tenant farmers.

One thing that most landowners shared was membership of the Church of Ireland. This was a product of the land settlements of the seventeenth century reinforced by the Penal Laws, legislation passed in the Irish Parliament to preserve the privileged position of the civil and religious elites. Between 1691 and 1775 Catholic landownership in Ireland is believed to have fallen from 22% to 5% of land, though the relaxation of the Penal Laws in the late eighteenth century resulted in a rise in the number of Catholic landowners.[3] By the late 1800s many landowning families had been in possession of their estates for centuries and over multiple generations. However, the ranks of the landed elite were augmented through new additions, notably businessmen who purchased estates and set themselves up as country gentlemen.

## 3.1.2 Institutions

The Church of Ireland, the state or established church until 1871, owned vast swathes of land in Ireland. Most of this land was in the possession of bishops and archbishops. Some of these diocesan estates were huge. For example, the property possessed by the archbishop of Armagh was mainly to be found in counties Armagh, Londonderry, Louth and Tyrone, with additional lands in counties Antrim, Cavan, Down and Monaghan. The usual practice of the bishops was to lease extensive tracts of land to major tenants, who in turned let the farms to their own under-tenants. A hugely valuable source for the tenants of church land is *Report of Her Majesty's Commissioners on the Revenues and Condition of the Established Church (Ireland)* [4082], HC 1867–8, xxiv (1868). Schedule I, Part 2 of this report is a rental of the lands of the archbishops and bishops. While many of those listed as lessees of bishopric lands were in possession of thousands of acres, a high number were in possession of much smaller areas and must have farmed these holdings themselves.[4] Parish clergy also possessed lands known as glebe, which provided them with a source of income.

Some estates were managed on behalf of charities. For example, Stearne's Charity was founded under the will (1744) of John Stearne,

Anglican bishop of Clogher, and was based on his estate at Middletown, County Armagh. Such estates were usually managed by trustees. Lands were used frequently to provide schools with an endowment, sometimes under the terms of the will of a landlord. The extensive Dr Michael Quane Papers in the National Library of Ireland include much material about endowed schools, including documentation about the occupiers of the lands attached to such schools.[5] Other institutions owning land included the Royal College of Physicians of Ireland.[6]

Trinity College Dublin was one of the largest landowners in Ireland, in 1843 owning nearly 200,000 acres or just over 1% of the island. The College lands were spread across 16 counties, ranging from 75,000 acres in Kerry to a mere 65 acres in Westmeath. As part of the scheme for the Ulster Plantation, Trinity College Dublin was granted extensive lands in three northern counties – Armagh, Donegal and Fermanagh, which in 1843 were calculated to extend to, respectively, 23,000, 63,000 and 10,500 acres. In addition to the College estates, the Provost of Trinity was in possession of 35,000 acres, principally in County Galway. In general the College lands were leased to middlemen, often in large blocks. In 1635 it was enacted that leases for College land could only be for a maximum of 21 years. It was the custom to allow annual renewals of 21-year leases on the payment of a fine.[7] The College lands in the nineteenth and early twentieth centuries are the subject of R.B. MacCarthy's volume, *The Trinity College Estates, 1800–1923: Corporate Management in an Age of Reform* (1992).

## 3.1.3 Companies

In the early seventeenth century the new county of Londonderry was created and so-named because of the involvement of the livery companies of London in its development. Until the early 1800s the usual practice of these companies was to lease their estates in their entirety to a middleman (or collective of middlemen). Two major works by James Stevens Curl – *The Londonderry Plantation, 1609–1914* (1986) and *The Honourable the Irish Society and the Plantation of Ulster, 1608–2000* (2000) – examine in some detail the activities of the London companies in this county. Curl's *Londonderry Plantation* includes chapters on each of the principal London livery companies. This volume is particularly useful in determining the succession of middlemen on the estates of these companies. An earlier volume of immense value is T.W. Moody, *The Londonderry Plantation, 1609–41: the City of London and the Plantation in Ulster* (1939; reprinted 2019). Elsewhere, land was owned by bodies such as the Lagan Navigation Company along the route of the Lagan canal in counties Antrim and Down.

## 3.1.4 The Crown

The Crown was in direct possession of lands in many counties in Ireland, though often the individual Crown estates may have been as small as a single townland. These ranged from lands attached to forts, such as Charlemont Fort in County Armagh, to properties that had been forfeited in 1641 or 1688 and not disposed of by the Crown. The Crown estates were managed by the Quit Rent Office, which in 1827 came under the direction of the Commissioners of Woods, Forests and Land Revenues of the Crown. The individual properties were generally let on long term leases, which expired or were terminated in the early 1830s. For information on QRO records, see the section below on the National Archives of Ireland and also Chapter 4.10 on emigration schemes from the Crown estates.

## 3.1.5 Publications on landed estates

As a browse through the Irish History Online database reveals, the number of published studies on landed estates in Ireland has increased considerably in recent times and only a selection is highlighted here. The work of W.E. Vaughan has contributed to a much richer understanding of the estate system in the nineteenth century, notably his volume *Landlords and Tenants in Mid-Victorian Ireland* (1994), as well as his shorter volume, *Landlords and Tenants in Ireland 1848–1904* (1984). W.A. Maguire wrote extensively on this subject area and his book *The Downshire Estates in Ireland, 1801–45* (1972) is a model study of a landed estate. Among his many publications on landed society, Anthony Malcomson, has written *Virtues of a Wicked Earl: the Life and Legend of William Sydney Clements, 3rd Earl of Leitrim (1806–79)* (2009).

Terence Dooley's volumes, *Sources for the History of Landed Estates in Ireland* (2000) and *The Big Houses and Landed Estates of Ireland: A*

*Research Guide* (2007) provide an introduction to the value of estate collections and other records for studying landed estates. Dr Dooley is the author of several other works that explore landed families and their properties, including *The Decline and Fall of the Dukes of Leinster* (2014). Further detailed studies include: Olwen Purdue, *The Big House in the North of Ireland* (2009), Peter Marson, *Belmore: The Lowry Corrys of Castle Coole* (2007) and William J. Roulston, *Abercorn: the Hamiltons of Barons Court* (2014). Local historical journals often include useful information relating to landed estates and Irish History Online can be very helpful in identifying articles of interest (see some examples below).

### 3.1.6 The role of agents

Land agents played a crucially important role in the management of landed estates, especially if the owner was an absentee. One of the best known land agents in Irish history is William Steuart Trench (1808–72). Born in County Laois, the son of a Church of Ireland clergyman, Trench was agent for the Shirley estate in County Monaghan from 1841 until his resignation in 1845. Drawing on the richness of the Shirley estate archive in PRONI, his activities are told in a series of articles in the *Clogher Record*.[8] In 1850 Trench became agent of the Lansdowne estate in County Kerry and retained this position until his death.

Within a year of taking up his appointment in Kerry, Trench introduced a far-reaching scheme of assisted emigration, which, in 18 months, resulted in over 3,000 people being sent to North America. In managing the estate, he introduced strict rules, among other things forbidding the tenants from marrying without permission. The regulations were intended to reduce destitution, and they did save people from starvation during periods of acute distress, but they produced a backlash, ensuring his continued notoriety. In addition, he introduced improvements to agriculture, forestry and fishing, and developed the infrastructure of the estate, building roads and harbours.[9] He was also agent for the Bath estate in County Monaghan and the Digby estate in County Offaly from, respectively, 1851 and 1857 onwards. In 1868 Trench published his autobiography, *Realities of Irish Life*.[10]

Trench's career is the subject of an exceptionally detailed study by Gerard J. Lyne, *The Lansdowne Estate in Kerry under the Agency of*

*William Steuart Trench, 1849–72* (2001). Other books looking at the work of land agents include Ciaran Reilly, *The Irish Land Agent: the Case of King's County, 1830–1860* (2014), in which the author identifies over 100 men who were agents in the county in the period under study. The Dublin-based land agency of Messrs Stewart and Kincaid is the focus of Desmond Norton's detailed study, *Landlords, Tenants, Famine: the Business of an Irish Land Agency in the 1840s* (2006). The agency was responsible for a number of estates across Ireland, including the property of Lord Palmerston in Sligo and Dublin.

## 3.2 Locating estate papers

The loss of records relating to the management of landed estates has been considerable. Some collections were destroyed accidentally in fires, floods or other catastrophes. For example, Shane's Castle, the seat of the O'Neills in County Antrim, was burned down in 1816, resulting in the loss of family and estate papers. Other records were obliterated deliberately – perhaps when it was felt that there was no more use for them. In other instances, estate papers were collateral losses through other actions, such as the burning of 'big houses' during the War of Independence and Civil War. In his study of nineteenth-century County Cork, James S. Donnelly remarks:

> Wastepaper campaigns have also wreaked havoc upon estate records, both the patriotic campaigns during the acute paper shortage of the Second World War (as many Cork solicitors sorrowfully told me) and the charitable ones since then. One church-sponsored paper drive in Cork city in the late 1950s claimed an enormous collection of documents from the South Mall firm of Hussey and Townsend, probably the largest land-agency concern in all of Ireland during the 1880s, with some ninety estates under its management.[11]

Having acknowledged that many collections do not survive, it is important to recognise that a vast quantity of estate material does exist in archives and libraries across the island of Ireland, as well as further documentation beyond these shores. The following sections consider this in more detail.

## 3.2.1 Published and printed guides

Many genealogical guides include information on the availability of landed estate papers. A helpful starting point is John Grenham, *Tracing Your Irish Ancestors* (5th edition, 2019). Chapter 13 of this book is titled 'County Source Lists' and provides a breakdown of records under various headings for each of the 32 counties of Ireland. One of these headings is 'Estate Records' where a summary listing is given of collections of estate papers held primarily in the National Archives of Ireland, National Library of Ireland and PRONI, as well as records that have appeared in print (e.g. in local history journals or genealogical publications). The county listing is arranged alphabetically by estate and includes the main categories of record with covering dates. The author has also indicated if the records concern all tenants or only major tenants and the civil parishes that formed part of the estate.

For relevant material prior to 1800 for Ulster, researchers should consult William Roulston, *Researching Scots-Irish Ancestors: the Essential Genealogical Guide to Early Modern Ulster, 1600–1800* (2nd edition, 2018). In addition to a chapter devoted to estate papers, Appendix 1 of this book identifies the estates with pre-1800 records in every parish in the nine counties of Ulster. Appendix 2 of the book runs to nearly 100 pages and lists in some detail the available estate records for all nine counties of the province. For the more substantial estates, a brief introductory paragraph is included and the available papers are presented under various headings, e.g. rentals, leases and maps. Information on estate collections can also be found in the county guides published by Flyleaf Press and the booklets issued by the North of Ireland Family History Society. See also A. Eiriksson and C. Ó Gráda, *Estate Records of the Irish Famine: a Second Guide to Famine Archives 1840–1855* (1995).

The Irish Manuscripts Commission (IMC) has published a number of volumes concerning family and estate archives. An early example is Edward MacLysaght, *The Kenmare Manuscripts* (1942), which explores the vast archive of the Browne family, ennobled as earls of Kenmare in 1801. The family's estates were principally in counties Kerry, Limerick and Cork, with other lands in counties Carlow, Kilkenny and Laois. As the editor notes in his introduction, the archive contains 'a remarkably full series of rental ledgers and estate account books, a considerable volume of correspondence … a very large number of conveyances, leases, etc'. MacLysaght's edition includes transcripts of many documents, including rentals.[12]

Other relevant IMC publications include John Ainsworth (ed.), *The Inchiquin Manuscripts* (1961), concerning the papers of the O'Brien family, earls of Inchiquin (among other titles), and available on the IMC website; and T.W. Moody and J.G. Simms (eds), *The Bishopric of Derry and the Irish Society of London, 1602–1705*, 2 vols (1968–83), which includes information of the management of the lands belonging to the Anglican bishop of Derry. More recently Anthony Malcomson has produced several volumes of calendars of important archival collections with significant estate material. These include: *Calendar of the Rosse Papers* (2008), *The Clements Archive* (2010), and, with Patrick Walsh, *The Conolly Archive* (2010).

The value of these publications lies in the way in which they draw attention to collections of records in disparate locations and present the data in an organised manner. For instance, the volume on the Conolly archive summarises papers in several different repositories, including the National Library of Ireland, Trinity College Dublin, the Public Record Office of Northern Ireland, the National Archives of Ireland and the Irish Architectural Archive, as well as some material in private possession. The Conolly estate collection relates to properties in counties Donegal, Dublin, Fermanagh, Kildare, Leitrim, Londonderry, Offaly, Meath, Westmeath, Roscommon, Waterford and Wexford, in addition to lands in England and Wales. The volume on the Clements archive also deals with collections of records now held in several different locations, while the estate papers concern properties at Mohill, Manor Hamilton and Newtowngore, County Leitrim, as well as lands in north County Donegal and 'Joyce's Country' in County Galway.

Mention should also be made of the IMC's annual publication, *Analecta Hibernica* (available on JSTOR), which provides summaries and transcriptions of original source material, some of which relate to the management of landed estates. Examples include John Barry, 'The Duke of Devonshire's Irish estates, 1794–1797', 22 (1960), pp 269–327; Sean Murphy, 'The Sligo Papers, Westport House, Co. Mayo: a report', 33 (1986), pp 15–46; and Brian Mac Cuarta, 'Sir Barnaby O'Brien's Irish revenues for 1629–31, Thomond rent, 1629 and Carlow tenants, 1639', 48 (2017), pp 31–72. See also the 'Survey of Documents in Private Keeping' series, published in no. 15 (1944), no. 20 (1958) and no. 25 (1967).

Many other journals and periodicals include transcriptions of original source material or discussions of significant collections of records. Chapter 1 highlighted the value of the Irish History Online database, listing published materials, as well as JSTOR (www.jstor.org), which provides access to a range of journals and periodicals. For example, the 2011 edition of the journal *Archivium Hibernicum*, published by the Catholic Historical Society of Ireland, includes a lengthy article by Luke McInerney, 'Documents from the Thomond Papers at Petworth House Archive [with index]'. This includes a helpful introduction to the material, transcriptions of a selection of documents and an appendix listing some of the pre-1641 Thomond Papers for counties Clare, Limerick and Tipperary in a private archive in Sussex, England.

The work of the Historical Manuscripts Commission (HMC) should not be overlooked. Established in 1869, this body identified documentary material in private possession, and published reports on its work, which included transcriptions or summaries of records. With regard to material of Irish interest, attention can be drawn to the *Calendar of the Manuscripts of the Marquess of Ormonde, Preserved at Kilkenny Castle*, published in two series totalling 11 volumes between 1895 and 1920. Some of the earlier volumes published by the HMC can be accessed online (e.g. Google Books, the Internet Archive and Hathi Trust).

As highlighted throughout this book, parliamentary papers include much invaluable information about farmers in Ireland. By way of example, 'The Third Report of the Commissioners for enquiring into the state of all Schools on Public or Charitable Foundations, in Ireland', printed in *Reports Presented to the House of Commons from the Commissioners of the Board of Education of Ireland* (1809), includes transcriptions of rentals of lands providing endowments for schools. These rentals may include all or some of the following: the name of the denomination of land, the name of the tenant, the tenure, the extent of the holding, and the annual rent paid. The lands contained in the report include portions of the estates of the late Earl of Ranelagh in counties Roscommon and Westmeath; the late Bishop

Pococke of Ossory; the late John Rogerson in counties Cork and Dublin; the late Dean Richard Stewart in County Louth; and the late Hon. Mrs Ann Hamilton in County Down.

## 3.2.2 Major archives in Ireland

### *National Library of Ireland*

The principal repository in the Republic of Ireland for landed estate papers is the Department of Manuscripts of the National Library in Dublin. It is important to be aware, however, that the NLI collections of estate papers include many records for what is now Northern Ireland. The National Library website hosts two principal catalogues, the Sources Catalogue (http://sources.nli.ie) and the Online Catalogue (http://catalogue.nli.ie). Both should be used in trying to identify relevant estate material. The Sources Catalogue is not exclusively limited to documents in NLI and can be a helpful guide to estate records held in other repositories. Estate records form the largest component within the Department of Manuscripts. In recent times considerable resources have been applied to cataloguing some of the more significant collections. These catalogues can be downloaded as PDFs from the NLI website, first by clicking on the link to Catalogues & Databases and then going to Manuscript Collection Lists and choosing the category Estate.

At present, over 60 Manuscript Collection Lists contain material relating to the management of landed estates. Usually, each one will begin with an introduction to the estate, which can provide information on the succession of owners and the manner in which the collection has been organised. The catalogues can go into great detail on the contents of the estate archive and many of them are upwards of 100 pages in length. For instance, the catalogue for the Conyngham Papers (Collection List No. 53), covering the family's estates in counties Clare, Donegal and Meath, runs to more than 200 pages. However, even this pales in comparison with the catalogue of the Lismore Castle Papers (Collection List No. 129) coming in at a colossal 874 pages. These records, created between 1586 and 1885, concern the estate in counties Cork, Waterford, Tipperary and Dublin owned by the Boyle family, earls of Cork and Burlington and the Cavendish family, dukes of Devonshire.

The value of the records of a land agency can be shown through the Kirwan of Tuam and Dalgin Papers (Collection List No. 142). The Kirwans of Tuam, County Galway, were land agents from the 1840s to the early decades of the twentieth century. The properties for which they were responsible included the Castlehacket, Ballinderry, Quansbery and Bermingham, Ballyglunin, Windfield, and Knocknagur estates (the Collection List includes details of the owners of these estates and the lands of which they were comprised). The items in this collection include rentals, rent receipts, letter books, diaries and maps.[13]

A very useful series of volumes in the National Library is titled 'National Library Reports on Private Collections'. While many of the sets of estate papers reviewed in these volumes have since been deposited in archives, others remain in private possession. NLI has created an extensive digital library, which can be accessed through its Online Catalogue. These include mid-nineteenth-century rentals of the estates of the Marquess of Sligo and the Earl of Leitrim and the Longfield Map Collection, dating from c. 1770–1840. Other items of interest include printed rentals for some estates produced in advance of a sale.

### National Archives of Ireland

A smaller collection of estate papers can be found in the National Archives of Ireland and a separate web page provides guidance on these.[14] There is as yet no comprehensive online catalogue to estate records in NAI. However, downloadable PDF descriptive lists are available on the NAI website for a number of collections of estate papers. One of the most significant is the collection of records relating to the Pembroke estate in Dublin and Wicklow, covering the medieval period through to the latter part of the twentieth century.[15] Finding aids for other collections are available in the NAI Reading Room. Other guides in the Reading Room include one titled 'Estate Maps and Rentals'. Estate papers can also be found in the Business Records archive in NAI.

Among the collections held by NAI are the records of the Quit Rent Office (QRO). Quit rents were paid to the Exchequer and derived primarily from the Cromwellian land settlement of the mid-seventeenth century. The QRO had a number of additional functions and was responsible for the management of the Crown estates in Ireland. In 1827 the QRO became a department within the Commissioners of Woods, Forests and Land Revenues of the Crown. With the absorption of the QRO by the Land Commission in 1943, its records were sent to the Public Record Office of Ireland and are now in NAI (some items of northern interest had earlier been transferred to PRONI).[16] A catalogue of the QRO records in NAI can be found on the Archives Portal Europe website (www.archivesportaleurope.net).

Of particular interest are the records relating to the management of the individual Crown estates. These comprise the type of records that a researcher could expect to find in any estate collection, including lists of tenants, maps and surveys, and estate improvement schemes. A listing of the estates for which there are records, including, for the sake of completeness, urban properties, is presented below (the reference for each begins QRO/4/3):

Kingwilliamstown, County Cork (/1)
Templeport, County Cavan (/2)
Kilcaskan, County Cork (/4)
Castlemaine, County Kerry (/5)
Ballykilcline, County Roscommon (/6)
Doon and Trust, County Galway (/7)
Irvillaghoughter [Ervallagh Eighter] and Boughil, County Galway (/8)
Glinsk, County Galway (/9)
Charlemont, County Armagh (/10)
Laggan [Legan] and Kiltullyvarry, County Roscommon (/11)
Mountjoy, County Tyrone (/12)
Kilconcourse [Kyle], County Offaly (/13)
Bantry Commons, County Wexford (/14)
Derryglogher, County Longford (/15)
Clonaltra Wood, County Westmeath (/16)
Hill of Forth [Forth Mountain], County Wexford (/17)
Barrack Hill, Wexford (/18)
North Gate Tower of Athlone, County Westmeath (/19)
Kinsale, County Cork (/20)
Ardfert Commons, County Kerry (/21)
Wicklow Town, County Wicklow (/22)
Monananig and Lackendarragh, County Cork (/23)
Kingsmountain, County Sligo (/24)

King's Island, Limerick (/25)
Passage and New Geneva, County Waterford (/26)
Chapelizod, County Dublin (/27)
Roebuck, County Dublin (/28)
Cruagh, County Dublin (/29)
Annaskinnan, County Westmeath (/30)
Cavanahanlon [Cavan O'Hanlon, Dorsy or Roxborough]
  and Drumaltamuck, County Armagh (/30)
Cork City (/31)
Waterford City (/32)
Limerick City (/33)
Galway City (/34)

## Public Record Office of Northern Ireland

As soon it opened in the 1920s, PRONI began to accession records relating to landed estates. The first three original documents in the catalogue (D1, D2 and D3) are early eighteenth-century maps of the Stewart estate at Cookstown, County Tyrone, while documents D5 and D6 are rent rolls of the Ward estate at Bangor, 1746–7. In addition to accessioning locally held estate material, PRONI archivists ventured far and wide in copying original documents held elsewhere, such as archives in England and Scotland. PRONI also took in significant collections of estate material from the rest of Ireland, in particular from counties Donegal and Monaghan.

What makes the estate records in PRONI stand out is the fact that most of them have been expertly catalogued making it relatively easy to discover what is available for a particular property by using the online PRONI eCatalogue. Detailed introductions have been prepared for many of the larger collections and these can be downloaded as PDFs from the PRONI website. Most of these introductions were written by Anthony Malcomson, a former Director of the institution, and they describe the history of the landowning family, the scope of the collection, and the way in which the records have been organised. Very usefully, some of them list the townlands in the estate.

## 3.2.3 Other archives in Ireland

### University archives and libraries

The Manuscripts & Archives Research Library of **Trinity College Dublin** holds extensive records relating to the property owned by the College, as well as some records relating to other Irish estates. The estate collections in **University College Cork Library Archives Service** include the Bantry Papers. The **University of Limerick Archives** holds several estate collections, notably the extensive set of records relating to the Dunraven estate contained in *c.* 120 boxes. Attention can also be drawn to the Timothy Looney Papers (P43), which were donated to the university in 2013. Timothy Looney (1914–90) was a local historian who amassed a huge collection of books, photographs, maps and documents. In 1960 he salvaged a major collection of papers from Shanbally Castle, County Tipperary, prior to its final demolition. The castle was the seat of the O'Callaghan family, ennobled as Viscounts Lismore. The documents preserved include rentals (1736–1902), accounts (1744–1943), estate correspondence (1814–1948), and maps and surveys (1715–1898). Smaller estate collections include those for Castle Hyde and Doneraile Court in County Cork and Castle Otway, County Tipperary.

### County archives, libraries and museums

Significant collections of estate papers can be found in a range of other repositories across the island. In many instances, catalogues of estate papers are available on the websites of these institutions, sometimes as downloadable PDFs. Some archives and libraries have copied or microfilmed material of relevance to their locality. For instance, the Local Studies Centre in **Clare County Library** (www.clarelibrary.ie) has microfilms of documentary material of local interest from the Petworth House Archives in Sussex, England. A number of local archives have made a selection of estate papers available online. For example, **Tipperary Studies**, based in Thurles, has created an extensive online digital library ((https://tipperarystudies.ie). Among the items that can be viewed are a rent roll of the estate of Lord Milton in County Tipperary, 1787–98, and a rental of the estate of Valentine Maher, Turtulla, Thurles (1839–43). **Limerick Archives** (www.limerick.ie/archives) has digitised and made available online a rental of the estate of Lord Viscount Courtenay (1762) and a receiving rental of the Devon estate (1861–2).

In Northern Ireland, **Armagh County Museum** has an important collection of estate records for properties mainly in County Armagh. Some of these have been made available online, including 'Abstracts from Rentals of the Archbishops of Armagh, 1615–1746' (SCA2.2014.1050).[17] In addition to rentals, this typescript document includes a survey of 1618 and information on leases, 1722–46; there is a lengthy index of personal names. There is also a digital version of the volume of maps of Richard Johnston's estate in counties Armagh, Down and Monaghan of 1731 (32.2007). Also in Armagh is **Armagh Robinson Library** (formerly Armagh Public Library), which has maps of the estate of Thomas Whaley, 1769 (P001497894) and the estate of the late Dr John Stearne, bishop of Clogher, 1820 (P001952346). **Newry and Mourne Museum** holds the Reside Collection, which includes estate rentals, some of which contain information from the first half of the eighteenth century, as well as leases, surveys and maps.

### Private archives in Ireland

Many records relating to the management of landed estates remain in private custody, often in the possession of the descendants of the landowning family. Others are in the vaults of solicitors' offices. Sometimes access to these records can be arranged. An important estate collection can be found in Birr Castle, County Offaly, home of the Earl of Rosse (https://birrcastle.com/archives). The records in this collection range from the early seventeenth century through to the present day. Access to the archives is by appointment only. A guide to the records in this collection is Anthony Malcomson, *The Calendar of the Rosse Papers* (2008), published by the Irish Manuscripts Commission. It is worth noting that Irish estate papers continue to come up for sale and that the catalogues produced by auctioneers, many of which can be viewed online, may draw attention to previously unknown documents.[18]

### 3.2.4 Archives beyond Ireland

A number of collections of records relating to the management of landed estates in Ireland are in repositories in Britain. This may be because the owner of the estate also possessed property on the other side of the Irish Sea. The National Archives (TNA) in Kew, London, is the official archive of the United Kingdom government and of England and Wales. In addition, there are hundreds of other local authority, university, institutional, business and private archives. A major resource with which researchers should become familiar is the Discovery catalogue hosted by TNA (http://discovery.nationalarchives.gov.uk). This vast database includes listings of archival materials from repositories across the UK and beyond.

For example, using the Discovery catalogue, it is possible to learn that the Cumbria Archive and Local Studies Centre in Whitehaven holds the Curwen Family of Workington Hall Papers, which include letters and other documents concerning Thomas Pottinger's estate at Mount Pottinger, Ballymacarrett, County Down, 1744–81. Details of leases, with rentals, 1810–22, of the Stoughton estate, County Kerry, are held by the Gloucestershire Archives. With regard to holdings of The National Archives itself, it may be noted that among its collections are records relating to the Castlemaine estate in County Kerry, part of the Crown estates in Ireland; the papers include surveys, dealings with tenants, assisted emigration, rentals, etc, 1822–55 (CRES 2/1539).

The principal Scottish repository is the National Records of Scotland (formerly the National Archives of Scotland and before that the Scottish Record Office), based in Edinburgh. A few collections of estate papers relating to Ireland may be found here. They include records of the Murrays of Broughton, Wigtownshire, and Cally, Kirkcudbrightshire, concerning the family's estate in the west of County Donegal (GD10). The National Records of Scotland also holds records of the Agnew estate at Kilwaughter, County Antrim, 1636–1712 (GD154/505–534). Estate collections found in Wales include the Powis Castle estate records in the National Library of Wales, which includes significant documentation relating to the Herbert estate in County Kerry – the manor of Mount Eagle Loyall. Bangor University Archives and Special Collections has papers concerning the estate of the Paget family, marquesses of Anglesey, in counties Down and Louth.

Further afield, Irish estate papers can be found in such institutions as the Huntington Library, San Marino, California, where there is an extensive collection of material relating to the Huntingdon estate in counties Fermanagh and Tyrone, as well as the Rawdon estate in counties Antrim and Down.[19] The Rare Book and Manuscript Library of Columbia University in New York City has a number of items relating to Irish estates (https://clio.columbia.edu). These include:

'Caleb Reeve, his booke of rents received in his life tyme out of his estate lyeing in the barony of Slaine and county of Meath in Ireland', 1695–8 – Ms MONTGOM 080

Account book showing receipts and expenditures of the Vesey family at Lucan, County Dublin, 1710–27 – Ms MONTGOM 088 Folio

Volume headed 'France Colclough Her booke of Resaits 1668', with further entries going up to 1750s – Ms MONTGOM 062 Folio

## 3.3 Online databases and resources

The **Irish Archives Resource** (https://iar.ie) allows researchers to search a selection of archival descriptions from repositories across the island. Both 'search' and 'browse' options are available. While it is by no means a comprehensive guide to Irish archives, it can provide helpful pointers. For instance, a search of the database reveals that papers of the Hanford Flood estate are held by the Kilkenny Archaeological Society. These cover the years 1897–1926 and comprise tenants' ledgers, estate valuations, an account and rental, and a significant collection of estate correspondence (444 items in four folders). The Irish Archives Resource also has a blog, which includes several articles relating to estate papers (https://blogiar.wordpress.com).

The **Landed Estates Database** (http://landedestates.ie) is a superb online resource covering all landed estates and historic houses in the provinces of Connacht and Munster from *c.* 1700 to 1914. The database is maintained by the Moore Institute for Research in the Humanities and Social Studies, National University of Ireland, Galway. The website of the database includes A–Z listings of estates, families and houses. The entry for each estate is broken down under the following headings (though there is not always information under each heading): Associated families; Description; Houses; Archival sources; Contemporary printed sources; and Modern printed sources. Under the Description heading there is a brief summary of pertinent details concerning the estate, such as the background of the landowning family, the extent of the estate, and the succession of owners.

The website includes a Google map with markers showing the location of each barony. By zooming in further the locations of the houses will be shown using green markers. The name of the house is linked to its entry in the database. Over 4,500 houses appear in the database with the information provided comprising the name of the house and a brief description of it (such as when it was built and by whom, and its current status) together with details on its location (townland, parish, Poor Law Union, district electoral division, barony, county, latitude and longitude coordinates and Ordnance Survey grid reference). For many of the houses there is also a photograph. More than 2,500 families are included in the database with biographical details of varying length of provided for each (as well as relevant families to which they were related).

The section on archival sources can be very helpful in identifying documents relating to the estate and where these can be found. Taking the Phibbs estate in County Sligo as an example, the database identifies material of interest in the National Archives of Ireland (including Encumbered/Landed Estates' Court rentals) and in Sligo County Library. The records in the County Library range from the first half of the eighteenth century through to the twentieth century and comprise deeds, leases, rentals and correspondence. By clicking on the link to the Sligo County Library it is possible to find a listing of over 90 collections of estate records held by the library. Through following the link on the homepage to Reference Sources it is possible to identify all of the archival sources (more than 150) in the database. The value of this website to tracking down relevant documentation for the south and west of Ireland is obvious.

In addition to the websites of the archives noted above, transcriptions and digital copies of estate papers can be found on many online platforms. Some of these are freely accessible to anyone, though others are behind a paywall and it may be necessary to subscribe to the website. Images and transcriptions of a selection of estate documents, along with an introduction to each item, can be found in the Small Sources series written by Jim Ryan and hosted on the Ancestor Network website (www.ancestornetwork.ie). Claire Santry's Irish Genealogy News website (www.irishgenealogynews.com) is an excellent way of keeping up to date with new records being made available online.

## 3.4 Identifying the relevant estate

Before delving into estate papers, it is first of all necessary to identify the collection of records relating to where your ancestor lived. There are various ways of doing this. First of all, estate collections tend to be identified by the surname or aristocratic title of the landowning family. However, it is important to keep in mind that non-titled landowning families could be elevated to the ranks of the aristocracy and that aristocratic titles themselves were subject to change. By way of example, an estate based around Dungannon, County Tyrone, was purchased by a Belfast merchant, Thomas Knox, in 1692. A subsequent Thomas Knox was created Baron Welles of Dungannon in 1781 and Viscount Northland in 1791. His son, the second Viscount Northland, who was also named Thomas Knox, was granted the earldom of Ranfurly in 1831. Therefore, in the records for this one estate there are leases issued by persons named Knox, Welles, Northland and Ranfurly. The many editions of *Burke's Peerage* are very helpful in understanding the various permutations in the names of titled landowners.[20]

As noted above, the relevant sections in the books by Grenham, *Tracing Your Irish Ancestors*, and Roulston, *Researching Scots-Irish Ancestors, 1600–1800*, can be helpful in identifying available records at county and parish level. For example, using Appendix 1 of the latter volume, the researcher can discover that the properties in Killeevan parish, County Monaghan, for which there are pre-1800 surviving records include the Blayney estate, the bishopric of Clogher estate, the Forster estate, the Ker estate, the Leslie of Glaslough estate, the Massereene estate and the Rossmore estate. In this instance, it is obvious that landownership in the parish was rather fragmented.

Occasionally a map of the townlands that formed an estate might appear in a publication on that property. As noted already, Irish History Online can be a useful way to determine if a book or journal article is available on a specific landed estate. There may even be published county maps showing the boundaries of estates. For example, the chapter by P.J. Duffy in the book, *Common Ground: Essays on the Historical Geography of Ireland*, edited by W.J. Smyth and K. Whelan (1998) includes maps showing the network of estates in the counties of Cavan and Monaghan, in the seventeenth and nineteenth centuries.

Another way to identify the owner of a particular townland is to examine the mid-nineteenth-century valuation known as Griffith's Valuation (discussed in more detail in Chapter 6) and note the most common name in the column headed 'Immediate Lessor' for the townland in question. While this may not always be the name of the owner of a landed estate, in many instances it will. For the researcher concentrating on the eighteenth century, however, there are clearly limitations with this approach. Although the family in possession of an estate in 1860 was often the same in 1760, and even in 1660, in many cases it will not be. Sometimes this will not be a problem, as the records of successive owners will be found together in the same estate collection.

Searching the online catalogues of the different archives holding estate collections is another way to try to identify if records exist for a particular townland. This approach is particularly worthwhile when looking for documentation in PRONI using the eCatalogue since many of PRONI's collections have been catalogued down to townland level. The Freeholders' Records database on the PRONI website is also worth checking since many of the registers will give the name of the freeholder's landlord (see Chapter 8 for more on freeholders). The Sources Catalogue (http://sources.nli.ie) hosted by NLI can also be very helpful. Even after trying these and other approaches, it may not be possible to identify the correct estate collection. Consequently, searches of a number of estate collections may have to be undertaken in the hope of finding relevant material. As highlighted already, it must be acknowledged that the records of many estates have not survived. Generally speaking, the larger the estate, the more likely it is that records survive, usually because facilities were created to store securely the papers relating to the management of the property. Conversely, the records of smaller estates, those in the 1,000–3,000-acre range, have a much poorer survival rate.

# Notes

1 For a careful analysis of this subject, see David Dickson, 'Middlemen' in Thomas Bartlett and D.W. Hayton (eds), *Penal Era and Golden Age: Essays in Irish History, 1690–1800* (Belfast, 1979), pp 162–85.

2 *Land Owners in Ireland. Return of Owners of Land of One Acre and Upwards, in the Several Counties, Counties of Cities, and Counties of Towns in Ireland ...* [C.1492] (HC, 1876). It was reprinted by Genealogical Publishing in 1988.

3 For a study of one family, see Karen J. Harvey, *The Bellews of Mount Bellew: a Catholic Gentry Family in Eighteenth-century Ireland* (1998).

4 The rental gives the acreage (not always included), rent and term – generally perpetuity or 40 years (for property in towns) or 21 years (sometimes giving the date the lease commenced), though annual tenancies and even some leases for lives are recorded.

5 The Quane Papers can be identified using the NLI Sources Catalogue (sources.nli.ie). Dr Quane wrote a huge number of articles on Irish schools, a listing of which can be found in the Irish History Online database.

6 Des Cowman, 'The Waterford estates of the Royal College of Physicians of Ireland (1703–1906)', *Decies: Journal of the Waterford Archaeological & Historical Society*, 71 (2015), pp 19–42.

7 W.J. Lowe, 'Landlord and tenant on the estate of Trinity College, Dublin, 1851–1903', *Hermathena*, 120 (1976), p. 6.

8 L. Ó Mearáin, 'Estate agents in Farney: Trench and Mitchell', *Clogher Record*, 10 (1981), pp 405–13; P.J. Duffy, 'Assisted emigration from the Shirley estate, 1843–54', *Clogher Record*, 14 (1992), pp 7–63; P.J. Duffy, 'Management problems on a large estate in mid-nineteenth-century Ireland: William Steuart Trench's report on the Shirley estate in 1843', *Clogher Record*, 16 (1997), pp 101–22.

9 From 1853 Trench was assisted by one of his sons, John Townsend. G.J. Lyne, 'John Townsend Trench's reports on the Lansdowne estate in Kerry, 1863–72', *Journal of the Kerry Archaeological and Historical Society*, 19 (1986), pp 5–64.

10 Gerard Lyne, in his biography of Trench for the *Dictionary of Irish Biography*, notes, 'The work displays considerable literary ability. As historical record, however, it is self-regarding, vainglorious, and unreliable.'

11 James S. Donnelly, *The Land and the People of Nineteenth-century Cork* (1975), pp 386–7.

12 A digitised version of this book is available on the IMC website (www.irishmanuscripts.ie/digital-resources). The archive has since been

deposited in the Public Record Office of Northern Ireland (D4151). Some documents relating to the estate can be found on the following website: www.muckrosshouseresearchlibrary.ie/Kenmare-Estate-Records.php.

13 The James Hardiman Library, NUI Galway, holds another collection of papers of the Kirwan family of Castlehackett, County Galway.

14 www.nationalarchives.ie/article/guide-landed-estate-records.

15 Deeds in section 2011/1 have been published in *Calendar of Ancient Deeds and Muniments Preserved in the Pembroke Estate Office, Dublin* (1891).

16 Fiona Fitzsimons, 'Quit Rent Office', *History Ireland*, 23:1 (January/February 2015): available online at www.historyireland.com/20th-century-contemporary-history/20th-century-social-perspectives/quit-rent-office.

17 https://visitarmagh.com/places-to-explore/armagh-county-museum/research-geneology/family-history.

18 By way of example, numerous estate records can be found on the website of the auctioneer Fonsie Mealy (www.fonsiemealy.ie/auction-results).

19 See Brenda Collins 'Sources for a seventeenth-century Ulster estate: the Hastings (Irish) Papers in the Huntington Library, California', *Familia*, 24 (2008), pp 145–54.

20 Earlier editions of *Burke's Peerage* can be found online on Google Books, etc.

# 4

# The range of records in estate collections

## 4.1 The potential and limitations of using estate papers

The previous chapter highlighted the importance of landed estate collections and discussed where relevant records may be found. This chapter will explore the documentation generated by the management of these estates. Some categories of estate papers are more useful to family historians than others. Title deeds are concerned with the legal ownership of an estate, and are generally of limited value to genealogists. The same can usually be said of mortgages. Wills and marriage settlements refer primarily to the members of the landowner's family. Nonetheless, in some cases such documents can contain invaluable information on the tenant farmers in the form of accompanying schedules (see examples in Chapter 5 on the Registry of Deeds). For the most part, however, the documents of greatest interest to genealogists are rentals, leases, lease books, maps, surveys, valuations, correspondence and manor court records.

While this chapter will be advocating strongly for estate papers as vital sources of information on farming families in Ireland, some difficulties need to be discussed to avoid giving the impression that research in them will always produce positive results. The reality is that many farmers are invisible in estate records. The most obvious reason for this is the fact that there will always be gaps of one form or another in surviving estate collections, never mind the fact that the papers for some estates are not available at all. Furthermore, estate papers may not name all of the farmers on a plot of land if they held a joint tenancy. Only one farmer might be named with the additional comment 'and partners' who, unfortunately, remain anonymous.

Another reason for the non-appearance of one's farming ancestors in estate papers relates to the hierarchy of land possession. As discussed in the previous chapter, many landlords, especially in the eighteenth century, leased large tracts of land to middlemen, who then let the land to the occupying farmers. There may be documents relating to the leasing of land to the middlemen, but not from the middlemen to those who actually farmed the land. Having acknowledged some of the limitations with regard to estate papers, it is important to emphasise that if relevant records do exist then these collections do offer huge potential for discovering more about one's ancestors.

## 4.2 Tenant farmers and tenure

From the farmer's perspective, security of tenure was arguably the most important aspect of the relationship between landlord and tenant. There were three principal ways in which a farmer held land from a landowner. The first was the lease, a written document that set out the terms on which the land was transferred into the possession of the farmer. In return, the landlord promised not to obstruct or impede the tenant farmer's 'enjoyment', as it was termed, of the farm. Two copies of the lease were usually prepared, with one copy retained by the landlord and the other by the tenant. Leases come in various formats and a detailed analysis of them is presented below.

Tenants could also be in possession of their farms on a yearly basis or 'at will'. In his detailed exploration of the Downshire estate, which was located mainly in County Down, with further lands in County Offaly, W.A. Maguire provided a succinct explanation of how the two differed:

> The essential difference between them was that whereas a yearly tenancy began on a certain date and ended a year from that date, a tenancy at will had no exact terminal date but continued so long as both landlord and tenant – in practice no doubt it was usually the former who ended it – wished it to continue.[1]

These tenancies have often been confused, even by landowners themselves, and often the term 'at will' was used in relation to all tenants without a written lease. In practical terms, there was often little difference between the two, though the farmer in possession of a yearly tenancy could expect six months' notice to quit his holding.

Some contemporaries made much of the differences in circumstances between a tenant with a written lease and one without. Appearing before a parliamentary commission in 1880, John Donnell of Dunnamanagh, County Tyrone, made the following observations on the farms in his district. Of Clogherny he commented: 'One portion of this townland is deeded, the other is in the occupation of tenants-at-will ... Three deeded farms which are in a far better condition than the others.' Rousky was entirely held by tenants with written leases, 'most of whom are industrious men, and have made great improvements.' In Drain Donnell observed that the farmers 'regret that their fathers and grandfathers did not take out leases renewable forever.'[2]

## 4.3 Tenant farmers and leases

Typically the items most commonly found within a landed estate collection will be leases issued by the owners of the estate to their tenants. In some estate collections the number of surviving leases can run to thousands. In considering the possibility that a farming ancestor might have been issued with a lease, it is important to pose the question: what proportion of tenants were in possession of a lease and did this change over time?

Here again, Maguire's analysis of the Downshire estate is helpful. Through an analysis of the estate records, he highlighted the fact that most of the tenancies in the estate were held by lease in the early 1800s. Of the nearly 1,400 tenancies in the Kilwarlin portion of the estate in 1816 almost 90% were held by lease. However, Maguire has also noted that few leases for farms in the estate were granted after 1830. Leases which expired were not renewed and the farmers became simply 'tenants-at-will'.[3] There is evidence of similar practices on other estates across the island. In his exploration of estate management in County Cork, James S. Donnelly noted that in the early 1800s most of the tenants holding farms directly from the proprietor rather than from a middleman were leaseholders rather than yearly tenants. However, between 1815 and 1845 annual tenancy became more usual.[4]

The disinclination of many landlords to issue leases as the nineteenth century wore on has been attributed to a number of factors. First of all, there was a change in the franchise with 40-shilling freeholders no longer able to vote after 1829 (see Chapter 8 for more on electoral records). This certainly had an impact on the granting of life leases (a prerequisite for voting). The emerging political consciousness, particularly among Catholic farmers, also made landlords reluctant to issues leases to people whose voting patterns they could not control as before. There were also economic factors, especially the agricultural depression following the end of the Napoleonic wars, which made it harder for tenants to keep up with the rent payments specified in their leases.[5]

Much illuminating information on the prevalence or otherwise of leases can be found in the *Returns showing the number of agricultural holdings in Ireland and the tenure by which they are held by the occupiers* (1870). The figures reveal that the vast majority of farmers across Ireland were only tenants-at-will – some 80% of all agricultural holdings were held in this way.[6] There were regional variations with nearly 90% of holdings in the province of Connacht tenancies at will, while in Munster the figure was 66%; the figures for Leinster and Ulster were approximately 75 and 83% respectively. While acknowledging that these figures are from the second half of the 1800s and do not necessarily reflect the situation half a century and more earlier, nonetheless, there are obvious implications for the likelihood of finding a lease issued to one's farming ancestor.

## 4.4 Robert Rolleston's lease of Gortavea

On 31 January 1835 my great-great-great-grandfather Robert Rolleston was issued with a lease for a farm in Gortavea, County Tyrone. He had only moved to this townland five years earlier (see Chapter 5). The lease was not one that had been created especially for him, but was rather one of hundreds of leases issued by the Abercorn estate at this time. Two copies of the lease exist, one in the Public Record Office of Northern Ireland (where it has been catalogued D623/B/12/224), and the other in my possession, having turned up in a solicitor's office in Strabane in 2004. The lease is a parchment document, measuring approximately 55 cm in length and 38 cm in breadth. It is a printed document with spaces left for details, such as the date, names, etc, to be filled in by hand. The paragraphs which follow explore the contents of the lease and consider the broader context of leases and leasing practices.

## 4.4.1 The parties to the lease

A lease will name the parties to it. On the one hand, there will be the lessor (or grantor), i.e. the landowner, and on the other, the lessee (or grantee), i.e. the tenant. Sometimes there may be more than one lessor, perhaps if the estate happened to be in the possession of trustees while the owner was a minor. There may also have been more than one lessee for on many occasions several tenants – perhaps related to each other – joined together to take a holding. In this instance, the lessor was James Hamilton, second Marquess of Abercorn, the owner of Gortavea and dozens of other townlands that together formed an estate of some 70,000 acres. The lessee was Robert Rolleston, who was described in the lease as a farmer, and who was in sole possession of his farm. Both parties signed the lease – the Marquess simply wrote Abercorn, while Robert signed his name in full, on this occasion spelling his surname Rollston.

While Robert was to enjoy possession of his farm for a further 19 years after the lease was issued until his death in 1854, there are instances of a tenant passing away before he even had a chance to sign the lease. In 1821 Lord Mark Kerr and Lady Charlotte Kerr leased a farm in Galboly, County Antrim, to Patrick McDonnell (PRONI, D2977/3A/4/59/7). The lease includes the following endorsement:

> ... this lease was first filed for Patrick McDonnell of Galboly who held the lands therein mentioned, but he having died without signing it, and his widow requesting that Henry Murphy of Galboly who is married to McDonnell's daughter, should get this lease. His name has accordingly been inserted in it, November 1835.

In 1824 a smallholding in Ballytober, County Antrim, was leased to Sarah Cruthers of Ballycronan, farmer and John Templeton, her son-in-law (PRONI, D778/832). Attached to this lease is a letter from Sarah Cruthers stating that she was unable through old age to go to Belfast to sign it and requesting that the lease might pass to Templeton on her death.

In some instances, a lease may include details of earlier deeds or occupiers of the holding. For example, an 1818 lease of 12 acres in Frankford, County Offaly, from Thomas Drought of Droughtville and Thomas Drought of Cappagolan to James Owens of Kinnity refers to the original lease dated 1742 and made to James Sissers (PRONI, D778/636). Taking another example, in 1827 the Marquess of Donegall issued a lease for a holding in Ballyalbanagh, County Antrim, to William Mackey; the deed references the original lease of 1775 from the Earl of Donegall to James Houston (PRONI, D300/2/1/2/10). An 1816 lease from Viscount Dungannon to William Brice of a farm in Moneyrea, County Down, refers to an action of ejectment against the previous tenant, John Lowry (PRONI, D778/632).

## 4.4.2 The location and extent of the farm

A lease will indicate the location and extent of the farm. Sometimes the location given will be no more specific than the name of the townland or subdivision of the townland. In the case of Robert Rolleston's farm, the lease stated that it was in the townland of 'Gortavey', manor of Donelong, parish of Donagheady, barony of Strabane and county of Tyrone. The Abercorn estate was divided into a number of manors, with Donelong the most northerly of these in County Tyrone. The extent of the farm in statute measure was 106 acres, 3 roods and 38 perches, 'be the same more or less' (there were 40 perches in a rood and four roods in an acre).

Although not the case here, a lease often provided a written description of the position of the holding within the townland. This may have been related to other landholdings and to natural features, such as rivers and bogs. For instance, in 1751 Francis McAwly of Frankford, King's County (Offaly), issued a lease to John Exham of two fields and a garden, called the 'Cow's pasture', bounded on the east by the old road formerly leading to Ballentloghan, on the north by lands of Francis McAwly himself, on the west and south by the holding of William Molloy (PRONI, D778/101). Sometimes a small map may be attached to the lease showing the location of the farm or a sketch of the farm might be included on the lease itself.

## 4.4.3 The term of the lease

The term of the lease – that is, the period for which the lease was valid – was specified. In this regard, there were two principal types of leases issued to tenant farmers.[7] First of all, there were leases for a determinate number of years. Such a lease would not expire until a specified period of time had elapsed. The number of years varied considerably, from fewer than five to upwards of 1,000. Leases for 21, 31 or 41 years were particularly common. As a result of the Penal Laws, for much of the eighteenth century the maximum duration of a lease issued to a Catholic was 31 years. Generally speaking, if the person to whom the lease was issued died within the set number of years the lease passed to his heirs, for example his son, for the remainder of the term.

In the second half of the seventeenth century life leases became increasingly popular. A life lease would not expire until certain individuals, identified by name in the lease, had died. The number of 'lives' inserted in a lease varied from one to four or even five, with three very common. Catholics were barred from receiving leases for lives for much of the 1700s; as a result of legislation passed in 1778 landlords were permitted to issue Catholics with life leases (up to a maximum of five 'lives').[8] Usually a life lease included a concurrent term of years. So one will find, for example, a lease for three lives or 21 years; the lease remained valid for whichever was of the longer duration. Unless the farmer was very unfortunate, the 'lives' usually outlasted terms of 21 or even 31 years.

Maguire's analysis the leases issued by the Downshire estate in County Down revealed that the possession of a lease for lives was certainly advantageous for the farmer. The average duration of 43 leases for lives concerning the Banbridge portion of the Downshire estate was 54 years – only six expired in less than 40 years, while 17 lasted for more than 60 years. Of the 180 leases for lives in existence in 1801 on the Kilwarlin portion of the Downshire estate 78 were still valid 36 years later with their average duration being 68 years.[9] For the tenant a lease for lives was a prized possession for it gave him and his family a greater degree of security of tenure. For the landlord the issuing of leases for lives not only created a solid and generally contented tenantry, it also allowed him to flex his muscles in parliamentary elections (see Chapter 8).

It would appear that in many instances – indeed, perhaps most instances prior to the nineteenth century – the choice of the lives was the privilege of the tenant. Since the tenant often named members of his immediate or wider family, such leases are very useful for genealogists. The ages of the persons named as lives were stated frequently, especially if they were children; this information is especially helpful in the absence of church registers. On very rare occasions the date of birth of one of the lives may appear in a lease.

Nonetheless, it must be acknowledged that very often the lives named in a lease were not family members. From the middle of the eighteenth century members of the royal family were often named as lives. Royal lives and 'ordinary' lives were sometimes used together. The tenants presumably did not have many objections to the choice of members of the royal family since these individuals, with a better diet and health care, were more likely to reach old age (the Prince of Wales (the future George IV), who was named as a life in many leases from the early 1760s onwards, lived until 1830). From the landlord's perspective, the choice of prominent public figures meant that it was easier to keep track of their status.

The leasing practices on an estate varied a great deal and depended, among other things, on the landlord's personal preferences and the circumstances of the time. It was also accepted that a landlord could not issue leases on better terms than he himself held his property. So someone, say a middleman, who was in possession of certain lands for a term of years could not issue leases for lives. In his study of County Cork, Donnelly noted that the enfranchisement of Catholics in 1793 resulted in many more life leases being issued. He noted that 83% of Lord Midleton's rental in 1828 was paid by tenants in possession of leases for three lives.[10]

In the mid-1700s the eighth Earl of Abercorn, a cautious landlord who had no particular desire to interfere in Irish politics, was reluctant to grant long leases to tenants on his estate in counties Donegal and Tyrone. His nephew and heir, the first Marquess of Abercorn, however, was politically ambitious and adopted the practice of issuing leases for one life to his tenant farmers (as well as including a concurrent term of years). This approach was continued by his own heir, his grandson the second Marquess. Therefore, the lease issued to Robert Rolleston in 1835 was for one life or 21 years. The individual named as the life was John James Hamilton Humphreys, the eldest son of John Humphreys of Milltown House, County Tyrone.[11] Humphreys senior was the agent for the Abercorn estate and a man who exercised considerable influence in the area for half a century. In this case the life in the lease is of little genealogical value. John James Hamilton Humphreys was aged 18 when the lease was drawn up and he lived for another 55 years before his death in London in 1890 – obviously a good choice of life for the farmers on the Abercorn estate issued with leases at this time.

One of the challenges for landlords and their agents was keeping track of the status of the lives named in leases. Many people named as lives emigrated to America or another part of the world. In addition, women named as lives acquired a new surname on marriage.[12] A lease to Edward McKeesick for land in Ballycormick, County Antrim, is endorsed: 'The life in this lease died in the Island of Jamaica in West-Indies and consequently this lease expired, at Nov. 1835' (PRONI, D2977/3A/3/2/4/5A). See below under Correspondence for examples of the pursuit of relevant information.

Some landlords introduced measures to deal with these eventualities. For example, in County Antrim in the early nineteenth century Lord and Lady Mark Kerr issued leases that stipulated that if the life named in the lease was absent from Ireland for three years at one time he would be considered as if actually dead. A clause in the lease to Robert Rolleston stipulated that if John James Hamilton Humphreys left the United Kingdom (at this time Great Britain and Ireland) without the permission of the Marquess of Abercorn then his life would be considered null and void and the lease would terminate at the end of the term of 21 years.

Depending on the terms of the lease, a lease for lives could be updated on the passing of each life by inserting a new name on the payment of a renewal fine. The renewals might have been limited to a certain number of lives, though often they were renewable forever. Such a lease was in effect a grant in perpetuity so long as the tenant wished to renew it. When a new life was added to the lease details of their age and relationship to the lessee might be included. John Ainsworth provided the following example of a renewable life lease, which at the time of writing, was in private custody.[13]

> Lease by Edward [Brabazon], Earl of Meath, to Talbott Keene of Dublin, gent., of a piece of land, with the new house and stables built on it, near Bray; for lives, renewable for ever, of tenant and of his sons Thomas and Christopher Keene. 1693.
> Renewed to Katherine Keene, the tenant's widow, for the additional life of Gilbert Keene, another son of the said Talbott Keene. 1700.

Renewed to James Medlicott of Ardscoll, County Kildare, esq., for the additional life of John Bagot (aged 7), second son of John Bagot of Nurney, County Kildare, esq. 1749.

Renewed to the abovenamed, for the additional life of James Medlicott, son of Edward Medlicott of Dunmurry, gent. 1759.

Renewed to the abovenamed, for the additional life of William Burgh of Bert, County Kildare, esq. 1762.

Renewed to the abovenamed, for the additional life of Frederick William Hoysted, son of James Hoysted of Foxhill, County Kildare, gent. on the death of Gilbert Keene, the last of the original tenant's family. 1764.

## 4.4.4 The payment of rent

A lease specified the rent that was due to the landlord by the tenant. The rent was usually paid twice a year on what were known as gale days. The rent generally stayed the same for the duration of the term, though in some instances there were incremental increases, which were specified in the lease. For example, a lease issued in 1713 for a farm in County Tyrone stated that the rent for the first seven years was to be £8 per annum, for the next seven years £9, and £10 thereafter (PRONI, D3007/A/13/3). The landlord's agent may have collected the rent in person or the tenant might have been required to bring it to the estate office.

The rent was usually a cash sum, though earlier leases often specified additional 'in-kind' payments, such as livestock, crops and so many days of service to the landlord. The currency was frequently specified since prior to 1826 separate English and Irish currencies were in use in Ireland (in 1701 the ratio was fixed at £108 6s 7d Irish to £100 English). Occasionally the landlord might waive the rent for a tenant in straitened circumstances or who had carried out some particular service for him. There are also examples of a small nominal rent, known as a peppercorn rent, being charged. In addition, there may also have been other payments expected of the tenant, such as receiver's fees (usually calculated as a percentage of the rent) which went to the agent or rent collector.

The rent payable by Robert Rolleston was set at £71 6s and 3½d. This was to be paid in two equal amounts on 1 May and 1 November. It was made clear in the lease that this sum was regardless of whatever others charges were liable on the land, such as parish and county taxes.

The lease also specified what would happen if Robert fell behind in his rent payments: the landlord reserved the right to enter the farm and remove anything that would allow him to recover the outstanding rent owed to him; ultimately the landlord had the power to repossess the farm. In reality, this approach was usually adopted on the Abercorn estate when the tenant was very far behind in his rent payments and there was little prospect of the arrears ever being paid. Nonetheless, there was always the threat that it could happen.[14]

## 4.4.5 The conditions to be fulfilled by the lessee

Leases included a broad range of clauses requiring the tenant to carry out, or desist from, various activities. The conditions to be fulfilled by the lessee could include the construction of a house on his property, often with clear instructions as to its dimensions, roof covering, etc. The creation of gardens and orchards could also be promoted through the clauses contained in leases. Leases often required the farmer to ensure that the boundaries of his farm were distinct and to erect appropriate fences or plant hedges if his farm was not already divided into fields. Tenants who did not fulfil the conditions imposed on them – which were often time-limited – were liable to a penalty of one form or another. A 1703 lease for Belgree, County Meath, included a covenant stipulating that a penalty of £5 per foot would be imposed for building a 'Popish Masse house or Presbiterian meeting house'.[15] Some leases included clauses that can be regarded as inducements to act or behave in a certain way. For instance, in a lease of 1700 granted by Viscount Charlemont the tenant was to have a reduction in some of his payments if he and his family and sub-tenants attended the Established Church on Sundays and other days appointed by the government (PRONI, D859/6).

The clauses in Robert Rolleston's lease included covenants forbidding him from removing manure from his farm, cutting turf without permission, and burning his land (an agricultural practice being discouraged at this time). He was not allowed to 'erect or build, or cause or permit to be erected or built, any huts or cabins' on his farm without the sanction of his landlord. Robert was required to 'as often as is necessary, perambulate, ascertain and make up the mears and bounds' of his farm, and 'keep, uphold and preserve the same'. One of the rights reserved by the Marquess was to enter the farm with 'horses and dogs, guns and nets, to hunt and hawk, fish and fowl'. Robert covenanted to preserve the game on his land and to prosecute poachers or other trespassers. An entirely handwritten clause in Robert Rolleston's lease stated that the Marquess of Abercorn reserved the right to enter the farm to cut a canal or other water course through it with the tenant being offered a proportionate reduction in his rent for any land lost as a result.

It was usual for the landlord to stipulate the mill to which the tenant was to take his corn (generally this referred to oats). In other words, the tenant could not take his corn to a mill of his own choosing, but rather to the mill his landlord directed him to use. In Robert's case, he was compelled to use the mill or mills within the manor of Donelong. At this time there were several mills in the manor of Donelong; the lease does not specifiy which of the mills he was to use, but the closest to his farm was at Drumgauty, a little over a mile away. Robert was expected to do 'suit and service' to the manor court of Donelong (see below for manor court records), though by this time the manor court system across Ireland was falling into abeyance and there is little evidence for the workings of the manor courts on the Abercorn estate in the early nineteenth century.

Tenants often wished to sub-let their property, or part of it, to a third party. A lease generally included a clause concerning the sub-letting of the holding. Sometimes this was strictly forbidden, though on other occasions it was allowed on the payment of an additional sum of money to the landlord. Robert Rolleston was not allowed to mortgage, grant or sub-let the farm without the written permission of the Marquess. He was permitted, however, to bequeath his farm under the terms of his will, but the lease stipulated that this was to one person only. If Robert did sub-let part of his farm to another without the sanction of his landlord the penalty was severe – he was to pay an additional £35 13s 2d on top of his existing rent.

## 4.5 Lease books

Lease books can be among the most useful of estate papers as far as genealogy is concerned. They record in summary form the information contained in the original leases, such as the name of the lessee, the date the lease commenced, the location and extent of the holding, and the rent payable on it. More detailed lease books can include the names of the lives in the life leases and the status of those lives (i.e. whether alive or dead and, if alive, where resident). Often covering an entire estate, they can be a much quicker way of finding information on a tenant farmer than searching for an individual lease.

There is a superb set of lease books for the Downshire estate produced in the late 1700s and 1800s (PRONI, D671/A/4). The early nineteenth-century lease book of the Kilwarlin portion of the estate in County Down serves as a good example. The details concerning each tenancy are in tabulated format (though the data provided do not follow the tabulation strictly), with the following information recorded: townland, tenant, acreage, term, commencement of lease, lives and ages when granted, rent and remarks. The column for remarks is particularly informative on the status of the lives in the leases. The following excerpts concern the lives in leases for the townland of Edenecullo (Edenticullo in Hillsborough parish):

> John Morrison died in 1787
> Ann Smith now the wife of John Walker late of Drumlogh went to
>     America in 1801
> Patrick Forde went to America 30 years ago
> Jacob and Jeremiah Smith in America – the latter heard from lately
> Agnes McClure (now Wright) lives in Cabra

The genealogical value of the information detailed is immediately apparent, especially for an era before deaths were officially registered and when there are very few records of emigration.

## 4.6 Rentals and accounts

Rentals, rent rolls or rent books – in practice, the terms are often used interchangeably – record the rent payments made by the tenants to their landlord. They are generally organised by year (rents were usually paid half-yearly) or with several years covered by the same document. In their simplest form they may only include the total value of the rents collected in each townland, or even just a list of names of tenants and the rent each paid. More usual will be rentals that name the tenants, identify the location of their holdings, and state the rent paid (which could include in-kind payments as well as cash sums). Still more detailed rentals can include such information as the terms on which the farms were held, e.g. 'at will' or by a written lease.

The format of a rental can range from a loose sheet of paper to a substantial bound volume, with the data on the tenant, his holding, the rent due and the rent paid laid out in columns across a double-page spread. The farms may be numbered and these numbers might relate to an estate map (which may or may not survive). The arrangement of the townlands within the rental can be alphabetical or geographical. Some rental volumes include an alphabetical index to the tenants. It should be noted that a rental may not record the names of all the tenants of a particular holding. Often the name of a tenant in a rental will be followed by the term 'and partners' or something similar. It may be the case that a later rental will name all of the partners, but it must be accepted that these 'silent' partners often remain unknown.

Details of the individuals named as lives in life leases may be found in some rentals. A 1774 rental for the Langford estate in Antrim gives the date each lease was granted and the terms of the lease (PRONI, D2624/4A). Many of these were issued in 1726 and usefully the rental includes the names of the lives in the original leases who were still living (quite a few in fact) in October 1775, almost half a century later. Further annotations reveal other details. For example, it was recorded that Mary Kelso, a life in a lease for a farm in Craigarogan, died in March 1776, while there was a note that Hugh Brown, a life in a lease for a farm in Ballymather, had written a letter home from Philadelphia on 20 September 1775 – clearly the family had produced this letter as evidence that Hugh was still alive (and, therefore, the lease was still valid).

Occasionally rentals may contain additional details such as a change in occupancy and the reason for this, or whether or not the tenants had fulfilled or failed to fulfil the covenants in their leases. Therefore, rentals can be helpful in identifying the circumstances in which a tenant left a farm. The following excerpts concerning the Mohill estate, County Leitrim, have been taken from a rental of the property of the Earl of Leitrim:

Clooncarne Anthony Kerrigan, 'Gone to America & left his wife & children in possession'

Garrett McDermott, 'John his son a leading Ribbonman[,] very troublesome people'

Corriscoffy    James Lannan, 'This man transported for stealing a horse[,] left a woman in possession'

Cashell    Patt Winter, 'Winter sold to Edwd Reilly who has been transported for firing at a policeman when detected breaking a House at night'

In the case of the above Edward Reilly, we can explore the circumstances of his removal from Ireland further through the Transportation Database available on the NAI website.[16] This reveals that Reilly, aged 23, was tried on 1 March 1847 for an assault on a dwelling house, and was sentenced to seven years' transportation. The ship transferring him to Australia was the *Hyderabad*.

Tenants who fell behind in their rent payments were said to be in arrears. Some rentals included columns to indicate how much the tenant owed in arrears, though separate listings of arrears were also maintained. A tenant who fell significantly behind in the payment of his rent was liable for eviction. Tenants were also evicted for failing to fulfil the clauses in their leases, while other removals were to clear land for an extension of the landlord's demesne or to create larger areas for grazing livestock. A note on the eviction of a tenant and the reasons for it may be recorded in a rental.

In addition, some estate collections include records relating specifically to evictions. For example, the papers deriving from the Brownlow estate in County Armagh include a volume from the 1830s listing ejectments served, with tenants' names and townlands, the amount of rent due, the date of the lease and the decree (D1928/E/1/1). 'Notices to quit' issued to tenants can also be found in some estate collections. For example, along with a rent arrears book, 1849–50, for the estate of Lucius O'Brien, Baron Inchiquin, in County Clare, there is a list of tenants under notice to quit (NLI, MSS 14,740–14,741). Among a collection of items in the King-Harman Papers relating mainly to the Newcastle property, Ballymahon, County Longford, is a return of the evictions, 1849–69 (PRONI, D4168/D/3/3). The ejectment books for the Fitzwilliam estate in counties Wexford and Wicklow are particularly extensive, covering the period 1845–86 (NLI, MSS 4972, 4992). The reasons for issuing notices to quit to the tenants of this estate included the non-payment of rent, sub-letting and poor farming practices.

Rentals may include additional notes or commentary about particular circumstances affecting the estate or even the country more broadly. The rental of the Red House estate in County Louth of 1849 was compiled during the Great Famine and includes a memorandum concerning the ability of various classes of tenant to cope with the present situation; the memorandum recommends the removal of a whole class of farmers/labourers, and enlarging the holdings of the most industrious farmers (PRONI, D4088/1/2/1). Rental volumes often have additional loose sheets of paper within them relating to various matters, such as letters and notices to quit. Within the rental volume of the manor of Derrywoon, County Tyrone, 1794–1809, is an undated sheet titled 'List of poor people in Derrywoon' (PRONI, D623/C/4/7).

Printed rentals are available for some estates and these were generally produced in advance of the sale of the estate or a major re-letting of the farms in it. Generally speaking, the information is presented in tabular format. Digital copies of some of these printed rentals can be viewed via the Online Catalogue of the National Library of Ireland (catalogue.nli.ie). An example is the document catalogued as 'Peremptory sale: rent roll of the estate of the defendant, James O'Reilly, Esquire … pursuant to the order of the 27th day of June, 1815, to be sold, or a competent part thereof … pursuant to notice in the public newspapers on Wednesday 24 January 1816.' This includes a rent roll for the townland of Baltrasna, County Meath, naming the tenants, giving the acreage of each holding, the rent, and the date and term of the lease. Similar rentals can be found in other archives. Limerick Archives has digitised a printed rental concerning certain lands in the Courtenay estate (P23/1). The rental names the lands, the tenants, and provides the dates and terms of the leases. The lives in the leases are named and in many instances their ages are given.

Rentals may also have been created for bogs or mosses and these were produced to keep a proper record of turf-cutting by the tenants. Bogs were valuable resources and turf was an important source of fuel for rural families. From the landlord's perspective, he could generate additional income from the rents charged for access to a bog and it also allowed him to control who could make use of it. The word turbary was used in connection with the right to cut peat or turf in a certain area of bogland. In the early nineteenth century the government established a commission which investigated how over one million acres of bog could be transformed into agricultural land. The minute book of the Commissioners for the Improvement of Bogs in Ireland, 1809–13, is in the National Archives of Ireland (Private Accession 1137/77), and has been published with other material in *Documents Relating to the Bogs Commissioners, 1809–1813*, edited by Arnold Horner (IMC, 2019).[17]

In addition to rentals, other sets of accounts appear within estate collections. Often these are of limited genealogical value and relate primarily to expenditure by members of the landowning family. Occasionally, however, items of real interest will turn up. The cash books maintained by the agent of the Caledon estate in counties Armagh and Tyrone include many references to monies advanced to the tenants to assist with improvements to farms, loans to buy livestock, and even donations towards funeral expenses (e.g. the cash book of 1845–50, PRONI, D2433/A/11/3). For instance, on 20 March 1845 Robert Lee received a donation of two shillings and six pence from Lady Caledon's account towards the cost of burying his child. A day later Sam Harvey was given 10 shillings from Lord Caledon's account to help pay his passage to America.

## 4.7 Maps, surveys and valuations

Maps form an important element in most estate collections and can vary from single sheets of parchment to substantial bound volumes. Early estate maps were often pictorial and included representations of houses, mills and other landscape features. Many early maps can be considered important works of art in their own right as the cartographer showed off his skills. Archaeological sites might also be shown, such as megalithic tombs and ringforts, some of which may have been destroyed subsequently through agricultural improvement schemes. As cartographic techniques became ever more sophisticated, so the accuracy of estate maps became ever greater and skilled surveyors were much in demand.

In the opening decades of the seventeenth century Thomas Raven was the foremost cartographer working in Ireland. He prepared maps of the estates of the London companies in County Londonderry in 1622, which include the names of the householders in the settlements founded by the companies. The originals are in Lambeth Palace,

London, but there are coloured replica drawings in PRONI (T510).[18] In 1625, Raven prepared detailed maps of Sir James Hamilton's estate in north-east County Down, which name many of the tenants. The original set of maps is in North Down Museum, but a copy is available in PRONI (T870). Other work carried out by Raven included a survey of the Essex estate in County Monaghan in 1634.[19]

Information on map-makers in Ireland and their maps can be found in a variety of publications. J.H. Andrews has written extensively on this subject and his books include: *Plantation Acres: an Historical Study of the Irish Land Surveyor and his Maps* (1985); *Shapes of Ireland: Maps and their Makers 1564–1839* (1997); and *Maps in those Days: Cartographic Methods before 1850* (2009). Brief biographical information can be found in Peter Eden (ed.), *Dictionary of Land Surveyors and Local Cartographers of Great Britain and Ireland, 1550–1850* (1975), and Sarah Bendall (ed.), *Dictionary of Land Surveyors and Local Map-makers of Great Britain and Ireland 1530–1850* (2 vols, 1997). See also Jacinta Prunty, *Maps and Map-making in Local History* (2004).

Estate maps served a number of useful purposes for those commissioning them. In the first place landowners were anxious to ensure that the boundaries of their estates were clearly known. With so much land changing ownership in seventeenth-century Ireland disputes over the limits of estates were inevitable. Likewise, it was essential that the individual holdings in an estate were known. Local knowledge was invaluable, but for landlords and their agents having accurate maps to hand was vital. Depending on the reasons for the production of a map, it was sometimes more important for them to know the boundaries of a farm, and the quality of the land contained within it, than the names of the occupying tenants, which in part explains why many sets of estate maps concentrate on the former and exclude the latter altogether. From a genealogical perspective of course, maps that name tenants and show the location of their farms are the most useful. The value of such maps lies in the fact that they can help a researcher to pinpoint where exactly an ancestor lived. This is especially helpful prior to the mid-1800s and the creation of the detailed maps of the Tenement Valuation (see Chapter 6).

Estate maps have been the subject of numerous investigations, the results of which have appeared in various publications, including local journals and histories.[20] Few are on the scale of the massive 300-page volume titled, *The Drapers' Company, Maps of the Estate: County of Londonderry, 1857–1858*, which was published in 2014 by the Ballinascreen Historical Society. This book reproduces in colour three volumes of maps held by the Drapers' Company in London. These maps were produced in an attempt to resolve discrepancies between an earlier survey of the estate and the Ordnance Survey maps of the area; in fact the new estate maps of the late 1850s were created using the most recent Ordnance Survey maps. The maps are hand-coloured to distinguish between the different holdings in each townland and the individual fields are numbered with reference tables correlating the fields and holdings to the tenants. The extent of each farm is given in both Irish and statute acres.

Due to their visual attractiveness, estate maps have featured prominently in digitisation projects. For example, Mayo Library has digitised several cartographic collections, including nineteenth-century maps of the Lynch Blosse estate in the baronies of Carra and Clanmorris, which can be perused via an excellent map viewer.[21] The extensive Longfield Map Collection of *c.* 1770–1840, which includes maps from every county in Ireland except Kerry, can be viewed on the NLI website. Wexford County Archive has made available a volume of maps of the Cliffe estate in counties Cork, Kilkenny, Meath and Wexford, dating from 1822.[22]

In addition to commissioning a set of maps of his property, a landlord might commission a written survey or valuation of it. Amongst other uses, this would be used as a guide to improving the estate in order to maximise the income from it, and may have been commissioned when leases were due for renewal. Often these surveys contain little of genealogical interest, as they concentrate on land quality and use. For example, William Starrat of Strabane worked extensively as a surveyor in west Ulster in the first half of the eighteenth century, but there is little information on the tenant farmers in his surveys. Nonetheless, while not containing the sort of detail that will allow the family tree to be extended, such surveys can provide a glimpse into the world of our forebears and should still be consulted.

Maurice Collis was a very active surveyor in the 1840s, producing data-rich statistical investigations of a number of estates, including the properties of the Grocers' Company and the Irish Society in County

Londonderry, the Ballyvaughan estate of the Duke of Buckingham in County Clare, and the estate of the Marquess of Londonderry in County Down.[23] Between 1839 and 1845 Collis prepared a detailed survey of the Trinity College Dublin estates, the results of which are contained in 16 volumes – 14 volumes for separate estates and two volumes of summaries (TCD, MUN/V/79). Collis went into great detail on many aspects of life on the estates and his survey includes details such as housing conditions, farm sizes, livestock, roads and sources of fuel. The data collected on the people living on the College lands is listed under the following headings: age, literacy, occupation, religion, sex and marital status.[24]

Other surveys and valuations, however, do contain much genealogical information. An extraordinarily detailed and extensive survey is the 'View of the archbishopric of Armagh', 1703 (PRONI, T848). The 'View' is a neatly written survey of the extensive property owned by the archbishop of Armagh which was prepared by Thomas Ashe at the beginning of the eighteenth century. These lands were mainly to be found in counties Armagh, Londonderry, Louth and Tyrone, with smaller portions in Antrim, Down and Meath. The information provided is of an incredibly detailed nature. The name of the tenant of each of the townlands is given, together with the names of the undertenants. In addition, the extent of the townland, the type of structures standing on it (such as dwellings, farm out-buildings, bridges, churches, taverns and mills), the degree of agricultural improvement, and antiquities are noted.

A very interesting volume, titled 'Observations made upon the Rt Honble the Lord Malton's estate in Ireland' (in County Wicklow) and dating from 1729, includes the names of the chief tenants and some fascinating commentary on the inhabitants (NLI, MS 6094). The following extracts are taken from it:

Mullins
It is a good farm for graising young cattle, and all inhabited by Romans except Henry Turner whose father was a Papist in King James' time and a Protestant in King William's.

Whiterock or Carrigalter
It was formerly sett to one Henry Manwaring who was the person that improv'd the farm and he hath a grand daur who was bred a

Protestant and will make a good tent for the farm. Her name is Jane Nevill.

Kockeen
The under tent [John] Patrickson is an industrious man, a good tent. Hath several sons, bred them all to industry. ... There are few better tents in the kingdom that Patrickson is.

A good example of a late nineteenth-century valuation is that of the Bruff estate in County Limerick, part of the property of Lord Carbery, prepared in the autumn of 1889 (PRONI, D3168/18/9). The archivist who catalogued this estate collection suggested that the valuation may have been carried out to ascertain 'fair rents' and dissuade the tenants from appealing to the Land Courts for a reassessment of their rent payments (see Chapter 9). The descriptive comments about the tenants are revealing of their circumstances, as the following excerpt shows:

James Dooley is a sporting character, and the only fine stock he had on the farm was a brace of the finest greyhounds I ever saw ... he has a very poor small house, mud walls, thatched, not at all suitable for a kennel for those beautiful dogs, though they and he, undoubtedly sleep together in it and are living and thriving.

## 4.8 Correspondence and tenants' petitions

The correspondence between a landlord and his agent can be of immense genealogical value. The best collection of eighteenth-century estate correspondence relates to the Abercorn estate in west Tyrone and east Donegal (PRONI, D623/A). Most of the letters were written by the eighth Earl of Abercorn and his estate agents, John McClintock, Nathaniel Nisbett, John Colhoun, John Sinclair, John Hamilton and James Hamilton. The eighth Earl was an absentee landlord who lived most of his life in London and only rarely visited his Irish estates. However, few absentee landowners can have known more about their estates as the Earl knew about his. The letters cover a broad range of subjects and relate to all aspects of the estate's management. The correspondence was transcribed primarily by Dr Brian Trainor, a former Director of PRONI, as part of his recuperation from an accident and the letters can now be read on the PRONI eCatalogue.[25]

Estate correspondence can be particularly interesting when it concerned the status of the 'lives' in a lease. On 1 May 1833 William Blacker, agent for the Gosford estate in County Armagh, wrote to a Mrs Whiteside in Dublin enquiring about two brothers named Robinson who had been named as the lives in a number of leases:

The reason why I am obliged to trouble you on the present occasion is that I see in some of Lord Gosford's leases the names of Andrew Robinson and Arthur Robinson brother, sons of James Robinson then of Markethill, these leases granted in the year 1760 and it appears the one was 7 years old at the time and the other 5 years old. On enquiry I find that Mrs McCreery of Markethill is the only person [who] could tell anything whatever about them. She says they both left this country for America about 35 years ago and that she never heard of them since but referred me to you for further information. I will feel obliged as soon as convenient that you will have the goodness to acquaint me when you last heard from them and whether they are dead or living. If alive as I should suppose they are not, they would be near about 80 years of age (PRONI, D1606/5/1).

A few days later a reply was received from John Whiteside, writing on behalf of his mother:

My mother has handed me your letter and after every enquiry she directs me to mention that her uncle Andrew she believes to be dead. Her uncle Arthur settled many years ago in London and attained some eminence as a medical man. A few years ago she heard he was alive and well. His address my mother cannot give but I apprehend enquiries might easily be made in London. He had retired from practice and was living in a genteel quarter of London with a son and two daughters. The Robinsons were all long livers. The Rev. John Robinson of Dublin who was much older than either of the brothers you mention only died here about one year since. My mother is in excellent health and begs to [be] remembered to you and her old friends in Markethill. She has 10 grandchildren and yet seems to be growing young.

In some instances, enquiries were pursued overseas in order to ascertain if a particular individual was still alive. Within the Antrim estate papers is a letter of 1875 from Charles Black in Chicago, confirming that he was the individual named as the life in the leases for farms in Kilmore, Glenariff:

> I believe & hereby certify that I am the life in the leases of the lands held by the tenants on the townland of Kilmore. I hope this letter will satisfy [the agent]. I have very good health thank God considering my age and hope to live for some time yet … many of my old friends who know my writing can satisfy … that this is written by myself (PRONI, D2977/3A/4/75/13).

Correspondence may also reveal details on the emigration of tenants from the estate for one reason or another. The following extracts from the copy out-letter-book of the agents of the Drapers' Company in County Londonderry provide an insight into the manner in which particular situations were dealt with (PRONI, D3632/G/5/2/2). On 1 April 1848 the agents wrote:

> In reporting upon Charles Kelly's memorial of Inniscarn on the 3rd of March last we made a mistake in our calculation of the amount it would require to take himself and large family to America. We stated we thought £15 would be sufficient with £10 he had of balance of sale of farm but the passage money will take about £40. Therefore if the Company will kindly add £15 more to what they have already been pleased to grant the entire of the family will be able to emigrate but if not he must leave a portion of them behind him which would be a dead weight upon this locality. We therefore respectively recommend an additional £15 to be allowed him. It would be a great matter to the estate to have so large a party removed off the estate.

However, on 23 May 1848 the agents wrote: 'The reason why we did not recommend more than £15 to be given to Charles Kelly of Inniscarn at first was that we had an expectation that his sons who were in America might send him some money which they have not done.'

Difficulties arising from the eviction of tenants can also be found as the following item of correspondence of 1882 from the copy out-letter-book of James Crossle, agent for the Verner estate in counties Armagh and Tyrone, reveals:

The farm of Donnelly in Ballynahaye was evicted more than two years ago on the expiration of the legal 6 months for redemption. We sold the land to a man named Dougan alongside of it who paid all the arrears and the balance was given to Donnelly and we hold his receipt for it. You will recollect some ruffians broke the tombstone in Aghnagar Chapel which Dougan had placed over his father and mother. We got him the price of it at last assizes, £7. They threatened to shoot him but he did not mind them; all are Romans (PRONI, D236/488/3).

The correspondence of an estate agent may occasionally be found separately from the other papers of an estate. For instance, NLI holds two registers of letters received by the agent of Marquess Conyngham in County Clare, 1868–87 (MSS 19,901–19,902), which are not part of the main estate archive held by this institution. Armagh County Museum holds the letter-books of the Boyle estate office in Armagh and these were used by Sean Barden in his book, *The Last Countess: an Exploration of an Estate Agent's Letters* (2002), the countess in question being Anna Lucy, the wife of the third Earl of Charlemont. The letters were written in the period 1890–99 and nearly all of them were penned by Hugh Boyle. The letter-books kept by the firms of solicitors acting on behalf of landowning families are another important source of information on tenant farmers. Through the letter-books in the collection of the law firm of Wilson & Simms, based in Strabane, I learned that in the 1890s my great-great-grandfather Thomas Roulston was threatened with eviction by the Abercorn estate for falling behind in his rent (PRONI, D2298/A–B).

Tenants' petitions comprise an important sub-category within estate correspondence.[26] These take the form of letters to the landlord, asking or even imploring him to consider a particular request, such as a rent abatement. The Shanbally Castle estate papers, found within the Timothy Looney Papers held by the University of Limerick Archives (www.ul.ie/library/looney-papers), include an extensive run of correspondence from or relating to the tenants from the 1890s and opening years of the twentieth century. The letters concern a range of issues, such as the payment of rents and applications for loans. Other letters concern disputes over such things as boundaries. These have been arranged alphabetically by the name of the tenant and in some cases there are upwards of 20 items concerning a single tenant (P43/209–378).[27]

Tenant application or petition books may be found in some estate collections. For example there is an extensive collection of these books for the Lismore estate, including an application book, containing requests for alterations or improvements to property within the estates of the Duke of Devonshire in County Waterford, 1861–3 (NLI, MS 7193). For the estate of Lord Farnham in County Cavan there are two volumes of summaries of applications and representations made by tenants and others, and decisions made in respect of these, 1832–60 (NLI, MSS 3117–3118).

The following examples, both dating from 1810, concern that part of the estate of Trinity College Dublin in the barony of Kilmacrenan in County Donegal. The College leased this property to the Earl of Leitrim, who in turn sub-let it to hundreds of farmers. In the summer of that year William Allen wrote to the Provost and Fellows, seeking their support in his dispute with Lord Leitrim, who was attempting to evict Allen from his farm (TCD, MUN/P/24/397). Allen claimed that he had spent over £600 in improvements to the farm, including building a flax mill. The previous Lord Leitrim had promised him a renewal of his lease, but he died before it was finalised. The other petition, dated 14 Sept 1810, was submitted by Hugh Magran, who stated that he had spent over £300 on improving his farm, including building a dwelling house and houses for his own undertenants, as well as tree plantations, etc (TCD, MUN/P/24/401). However, although he had held a lease from the previous Earl, he had been turned out of his holding by the current Lord Leitrim.

In addition to petitions by or on behalf of a single tenant farmer, there are also numerous examples of petitions submitted by associations of tenants. These may have been prompted by difficult circumstances caused by harvest failure or other natural disaster and often the tenants sought a reduction in their rent. In October 1903 around 50 tenants on the Callowhill estate in County Fermanagh owned by the Earl of Erne signed a petition in which they stated that

> ... this year 1903 has been the worst for the farmer in living memory and ... it will be almost impossible to make ends meet. In view of the continuous rain in the spring, summer and harvest, crops have been lost; potatoes, hay and turf lost to the farmer – potatoes a complete failure. No sale of livestock at anything like a paying price; the prospect is dismal; not feeding stuff to keep them to the spring. We

... humbly put before your Lordship that ye may give a reduction in the rent at the coming gale day ... (PRONI, D1939/11/10/3).

Around 1790 the Rt Hon. John Foster received a petition signed by some 100 'buyers of grain and farmers attending the Market of Drogheda' (PRONI, D562/1426). The signatories were protesting at a proposed legislation which would require sellers of grain to bring as a sample a barrel at least instead of the customary pocketful. Other petitions to a landowner may have been prompted by a desire to improve facilities of one form or another available to the tenants. Returning to the Trinity College archive, in June 1860 the College received a petition from 49 householders of Laghey in the barony of Tirhugh, County Donegal, requesting assistance in establishing a school (TCD, MUN/P/24/460).

Landowners and their agents responded in various ways to the petitions they received, sometimes granting the requests in whole or in part, or on other occasions simply ignoring them. There may be records to indicate the decisions made (as in the case of the Farnham estate noted above). A fascinating document is the detailed report by Richard Wilson, agent for Lady Londonderry in response to a petition from the tenants of the Glencloy area of County Antrim alleging that their rents were higher than Lord Antrim's tenants, 1862; the report gives details of the circumstances and holdings of each of the tenants who signed the petition (PRONI, D2977/5/1/8/51).

Communications between farmers and landlords could also be in the form of proposals from the former for new or renewed tenancies. Dating from c. 1730 is a summary of the proposals received from tenants of the Balfour estate for lands where the leases had expired (PRONI, D1939/17/10/58). For instance, Francis Graham indicated that for a farm in Coolaran he was prepared to 'build a house of lime and stone, forty foot long & ten foot in side wall, the front well shafted, together with convenient offices', as well as enclose the farm and plant an orchard of half an acre in extent within three years. Proposals from tenants can also be found within the surviving records of the Grandison estate in County Waterford, 1726–64 (PRONI, T3131/C/6). One of the tenants, John Sisson, offered, in 1726, £23 rent for a 31-year lease of that part of Dromannabeg and the slate house in 'Dromanna' in which he lived 'to get a Letle bread in my old age'. The papers of the

Listowel estate in County Kerry include a list of 50 proposed tenants, giving character sketches, 1829 (PRONI, D585/53).

On special occasions in the life of the landowning family the tenants could come together to make a presentation to mark this. Among the Dufferin Papers are addresses from the Killyleagh tenantry in County Down offering congratulations on Lord Dufferin's forthcoming marriage, his appointment as Governor General of Canada, and welcoming him home on his return from Canada, 1862–79 (PRONI, D1071/H/B/K/106/1–4). When the Duke of Abercorn was appointed Lord Lieutenant of Ireland in 1874 (the second time he had held this position) the tenants of 'the ancient manor of Dunalong' presented him with a bound, illuminated address, containing their signatures.[28]

## 4.9 Manor court records

Many estates enjoyed the status of a manor as the result of the issuing of a royal patent. Under the provisions of such a patent, the landlord was empowered to hold manor courts to regulate the affairs of his estate. Tenants were obliged, under the terms of their leases, to attend the manor courts as directed. Disappointingly, only a relatively small number of manor court records exist. A good introduction to the subject is Ian Montgomery's article, 'The manorial courts of the earls of Antrim' in *Familia*, 16 (2000), pp 1–23, which discusses the range of manor court records and the functions of these courts.[29]

The court leet, also known as a 'view of frank-pledge', was originally a meeting of the freeholders of the manor called to exercise criminal jurisdiction. With the development of the criminal justice system and the rise of the magistracy, the importance of the court leet declined so that it became an administrative body. The court baron dealt with a range of civil actions, ranging from the recovery of small debts to trespasses and claims for damages. Usually a limit of 40 shillings was placed on the claims that the court could deal with. However, if a landlord wished to extend the power of his court he could have it made a 'court of record', which could deal with larger claims. The courts were presided over by an official called a seneschal who was appointed by the landlord. The courts may have been held in a purpose-built structure or other public building, but often they were held in private homes or in the open air.

The late seventeenth-century manor court records for the Thomond estate are a remarkably detailed set of documents. Covering the years 1666–86, the originals are found in the Petworth Papers, preserved at Petworth House and accessible through the West Sussex Record Office in Chichester (ref. MS C 10/7). They have been transcribed and published: S.C. O'Mahony, 'The manor courts of the Earl of Thomond 1666–1686', *Analecta Hibernica*, 38 (2004), pp 135–220.[30] The Thomond estate was huge, comprising eight manors in County Clare and one each in counties Limerick and Tipperary. In total, some 1,500 householders are named in these records, ranging from the tenants who sat on the jury to the plaintiffs and defendants. Addresses are also given, and occasionally status, e.g. 'gent', and occupation.

The panel from which the jury was drawn had to attend every meeting of the court; unless excused, absence resulted in a fine. Generally speaking, there were 10–15 jury members, with several individuals excused from jury service, and lists of absentees with the fines imposed on them. The matters that came before the courts included: the destruction of Lord Thomond's woodland; the alienation of lands by tenants; and the failure to fulfil covenants in leases, such as requirements to build houses, plant orchards, improve lands and grind corn at the manor mill. Disputes between tenants, sometimes culminating in fights and assaults, were also dealt with. The death of a tenant might be noted. For instance, at a court held at Killadysert on 15 October 1672 for the manor of Cruovraghan the following entry was made: 'We find Mathew Cuingam, tenant to the said earl in the lands of Erbull, is dead, and the land now in the possession of his wife'.

In the early nineteenth century questions were asked about the purpose and effectiveness of these courts and there were calls for them to be discontinued. The *Report from the Select Committee on Manor Courts, Ireland* (1838) revealed that there were just over 200 such courts across the island at that time with over half of them in Ulster. However, it was clear from the report that the manor court system was only a shadow of what it had once been. Manor courts were abolished officially in Ireland in 1859, though it would appear that at least one, Lisburn (Killultagh), continued to exercise a number of functions for some time after this.

The following is a summary listing of a selection of surviving records relating to manor courts in Ireland:

*Antrim estate, County Antrim*
Very extensive material relating to the manor courts of the Earls of Antrim (Dunluce, Glenarm and Oldstone or Kilconway), 1742–1847 – PRONI, D2977/23
J.B. Hamilton (ed.), *Records of the Court Leet for the Manor of Dunluce in the County of Antrim held in the Town of Ballymoney, 1798–1847* (1934)
Manor court account book relating to Cushendall, Ballycastle, Ballintoy, Bushmills areas, 1845–59 – PRONI, D2148/4

*Armagh archbishopric estate, County Armagh, etc*
T.G.F. Paterson (ed.), 'The Armagh manor court rolls ... 1625–1627', *Seanchas Ardmhacha*, 2:2 (1957), pp 295–322
Return of tenants of the town and manor of Armagh at a manor court, 1714 (typescript with an index) – Armagh County Museum, 28.2014.84; PRONI, DIO/4/22/1/1 (see also NLI, MS 3922, MS 7371)

*Brownlow estate, County Armagh*
Estate court books for the manor of Brownlowsderry, 1776–1847, and manor of Richmount, 1816–34; seneschal's court books for the manor of Brownlowsderry, 1827–32, and manor of Richmount, 1827–31; manor court manuscript copy out-letter-book, 1839–47 – PRONI, D1928/J

*Caledon estate, counties Armagh and Tyrone*
Manor court book of the Caledon estate, 1839–59 – D266/336

*Cashel, County Antrim*
Extracts from the manor court book of the manor of Cashel (Portglenone area), 1770–1825, printed in R.M. Sibbett, *On the Shining Bann: Records of an Ulster Manor* (1928), pp 78–143

*Donaghadee, County Down*
Court leet books of the manor of Donaghadee, *c.* 1770–91, 1792–9; volumes recording the business done at the Three Weeks Court of Record in and for the manor of Donaghadee, 1771–83, 1800–10 – PRONI, MIC321/1–4

*Doneraile, County Cork*
Papers relating to the manor court at Doneraile, 1814–31
 – NLI, MS 34,130/7

*Fleetwood, County Cork*
Copy of the court leet minute book of Fleetwood manor, 1765–1846
 – NAI, M 4921

*Fortescue, County Antrim*
Court book of the manor of Fortescue, Galgorm, 1811–45
 – PRONI, D822/1

*Goldsmiths' Company estate, County Londonderry*
'The severall inhabitants in the Mannor of Goldsmiths which was
    summoned to appear at a Court Leet held at New Buildings for the
    said mannor the 19th day of April 1716' – PRONI, MIC9B/12A

*Gormanston estate, counties Dublin and Meath*
Proceedings at the manor court of the 11th Viscount Gormanston,
    1772–87 – NLI, MS 44,455

*Killultagh, County Antrim*
Proceedings of courts leet, manor of Killultagh, Lisburn, 1853–85
 – PRONI, D427/23–4

*Lismore, County Waterford*
Volume of cases brought before the manor court of Lismore, 1837–41
 – NLI, MS 7204

*Mallow, County Cork*
Proceedings of the court leet of the manor of Mallow, 1622–5
 – NLI, MS 762

*Martry, County Meath*
Marion Rogan, 'The manor courts of Martry in County Meath: law
    and order on the Tisdall estate 1789 to 1792' in Brian Casey (ed.),
    *Lords, Land & Labourers: the Big Houses & Estates of Royal Meath*
    (2016), pp 71–91

*Mount Eagle Loyall, County Kerry*
Records of the courts baron and courts leet of the manor of Mount
    Eagle Loyall, including abstract of forfeitures, 1676–8; warrants for

levying fines with schedules of fines, 1676–80, and presentments, 1680 – National Library of Wales, 15473–84

*Rathfriland, County Down*
Process book of the civil bill court, in the manor of Rathfryland [sic], 1821–49; court book for the manor of Rathfryland, 1818–21 – PRONI, D875/6–7

*Salters' Company estate, County Londonderry*
List of the inhabitants of the Salters' estate (Magherafelt area) who ought to attend courts leet and baron, 1752, names arranged by townland – D4108/15F
Manor court book for the manor of Sal, 1837–42 – PRONI, D4108/1/23A

*Shirley estate, County Monaghan*
Manorial court book(?), recording arbitration and other decisions in disputes between landlord and tenant and between tenant and tenant, *c.* 1843–1848 – PRONI, D3531/M/6

*Thomond estate, counties Clare, Limerick and Tipperary*
S.C. O'Mahony (ed.), 'The manor courts of the Earl of Thomond 1666–1686', *Analecta Hibernica*, 38 (2004), pp 135–220

*Tullamore and Croghan, County Offaly*
Court books of the manor of Tullamore and Croghan, courts leet, 1765–1816, courts baron, 1795–1816 – NAI, M 5284–6

*Tyconnett and Seaforde, County Down*
Report of proceedings at a court leet of the manor of Tyconnett and Seaforde, 1810 – NAI, M 4939

## 4.10 Emigration schemes

As has been demonstrated already, estate records contain much information about the emigration of farming families to another part of the world, including the assistance offered by landlords to help some of their tenants emigrate. Patrick Duffy has observed: 'Emigration schemes may be represented as a management device to reduce the pressure on the land resources, to try to instigate some element of improvement on estates, and, of course, to reduce tax liability for impoverished tenants.'[31] Estates assisting significant numbers of people to emigrate in the mid-nineteenth century included the Fitzwilliam estate in Wicklow (6,000 1847–56), the Wandesforde estate in Kilkenny (5,800 1840–55), the Lansdowne estate in Kerry (over 3,300 1850–53), and the Palmerston estate in Sligo (some 4,300 1847–50).[32]

The papers of the Shirley estate in County Monaghan document some 1,300 people who were helped to emigrate from the estate to America, Canada, England and Australia between 1843 and 1854 (PRONI, D3531/P). The assistance offered to departing tenants could have included items of clothing, such as trousers, gowns, coats and shoes, as well as food, e.g. oatmeal, bacon, coffee (and a coffee pot) and sugar.[33] Exceptionally detailed records relating to the emigration of families from the Fitzwilliam estate in County Wicklow survive from the mid-1800s (NLI, MSS 4974–4975, 18,524) and these have been utilised by Jim Rees in several works, including *Fitzwilliam Tenants Listed in the Coolattin Estate Emigration, 1847–56* (1998) and *Surplus People: The Fitzwilliam Clearances, 1847–1856* (2000), reprinted as *Surplus People: From Wicklow to Canada* (2014).

Emigration schemes on the Crown estates were carried out in the mid-1800s under the direction of the Commissioners of Woods, Forests and Land Revenues of the Crown, whose office was in London and under whom the Quit Rent Office (QRO) in Dublin had operated since 1827. Some documentation relating to these schemes was sent to the QRO after the transfer of Crown land revenues to the Irish Free State in 1923. With the absorption of the QRO by the Land Commission, the QRO records were sent to the Public Record Office of Ireland (now NAI) in 1943. Material relating to the emigration schemes is available for the following estates: Ballykilcline, County Roscommon; Boughill, County Galway; Kilconcouse, County Offaly; Kingwilliamstown, County Cork and Castlemaine, County Kerry. The records include lists of potential emigrants, receipted accounts of shipping agents and correspondence. Between 1847 and 1852 over 1,100 people left the Crown estates for North America. For the individual migrants the data comprises name, age, family relationships, dates of departure and arrival, and personal details, such as 'very poor'.[34]

## 4.11 Miscellaneous records

Numerous other records can be found within estate collections that do not fit easily into any of the above categories. The records of the Shirley estate in County Monaghan include a number of interesting items that have been categorised under the heading 'Miscellaneous Volumes' in PRONI. For instance, the 'Shirley estate loan book' of 1827–45 (D3531/M/4) records the names and addresses of tenants, the sums lent to them, and the purposes for which the loans were made. The latter included such things as 'to buy a cow/horse' and 'to purchase land' (which must refer to 'buying' the right to occupy a holding, rather than an outright sale). Other loans were made to assist a family member to emigrate. For example, in 1840 William Babington of Knocknecran was loaned £14 'to send his son to America'.[35]

Many landowners provided incentives to their tenants to improve their farms through granting premiums for excellence. For example, PRONI has a photocopy of a memo from Robert O'Neill and Hugh Martin to Lady Londonderry listing the awards in the farm competition for the Carnlough estate, 1856 (D654/N/5/8). This includes the names of the prize winners in the different categories. For instance, first prize in the category 'First Class Farms' went to John McGarrell in Drumcrow, while the runners up were Charles Anderson and James Robinson, both of Culcrum. Other prizes were awarded for livestock and crops. John Watt of Drumcrow won the prize for the 'best selected manure heap'. Some landlords encouraged their tenants to take part in agricultural improvement societies (discussed in Chapter 11). Among the papers of the O'Hara estate in County Sligo is a hand-written list of tenants of Charles King O'Hara 'who received premiums from the Agricultural Society', 1843–5 (NLI, MS 36,350/20).

The involvement of landlords in many aspects of local life meant that their personal archives include material from a broad range of local initiatives and institutions. For instance, records relating to the Meade estate in County Down include documentation deriving from the Rathfriland dispensary, including a list of tenants receiving treatment, 1829–30 (Norfolk Record Office, MEA 5/73). The Jackson Trust was established through the will of Richard Jackson (1722–87), the conscientious owner of the Forkill estate in south

County Armagh. His will proved complex and required an act of parliament and the appointment of a board of trustees to fulfil its instructions. Among the records of the Jackson Trust now in PRONI is a set of bound volumes of accounts relating to the Old Farmers Fund, 1791–1822, 1823–55, 1883–2003 (D4338/3/3/1–3). This fund provided a small annual subvention to elderly farmers judged to be in need. The last 'old farmer' continued to receive a grant until his death in 2006. Other records of the Trust in PRONI include minute books and correspondence.[36]

# Notes

1 W.A. Maguire, *The Downshire Estates in Ireland* (1972), p. 108.
2 *Irish Land Act Commission, 1880. Minutes of Evidence*, pp 374–5.
3 Maguire, *Downshire Estates*, p. 129.
4 James S. Donnelly, *The Land and the People of Nineteenth-century Cork* (1975), pp, 10–11, 63.
5 Maguire, *Downshire Estates*, pp 129–31.
6 This calculation excludes lands owned in fee simple – even if these lands are included, the figure is still 77%.
7 A small proportion of farmers were in possession of their holdings by virtue of a fee farm grant, which was in effect a lease in perpetuity. In the early 1600s, as part of the scheme for the Plantation of Ulster, landowners were obliged, under the terms of their patents, to lease a proportion of their lands in fee farm, the thinking being that those who received such grants would become the backbone of the tenantry, individuals who were secure in their title and ready to invest in their lands. Fee farm grants continued to be issued from time to time by many landlords. Generally speaking, later fee farm grants were issued in return for an up-front payment, which could be quite substantial, and were often created in response to financial difficulties for the landowner or to stimulate urban development.
8 Donnelly, *Land and the People ... Cork*, p. 10.
9 Maguire, *Downshire Estates*, pp 117–25.
10 Donnelly, *Land and the People ... Cork*, pp 10–12.
11 The surname is spelled Humphrys in the deed. The family home, Milltown House, later became my secondary school, Strabane Grammar School.

The best known child of John Humphreys was the hymn-writer Cecil Frances, who married Rev. William Alexander, a Church of Ireland clergyman who went on to become bishop of Derry and archbishop of Armagh. As an aside, William Alexander attended the Classical school in Strabane run by Rev. Thomas Rolleston, brother of my great-great-great-grandfather Robert.

12 For a case study of the ramifications of this, see 'The lives lease system and emigration from Ulster: an example from Montgomery County, Pennsylvania' by Peter Roebuck, published in *DIFHR*, 18 (1995), pp 75–7.

13 John Ainsworth, 'Sidelights on 18th century land tenure', *JRSAI*, 79 (1949), pp 186–7.

14 For more on the subject of evictions, see Chapter 2 of W.E. Vaughan, *Landlord and Tenant in Mid-Victorian Ireland* (1994).

15 Ainsworth, 'Sidelights on 18th century land tenure', p. 189.

16 http://findingaids.nationalarchives.ie/index.php?category=18&subcategory=147.

17 A marvellous set of maps produced for the Bog Commissioners has been digitised and made available online through the Bord na Móna website (www.bordnamonalivinghistory.ie/maps).

18 These maps and the names of householders were published in *Londonderry and the London Companies*, ed. D.A. Chart and published by the Public Record Office of Northern Ireland in 1928.

19 Patrick J. Duffy, Farney in 1634: an examination of John [sic] Raven's survey of the Essex estate, *Clogher Record*, 11:2 (1983), pp 245–56.

20 For example, James Garry, 'The Chester estate map 1856: tenant farms in Carstown, Newhouse, Milltown, Galroostown and Priorstown, County Louth', *Seanchas Ardmhacha*, 18:1 (1999/2000), pp 134–62.

21 www.mayo.ie/library/local-history/maps.

22 http://wexfordcountyarchive.com/our-collections/estate-paper-collections/cliffe-estate-survey.

23 Alan Gailey, 'Local life in Ulster 1843–1848: the statistical surveys of Maurice Collis', *Ulster Local Studies*, 9:20 (Summer 1985), pp 120–27.

24 F.J. Carney, 'Pre-Famine Irish population: the evidence from the Trinity College estates', *Irish Economic and Social History*, 2 (1975), pp 35–45.

25 W.H. Crawford, *The Management of a Major Ulster Estate in the Late Eighteenth Century: the Eighth Earl of Abercorn and his Irish Agents* (2001).

26 Irish material can be found in Rab Houston, *Peasant Petitions: Social Relations and Economic Life on Landed Estates, 1600–1850* (2014).

27 https://specialcollections.ul.ie/shanbally-castle-papers.

28 The original document was catalogued by PRONI as D623/E/1 and then returned to donor, but not before it had been microfilmed (MIC18/12).

29 Richard McMahon, 'Manor courts in the west of Ireland before the Famine', in D.S. Greer and N.M. Dawson (ed.), *Mysteries and Solutions in Irish Legal History: Irish Legal History Society Discourses and Other Papers, 1996–1999* (2001), pp 115–60.

30 See also Raymond Gillespie, 'A manor court in seventeenth-century Ireland', *Irish Economic and Social History*, 25 (1998), pp 81–7.

31 Patrick J. Duffy, '"Disencumbering our crowded places": theory and practice of estate emigration schemes in mid-nineteenth century Ireland' in P.J. Duffy (ed.), *To and From Ireland: Planned Migration Schemes c. 1600–2000* (2004), p. 83.

32 Ibid., p. 84.

33 These records have been analysed in detail by Patrick J. Duffy, 'Assisted emigration from the Shirley estate, 1843–1854', *Clogher Record*, 14:2 (1992). See also Trevor McClaughlin, Stephanie James and Simon O'Reilley, 'Migration to Australia mid-nineteenth century; emigration from the Shirley estate at the time of the Famine', *Clogher Record*, 20:2 (2010), pp 287–334.

34 For more of these records, see Eilish Ellis, 'State-aided emigration schemes from Crown estates in Ireland, c. 1850', *Analecta Hibernica*, 22 (1960), pp 328–94.

35 Other items in PRONI listed under D3531/M include account books of the Carrickmacross Savings Bank, 1831–49, estate improvement books, 1844–78; and receipts from the Carrickmacross market tolls, 1876–1904.

36 https://jacksoncharitabletrustforkhill.com.

# 5

# Finding farmers in the Registry of Deeds

The Registry of Deeds in Dublin is unlike any other archive in Ireland and few research experiences surpass a day spent in it. Founded over three hundred years ago, its collection survives intact. One experienced researcher described the Registry of Deeds as the 'most important single source of genealogical information for the eighteenth century'.[1] The immense genealogical value of the institution in the nineteenth century is also apparent, and for those pursuing farming ancestors it is an archive of huge significance. The Registry of Deeds continues as a government office today and is now under the Property Registration Authority.[2] This chapter provides an overview of the registration process, the indexes to the deeds, the range of material and the usefulness of the Registry of Deeds in researching farming ancestors.

## 5.1 The creation of the Registry of Deeds

The Registry of Deeds was established by an act passed in the Irish Parliament in 1707. The aim of the act was to provide one central office in Dublin 'for the public registering of all deeds, conveyances and wills that shall be made of any honours, manors, lands, tenements or hereditaments'. Furthermore, its purpose was 'for securing, purchasers, preventing forgeries and fraudulent gifts and conveyances of lands, tenements and hereditaments, which have been frequently practised in this kingdom, especially by Papists, to the great prejudice of the Protestant interest thereof.' By this it can be seen that the legislation that created the Registry of Deeds was part of the Penal Laws that were designed to preserve the privileged position of the Anglican elite by restricting the rights of Catholics.

The Registry of Deeds opened in 1708 and the first deed was registered on 29 March at 5 o'clock in the afternoon. This was a lease and release[3] dated 26 and 27 March 1708 of the lands of Stephenstown and Ballinscala, estimated at 383 acres, and part of the lands of ffanstowne, containing 105 acres, in the barony of Coslea, County Limerick. The parties were the Earl of Bellomont and Connell Vereker of Ballinscala. The latter was to hold the lands for the duration of three lives, the lives being Vereker himself, his eldest son Henry, and his brother Henry, while the rent was set at six shillings and six pence per acre (or £158 12s in total). It was to be another week before the second deed was registered and this concerned lands in County Monaghan owned by the Cairnes family.

Whatever may have been intended by the framers of the original legislation, in practice registration was not compulsory and it must be realised that the registered deeds represent only a proportion of all land transactions executed since the early 1700s. Even so, the sheer number of deeds registered is incredible. By the early 1750s more than 100,000 deeds had been registered and by the end of the century this figure had increased to nearly 350,000. By 1832, when the numbering system changed, the total was approaching 600,000.

## 5.2 The registration process

The registration process can be summarised as follows: a deed was drawn up between two or more parties; one of those parties felt that it would be advantageous to register the deed in the Registry of Deeds in Dublin; a duplicate (though not necessarily a complete transcription) of the original deed was made, and this copy, known as a 'memorial', was verified by a Justice of the Peace; the memorial was then taken to the Registry of Deeds; here the memorial was given a unique reference number and was copied into a transcript volume by a clerk. The memorials were retained and these are stored in the vaults at the Registry of Deeds. Researchers should be aware that if a copy of a deed is ordered the item provided will be a copy of the memorial, not a copy of the entry in the transcription book (unless the memorial is missing).

The transcript volumes are large and cumbersome tomes, especially in the case of the 1708–1832 books. Several transcript volumes may have been in use simultaneously, meaning that the deeds registered in one particular year may be found in several different volumes. While registration generally took place fairly soon after the date of the transaction, it is not unusual to find deeds registered many years later, perhaps because of concerns about an impending legal dispute over title to the property in question.

## 5.3 The indexes

Two indexes to the transcripts of the memorials are available: an index of grantors and a lands index.

### Index of grantors

Until 1833 the index of grantors provided no more than the surname and the forename of the grantor, followed by the surname only of the grantee, and then the volume, page number and memorial number. It is important to emphasise that the names listed alphabetically in this index are those of the person transferring the land rather than the individual to whom the property was transferred. Unfortunately, there is no index to grantees. Aristocrats tend to be listed under their title rather than their surname. Some of the volumes will include 'Names that admit of different spellings', listing alternative renderings of particular surnames.

From 1833 onwards the index of grantors includes the full name of both the grantor and the grantee. Information is also provided on the property affected by the deed. A column headed 'First Denomination' generally states the townland, while there are also columns for the 'County, City or Town' and the 'Barony or Parish'. These details are followed by three further columns giving the year the deed was registered, the volume of the transcript volume and the number of the memorial within that volume.[4]

### Lands index

The lands index is organised by county, with one or more counties per individual index volume.[5] The sequences of years covered by the indexes vary. For the first century or so, the periods run 1708–38 and 1739–1810. So, for example, volume 63 of the lands index includes deeds registered for counties Westmeath, Wexford and Wicklow, 1708–38. In the nineteenth century the sequences of years are much shorter. The volumes for the 1860s, for instance, are organised as follows: 1860–61, 1862–4 and 1865–9.

Within each county section in an index volume, the entries are arranged alphabetically, but only with regard to initial letter. Prior to 1833, each index entry gives the surnames of the parties, the name of the denomination of land, and the volume, page number and memorial number. The page number, incidentally, is the first page on which the memorial appears; the transcription itself could run from half a page to upwards of a dozen pages. There is a column for the name of the barony and parish, though this is not always filled in; occasionally the name of the manor in which the property is located is given here.

The format of the lands index from 1833 onwards is along similar lines to the earlier arrangement. A significant difference, however, is that within each county the lands are subdivided by barony. It is important, therefore, to know the barony in which the townland is located. The columns are headed: lands; parish (not always completed); grantors (including forenames); grantees (including forenames); year of registry; transcript volume number; and memorial number and page of book.[6]

## 5.4 The range of documents registered

The legislation that created the Registry of Deeds was framed in such a way that it allowed for a range of different documents to be registered so long as they were concerned with the transfer of 'lands, tenements and hereditaments' (i.e. property that can be inherited) from one party to another. The legal jargon used means that it can be difficult to understand the exact purpose of the deed. A deed introduced as a 'lease and release' could have been a mortgage, while a deed described as a 'bargain and sale' may have been a lease. Furthermore, some deeds have many different parties and understanding how each of them relates to the transaction can be challenging. However, after reading through the contents of a memorial it is usually possible to at least get the gist of what the framers of the deed intended. In any case, the genealogical information contained in the deed is often more important than the nature of the transaction itself.

### Leases

Outright sales of property were rare: a landowner usually wished to retain some interest, however minimal, in the land that was being transferred to the grantee. More common than transactions relating to the sale of property are deeds concerning the leasing of land. Often these were between persons of relatively similar social standing, rather than the landlord-tenant relationship. In fact, registered leases from landlord to tenant are not as common as might be hoped. For one thing, the legislation of 1707 specifically stated that it did not extend to leases 'for years not exceeding twenty-one years, where the actual possession goeth along with the said lease'. (In practice, however, many shorter leases were registered.) Therefore, for many landed estates there are either no registered leases at all or else very few.

For some estates, however, there are useful runs of leases in the Registry of Deeds. For example, for the manor of Ardstraw in County Tyrone, held by the McCausland family from the bishop of Derry in the early eighteenth century, there are over a dozen registered leases from the 1720s containing the names of around 100 tenant farmers.[7] Information on the occupiers of churchlands in the eighteenth century is usually very hard to come by, making this collection all the more valuable. The fact that the McCauslands were perpetually in financial difficulties and uncertain of their future may account for the registration of so many of these leases.

### Marriage settlements

A marriage settlement was the agreement made between the families of the prospective bride and groom prior to their wedding. The main aim was to provide financial security to the bride should she outlive her husband. The information in this type of deed varies, but can include the names and addresses of a large number of people from the two families involved. The first two parties to the deed will typically be the groom and the father of the bride. If the latter was dead, then the bride's guardian will be named. While marriage settlements were commonplace among the upper classes, they were also used by tenant farmers of a certain status. Many marriage settlements were registered in the Registry of Deeds.

A good example is the settlement that was drawn up on 5 September 1766 in advance of the marriage between Joseph McFarland and Catherine Johnston, both from County Tyrone (book 257, page 26, memorial no. 165140). The parties to the settlement were:

1) Andrew McFarland of Droyt [Droit, Lower Bodoney parish], on behalf of his son Joseph;
2) Audly Colhoune of Strachalter [Strahulter, Ardstraw parish], on behalf of Catherine Johnston, daughter of John Johnston of Cashell [Cashel, Lower Bodoney parish] and granddaughter of Audly Colhoune.

Under the terms of the settlement, Andrew McFarland granted to Joseph for the term of five years: two acres of 'plow land', with horses and other implements needed to plough the land; two cows with grazing for them; and a house and garden. In addition, Andrew granted Joseph one third of his farm, with two milk cows, and grazing rights for those cows, as well as a horse and a number of sheep. On his part, the bride's grandfather, Audly Colhoune, granted Joseph various properties of his in the village of Newtownstewart in perpetuity.

## Wills

The legislation that established the Registry of Deeds provided for the registering of wills of testators who died after 25 March 1708. A will can be easily identified in the index to grantors by the phrase 'His Will' or 'Her Will' appearing where the surname of the grantee would otherwise have been written. A will may have been registered if there were concerns that it was going to be contested. Some of the wills were transcribed in full, while others were recorded in a more abbreviated format. As discussed elsewhere in this book, nearly all testamentary papers prior to 1858 were lost in the destruction of the Public Record Office of Ireland in 1922. Therefore, the wills registered in the Registry of Deeds form an invaluable set of documents that, in most cases, do not exist anywhere else.

The Irish Manuscripts Commission has published three volumes of abstracts of over 2,000 wills registered between 1708 and 1832 (P. Beryl Eustace and Eilish Ellis (eds), *Registry of Deeds, Dublin: Abstracts of Wills*, 1954–88). These abstracts provide the names, addresses and occupations of the various individuals recorded (e.g. beneficiaries and witnesses) and the testator's property that was mentioned in the will. The volumes can be downloaded as PDFs from the website of the Irish Manuscripts Commission (www.irishmanuscripts.ie).

By way of example, the Registry of Deeds has a transcription of the will of Hugh Gartlany, a tenant farmer at Cullenstown, Darver parish, County Louth (book 354, page 99, memorial no. 236714). The will was dated 8 May 1783 and registered on 31 May following – a much shorter interval between the two than was usually the case. The family members named in the will were: his wife Madlin, son Nicholas, stepsons John and Patt, daughters Ann (married to Conry), Mary, Catherine, Rose and Margaret (married to Thomas Rooney of Peppardstown). The actual will provides information on the bequests to these individuals. As was typical in wills of this period, the testator specified his preferred place of burial – the churchyard of Dromiskin.

### Mortgages, rent charges, bills of discovery

In the era before the creation of a reliable banking system, mortgages were commonly used as a ready means of raising capital, particularly by merchants and those seeking to acquire additional land. Mortgages can usually be recognised by the inclusion of the rate of interest and a clause of redemption, though these may not always appear in the memorial. Rent charges were annual payments issuing from specified lands and were used to pay off debts or to provide for family members without an adequate income. Bills of discovery were issued against Catholics holding lands on terms forbidden under the Penal Laws. The Protestant filing the bill was able to claim the lands affected. In many cases the bill was filed by a Protestant friend of the Catholic concerned in order to pre-empt a less sympathetic discovery.

## 5.5 The value of research in the Registry of Deeds

A popular misconception of the Registry of Deeds is that it is of little value for those researching families below the level of the elite. In actual fact, a significant number of deeds, even in the first half of the eighteenth century, concern directly or make reference to tenant farmers, including farmers of Catholic background. At the same time, it must be acknowledged that large swathes of Irish society, for both economic and social reasons, will generally not be found in the Registry of Deeds.

In terms of their genealogical value, the registered deeds provide the researcher with names, addresses and occupations of the parties involved. Sometimes several generations of the one family can be found in a single deed. Deeds will also include the names, addresses and occupations of those who acted as witnesses and these may provide other avenues of research. Two sets of witnesses will appear: one set witnessed the original transaction, while the other witnessed the memorial. At least one of the witnesses to the memorial had witnessed the original deed.

Occasionally deeds that have no apparent relevance to tenant farmers can contain much of interest. For example, the marriage settlement of 1734 involving Lord Mountjoy included a list of over 50 tenants on his Newtownstewart estate in County Tyrone (though unfortunately without townlands), details that are not available from any other source (book 77, page 1, memorial no. 52432).[8] An extraordinary deed concerns what had been the De Clifford estate (and subsequently the Ker estate) in and around Downpatrick, County Down, and dates from 1839 (year 1839, vol. 19, memorial no. 292). After several pages of complex legalese involving numerous parties, the memorial sets out in astonishing detail a schedule of the tenants and tenancies on the estate. The details provided include the names of the lessees, the dates of their leases, the tenure (and if the lease was for lives, the names and ages of those lives in 1833), the statute acreage of the holding and the rent payable. In all, there are the names of over 1,000 tenants on the estate.

A further excellent example of this is a deed, seemingly a mortgage, of 1845 concerning the property of Sir Samuel O'Malley of Kilboyne Castle, County Mayo (year 1845, vol. 19, memorial no. 79). The lands in question comprised the Carrowmore and Caher and the Clare Island estates in the barony of Murrisk, the Castleaffy and Rosehill estates in the barony of Burrishoole, and the Kilboyne estate in the barony of Carra, plus some other smaller areas, all in County Mayo. The accompanying schedule, arranged by townland and then by townland subdivision, lists over 300 tenants. Tenure is also indicated, with most farmers tenants-at-will, though a proportion were in possession of a lease issued in 1801 for one life (the name of the life is often given).[9]

In many instances, the Registry of Deeds can compensate for the absence of records relating to the management of certain estates. When I was writing a history of my home parish of Donagheady in County Tyrone one of the gaps in source material was the virtual absence of eighteenth-century papers for one of the major estates, that of the Hamiltons of Dunnamanagh. However, from the mid-1700s onwards this family issued numerous leases for lives (some of them renewable forever) and a high proportion of these were registered in the Registry of Deeds. Therefore, it was possible to explore aspects of estate management as well as the lives of the tenant farmers thanks to this archive.

The following examples explore in more detail two deeds involving tenant farmers and show how these can provide greater insights into the individuals concerned as well as answer important questions about those families.

*Example 1: an eighteenth-century deed*

The first example is of a deed that was registered on 19 November 1767, the reference to which is book 260, page 142, memorial no. 168079. This deed was drawn up on 17 November 1762 – so fully five years before it was registered – and the parties to it were as follows:

1) Jane Wilson, widow; James Mawhiney and his wife Margery (née Wilson); Jane Wilson the younger, spinster, all of Lemnaroy [Termoneeny parish], County Londonderry;
2) George Wilson of Ballyriff [Artrea parish], County Londonderry, farmer.

The deed revealed that in consideration of the sum of £60 paid to them by George Wilson, the two Jane Wilsons and James and Margery Mawhiney leased to George Wilson the farm of land in the townland of Lemnaroy which had belonged to Arthur Wilson, now deceased (the late husband of the older Jane and father of the younger woman, though not identified as such). The lease was for 12 years.

The farm in question formed part of the estate of the Vintners' Company, one of the London livery companies that had been granted lands in County Londonderry in the early seventeenth century. Rather than manage the property directly, however, the company had adopted the practice of leasing its estate to a middleman. In 1762 the heirs of the Right Hon. William Conolly held this estate from the Vintners. The deed involving the Wilsons and Mawinneys alludes to this situation, noting that George Wilson was expected to pay £4 4s

10*d* annually to Conolly's heirs. This sum was 'the proportionable part of the rent' of the farm in Lemnaroy that was paid by Arthur Wilson under the terms of a lease issued to him and several other farmers by William Conolly on 1 April 1734.

Very usefully the deed explains why it had been drawn up – the Wilsons and Mawhineys 'intended going to America'. Furthermore, they promised that if they did not return to Ireland at the end of the 12 years, or within two years of the expiration of the lease, then George Wilson, for a further sum of £60, could continue in possession of the farm for the duration of the lease issued by Conolly in 1734. It ought to be pointed out that deeds specifically mentioning the planned emigration of people to another part of the world are rare. On the other hand, it is not particularly unusual to find a deed referring to an individual living in America or elsewhere, who had a residual claim on property in Ireland.

One of the witnesses to the deed was Morgan Wilson of Lemnaroy, farmer. The other witness was William Doherty of Magherafelt, who died in the period between the drafting of the deed and its registration. Morgan Wilson also witnessed the memorial and to this was appended the following statement by him: 'I Morgan Wilson abovenamed do solemnly, sincerely and truly declared and affirm that I now am and for the space of three years last past and upwards have been one of the people called Quakers …'. This statement may have been prepared to address the issue of the Quaker refusal to swear oaths.

As noted above, wills were sometimes registered in the Registry of Deeds and as it turned out the will of Arthur Wilson of Lemnaroy was one of them. A transcript of his will appears in book 200, page 238, memorial no. 133004. The will was dated 11 June 1759 and was registered on 23 July following. Under the terms of his will, Arthur bequeathed to his wife Jane and his daughters Margery and Jane his farm in Lemnaroy, to be possessed by them in three equal parts. Margarey seems not to have been married at this stage for there is no mention of her husband, James Mawhiney. Other family members make an appearance in this will, including his son Thomas (who was left 'five shillings and five pence and no more') and two sons-in-law, Thomas Faucet and Charles McKaghey (their wives are not named). Morgan Wilson, identified as the testator's brother, was one of three men appointed executors.

## Example 2: a nineteenth-century deed

The second example relates to my own family and shows how using the Registry of Deeds allowed me to discover when my great-great-great-grandfather, Robert Rolleston, relocated to the farm we still possess in the townland of Gortavea, Donagheady parish, County Tyrone. Moreover, the deed in question also provided his place of residence before moving to Gortavea, a detail that was hitherto unknown. Through a search of the lands index, a deed concerning the townland of Gortavea where the parties were named as Hamilton and Rolleston was identified. The full index reference to this deed was book 859, page 311, memorial no. 573311.[10] Turning to the deed in question, it was described as 'an indenture of assignment' and was dated 25 February 1830. The parties were named as:

1) Jane Hamilton of Gortavea, widow of James Hamilton, farmer;
2) John Hamilton of Loughash, County Tyrone, eldest son of James and Jane;
3) Thomas Hamilton of Gortavea, second son of James and Jane;
4) Robert Rolleston of Gannaghan, County Tyrone, farmer.

The witnesses were named as William Hatrick of Creaghcor, who farmed near Gortavea, and William Glasse of Strabane, an attorney at law. Under the terms of this deed the Hamiltons transferred their property in Gortavea to Robert. It was not an outright sale for the land in question was owned by the Marquess of Abercorn and the Hamiltons were simply tenant farmers. However, in a sense the Hamiltons were 'selling' to Robert the right to occupy the farm, a practice known as Tenant Right (see Chapter 9 for more on this contentious issue). The memorial does not, in fact, specify the sum of money that Robert paid the Hamiltons. On disposing of their farm in Gortavea, the Hamiltons moved across the River Foyle to County Donegal and took up residence on a farm in the townland of Maymore – less than a mile as the crow flies from Gortavea – where their descendants continue to farm to this day. The deed was registered on 21 May 1830.

Thanks to the identification of the deed in the Registry of Deeds we discovered that Robert was 'of Gannaghan' in County Tyrone at the time he acquired possession of the farm in Gortavea. But where was

Gannaghan? There was a clue in Robert's funeral card, which still survives. This stated that his body was to be removed to Castlederg, nearly 20 miles from Gortavea, for burial on 21 January 1854. A little over a mile south of the town of Castlederg is the townland of *Ganvaghan* – strictly speaking three townlands named Ganvaghan Hemphill, Ganvaghan Kyle and Ganvaghan Semple. Some further research indentified a Roulston farm in the first of these in the early nineteenth century. What had prompted Robert Rolleston, who, in 1830, was in his late forties, to make this move? This has still to be fully established, but he may have been a younger son and the relocation to Gortavea provided him with an opportunity to acquire a farm of his own.

## 5.6 Access to the Registry of Deeds

Initially, the Registry of Deeds was located in a private house in Dublin, before new premises were acquired in Lower Castle Yard. In 1805, the registry was transferred to Inns Quay, which was convenient to the Four Courts. Since the early 1830s the Registry of Deeds has been located in a large Georgian building in Henrietta Street (the main entrance faces on to Constitution Hill). The Registry of Deeds is open to the public free of charge each week from Monday to Friday. Researchers sign in at the reception desk and then make their way to the top floor of the building where the indexes and transcript volumes are available for inspection. Information can be noted down from these volumes, but photography is strictly forbidden; copying facilities are available.

For those unable to visit the archive, there are alternatives. As a result of the efforts of the LDS, microfilms of the indexes and memorial volumes have been available for some time in various archives. A recent and hugely significant development has been the release online of digital scans of these microfilms through FamilySearch.org; the collection is titled 'Transcripts of memorials of deeds, conveyances and wills, 1708–1929'.[11] Searching the digitised files can be a slow process and requires some patience and perseverance. However, the initiative has opened up access to this archive for researchers worldwide.

The Registry of Deeds Index Project (http://irishdeedsindex.net) has been running for a number of years and many thousands of index entries have been created (at the time of writing, over 400,000 index records from over 40,000 memorials). It is possible to conduct a search by personal name and place-name and browse the database of records. Unlike the personal name indexes in the Registry of Deeds itself, which are restricted to the grantor, this database can be used to search for any of the individuals found in a memorial, including witnesses and those mentioned incidentally. Usefully, links have been provided to the digital version of the relevant transcription volume hosted on FamilySearch.org (sometimes to the start of the volume and on other occasions to the actual page on which the memorial begins).

## 5.7 The Land Registry of Ireland

The Land Registry was established in 1892 following the passing of the Local Registration of Title Act in 1891. It is important to bear in mind that the Land Registry and the Registry of Deeds are 'mutually exclusive'. The critical difference between them is that documents are registered in the Registry of Deeds and title is registered in the Land Registry. With the transfer of ownership of tens of thousands of acres under the land acts, the government was anxious to protect its considerable investment in land purchase schemes (see Chapter 9). Deeds submitted to the Land Registry as evidence of title were filed and the relevant details were recorded on folios which in turn comprise the registers kept by the Land Registry. In addition, there are maps showing the location of properties. The Land Registry is now part of the Property Registration Authority (PRA) and fuller information on its work and range of services can be found at www.prai.ie/land-registry-services.[12] In addition, the PRA maintains the website Landdirect.ie (www.landdirect.ie), which provides access to the digital Registry map (for free) and the folios (for a fee).

## 5.8 The Land Registry and Registry of Deeds in Northern Ireland

With Partition, new offices of Land Registry and Registry of Deeds were established in Northern Ireland and these are currently part of Land & Property Services within the Department of Finance. More information on the products and services offered by these bodies can be found at www.finance-ni.gov.uk/topics/land-registration. In addition to a names index, the Registry of Deeds in Northern Ireland once maintained a lands index, but this ceased in 1949. The lands index 1923–49 is available in PRONI (RODB) and is organised by county and barony, with separate indexes for deeds omitting the name of the barony.

# Notes

1  Jean Agnew, 'How to use the Registry of Deeds', *Familia*, 6 (1990), p. 78. Other helpful studies of the Registry of Deeds include: P.B. Phair, 'Guide to the Registry of Deeds', *Analecta Hibernica*, 23 (1966), pp 257–76; John Grenham, *Tracing Your Irish Ancestors* (5th edition, 2019), chapter 9; and Brian Nugent, *A Guide to the 18th Century Land Records in the Irish Registry of Deeds* (2013).

2  For more details on its current services, see www.prai.ie/registry-of-deeds-services.

3  This term is found frequently in the Registry of Deeds prior to 1845. It could be described as a legal sleight of hand and was designed to avoid some of the the obligations associated with certain categories of land conveyancing. A recent article that is very helpful in understanding the legal basis of Irish land transactions is Peter J.F. Coutts, 'Understanding property transactions in Ireland, I: legislative and historical context', *The Irish Genealogist*, 15:3 (2020), pp 387–412.

4  In the early years of the new indexing system the final column was titled, 'No. of Memorial and Page of Transcript Book', though in practice the only number written in this column was that of the memorial. Subsequently, the title of the column indicated that it was only the memorial number that needed to be entered.

5  Deeds relating to corporate towns are indexed separately from the rest of the deeds for a particular county.

6  Again, only one number appears in the column for memorial number and page of book and this is the memorial number. There will also be a final column giving the page in the day book, but this has no relevance for researchers.

7  Summaries of these were published in *DIFHR* 24 (2001), p. 84.

8  These names were published in *DIFHR*, 24 (2001), p. 84.

9  The names from the deeds concerning the De Clifford and O'Malley estates can be found on the excellent website of the Registry of Deeds Index Project (https://irishdeedsindex.net/search/memorial_list_big.php).

10 In actual fact the transcription of the memorial begins on page 310 of the volume.

11 The direct link to it is www.familysearch.org/search/catalog/185720? availability=Family%20History%20Library.

12 According to the Property Registration website: 'By international comparison, Ireland has a very extensive and well developed system of land registration. Since the foundation of the Land Registry in 1892, there has been a gradual, ongoing and continuous programme of movement away from the older and limited system of recording deeds (in the Registry of Deeds), to the more modern, flexible and comprehensive 'title registration' system provided through the Land Registry. 93% of the total land mass of the State and almost 90% of the legal titles in Ireland are now registered in the Land Registry.'

# 6

# Finding farmers in valuation records

## 6.1 TITHE VALUATIONS

### 6.1.1 Early tithe records

The collection of tithes to support the clergy of the Established Church was a hugely contentious issue in Ireland, where more than 85% of the population claimed no allegiance to this religious denomination. In the 1760s, one commentator defined tithes as 'the tenth part of the increase yearly arising and renewing from the profits of lands, the stock upon lands, and the personal industry of the inhabitants.' However, the ways in which tithes were paid varied considerably across the island, with tithes levied on some crops in certain areas, and not in others. For instance, the tithing of potatoes was particularly associated with Munster and south Leinster, though it was found in other parts of the island as well. Furthermore, from 1735 onwards pastureland was exempt from tithes.

Tithes were also resented because of the manner in which payments were frequently demanded. In his 1725 report of the estate of the Ironmongers' Company of London in County Londonderry, Isaac Pyke wrote that tithes were collected from the farmers 'in so rigorous a manner as is not known and scarce would be believed in England, so that I do not wonder they have so few converts from ye Roman Catholic religion to ye Church and yet Presbyterians have so many' (London Metropolitan Archives, MS 17,275). An approach by at least some of the clergy was to lease the right to collect tithes to an outsider, thus absolving themselves of having to do this.[1]

Comparatively few records naming tithe-payers survive from before the early 1820s, when the system was changed. Examples include a tithe roll of Finglas parish, County Dublin, 1717 (PRONI,

D562/473); a 'View Book of Great Tythes' for the Deanery of Down, covering lands in the parishes of Tyrella, Bright, Ballee, Ballyculter and Down, County Down, 1732 (PRONI, D1145/D/1); a book of vicarial tithes for the parish of 'Ballywoolen' (Ballywillin), counties Antrim and Londonderry, 1783 (PRONI, D668/B); and a valuation of the corn tithes of Newcastle, County Wicklow, 1792–6 (NLI, MS 3,980). A tithe book for the parishes of Ardmayle and Ballysheehan in County Tipperary, 1790–1801, has been made available online by Tipperary Studies.[2] It lists tithe-payers by townland with details of valuations and payments. There are occasional comments about the tithe-payers, such as 'dead', 'ran away', 'in England' and 'admitted a pauper'. The Sources Catalogue (sources.nli.ie) is one way to search for earlier tithe records, as is the PRONI eCatalogue.

## 6.1.2 Reform of the tithe system

Demands for reform of the tithe system increased in the early 1800s and in the spring of 1823 a bill was introduced to Parliament at Westminster which attempted to resolve the tithe issue by replacing the payment of tithes on produce with a composition. What was proposed can be summarised as follows: upon application the lord lieutenant of Ireland could establish a 'special vestry' in a parish; this application could be made in the name of the Anglican clergyman or five individuals occupying lands worth £20 a year each; the membership of the special vestry was made up of those paying the highest tithes; those gathered in the special vestry voted on whether to proceed with a tithe composition; if a majority wanted a composition, the clergyman and parishioners appointed a commissioner to assess the value of it.

While the process was hardly straightforward, the end result was to simplify the many different payments on produce into one single monetary payment. It was fairer to farmers and cottiers growing potatoes and oats since pastureland was now to bear the same rate per acre as tillage, and the main beneficiaries were those holding only a few acres. The Tithe Composition Act received royal assent on 19 July 1823. According to the historian James S. Donnelly, the 1823 Act 'possessed numerous defects, but it was arguably the first significant social reform conferred on Ireland by the British parliament since 1800.'[3]

Of some significance was the fact that the procedure was made voluntary, rather than compulsory. If either the clergyman or the special vestry opposed a composition the matter could not be proceeded with. The result was that while over 1,000 applications for a special vestry had been received by March 1824, in many of these parishes no agreement over a composition had been reached. In order to try to remedy this, an amending act was passed in July 1824 which allowed the lord lieutenant to intervene to resolve outstanding issues. A further act of 1832 gave the lord lieutenant the power to compel a tithe composition in a parish where a voluntary composition had not taken place. Finally, in August 1838 an act of parliament was passed which converted tithes into a rent charge with the landlord, rather than the tenant, given the responsibility for paying this.

## 6.1.3 Tithe applotment books

The practical outworking of the legislation of 1823–4 was a comprehensive valuation of land liable for tithes. The results of this valuation are found in the tithe applotment books, which are organised by parish and diocese. The original volumes for parishes in Northern Ireland are held in PRONI (where they are catalogued with the prefix FIN/5/A), while the books for the Republic of Ireland are in the National Archives in Dublin. The books themselves come in different shapes and sizes – usually in portrait format, sometimes tall in height and narrow in width – and vary in the way in which the data is presented. A statement may be included on the events that led to the tithe valuation being undertaken in a particular parish, along with documents relating to this. Occasionally, there may be more than one tithe book for a parish, with a second dating some years after the first.

In their most basic format, tithe applotment books list the names of the tithe-payers by townland giving the monetary value of the tithe payable by each individual. Other details recorded include the acreage possessed by the tithe-payer, which may be broken down in terms of quality and use (e.g. the proportion that was arable or pasture), and the total valuation of each holding (from which the tithe was calculated). The acreages in the tithe applotment books are generally in the Irish, or plantation, acre, with the Scottish Cunningham acre used in some northern areas.[4] The small size of many of the holdings listed indicates that the plots of land held by cottiers were often included, at least in certain areas (see Chapter 13 for more on cottiers).[5]

The volume for Carrick-on-Suir parish, County Tipperary, of 1834 is an example of a tithe book that breaks down agricultural activity, including the crops grown, on each holding. Some tithe books give the name of the landlord of each townland, providing useful clues for research using estate papers. Occasionally some additional details may be given about the tithe-payer. For instance, three tithe-payers named John Tomelty in Bankmore in the parish of Ballyphilip, County Down, were distinguished by the nicknames Geordy, Willy and Hance (PRONI, FIN/5/A/45A). If the tithe-payer was not resident in the townland, his actual abode may be given. In rarer instances, familial relationships might be stated. More common is for a widow to be identified as such.

Accompanying maps are rare, though attention may be drawn to maps for at least some of the townlands in the parish of Drumlease, County Leitrim, showing the boundaries of individual holdings.[6] For Rasharkin, County Antrim, there are later Ordnance Survey maps annotated to show plot boundaries (corresponding with the numbered entries in the tithe book) for part of this parish (PRONI, FIN/5/B/2/27).

## Online access

A transcription of the tithe applotment books for the Republic of Ireland along with page images is available on the website of the National Archives (genealogy.nationalarchives.ie). The page images are from the microfilms of the tithe books.[7] The NAI database allows the user to search by the name of the tithe-payer as well as by townland, parish and county. There is also a browse facility, which is particularly useful if looking for a name that *should* be there but is not. For instance, a Joseph Grier ought to have been listed in Newtowntully, Tullymore townland, Tullyfern parish, County Donegal. However, searching for this name produced no results. However, by using the browse function, and drilling down from county to parish to the smaller land units, all of the tithe-payers in Newtowntully can be identified, one of whom has been transcribed erroneously as Joseph *Green*.

Other indexes (though not page images) are available on Ancestry.com and on RootsIreland.ie (mainly northern counties). PRONI has created digital versions of the tithe applotment books for Northern Ireland and these can be downloaded as PDF files from its website (nidirect.gov.uk/proni). The relevant volume can be identified through the PRONI eCatalogue and downloaded by selecting 'View' in the Digital Record column. Note that most of these files are huge (upwards of 100 MB). Documentation relating to the collection of tithes, including in some instances lists of names of parishioners, can also be found in the Chief Secretary's Office Registered Papers in NAI (see Chapter 10).

### Gaps and absent tithe books

In searching for an ancestor in the tithe applotment books, it is important to bear in mind that not all agricultural land in Ireland was tithable. This included certain lands in the direct possession of the Church of Ireland, for example glebe lands held by the parish clergy. This means that usually one or more townlands are missing from every tithe book. However, for a number of parishes there are no tithe applotment books at all. For a consideration of absent tithe books across the island of Ireland, see Valerie Adams and Brian Trainor, 'Tithe applotment books Ireland 1824–38: gaps in the archive', *Familia*, 1 (1985), pp 97–103. The absence of a tithe book for a parish could be down to any one of a number of reasons. For historical reasons, some parishes were tithe-free. In other instances, the parish was part of a larger ecclesiastical union and the tithe records may be found under the name of a different parish. There may be substitutes for the absence of tithe books. For instance, there is no tithe book for Donagheady, County Tyrone, but there are documents relating to the composition of tithes for some townlands in the parish (NLI, MS 17,990).

### 6.1.4 Tithe defaulters

There was strong opposition to the new system of collecting tithes, especially from among the graziers and dairy farmers, many of whom now found that they had to pay tithes, having been previously largely exempt. Growing discontent led to the 'Tithe War' that began in 1830/31, which resulted in the widespread refusal to pay tithes.[8] A

Clergy Relief Fund was created in 1832 to support Church of Ireland ministers affected by the agitation. To benefit from this fund clerics had to submit schedules naming those who had defaulted on their tithe payments. Nearly 130 lists of tithe defaulters containing some 29,000 names (with addresses) survive in the Official Papers Miscellaneous Assorted (OPMA) series in the National Archives (see Chapter 10). Coverage is best for counties Kilkenny and Tipperary, with some material also available for counties Carlow, Cork, Kerry, Laois, Limerick, Louth, Meath, Offaly, Waterford and Wexford. Around half the returns also include the occupations of the tithe defaulters.

A list of the surviving returns is found in Suzanne C. Hartwick's article, 'The Clergy Relief Fund, 1831: tithe defaulters' in *The Irish Genealogist* (vol. 8, 1990). Online access to the names is provided by Findmypast. The schedule of tithe defaulters for a parish is worth checking even if the tithe applotment book itself is available because some people will appear in the former who are not listed in the latter. For instance, a Martin Barron of Knockbodley townland, Graiguenamanagh parish, County Kilkenny, is recorded as a tithe defaulter, but his name does not appear in the tithe book. Surnames variations may also be found. A tithe defaulter called James Corcoran in the same townland of Knockbodley is named James Corrigan in the tithe book.

## 6.2 THE VALUATION OF IRELAND

### 6.2.1 The work of the Valuation

The Valuation of Ireland was established by an act of parliament in 1826 and as a result every acre on the island was valued between 1830 and the mid-1860s. It was introduced to try to create a uniform system of local taxation across the entire country. The Valuation was headed by Sir Richard Griffith, a towering figure who set high standards and was not slow to criticise what he considered to be inadequate work. The definitive publication on the Valuation is Frances McGee, *The Archives of the Valuation of Ireland, 1830–65* (2018) and researchers who wish to delve more deeply into this subject will find much of interest in it. It is important to appreciate from the start that the innovative nature of the Valuation meant that it was subject to various revisions over the years – this is where Frances McGee's book is exceptionally helpful.

Initially, the work was carried out under the aegis of the Townland Valuation – which used the townland as the basic unit for the purposes of valuation. Under the Townland Valuation each townland was divided into a series of 'lots'. To begin with, these 'lots' were not based on individual farms, but were rather distinguished on the basis of their use and quality. (The Instructions issued in 1839 specified that lots were to correspond with farms.) Each of these lots was given a number, which allows its location to be found on a Valuation map (see below). The succinct descriptions of each lot might include phrases such as 'chiefly meadow', 'boggy pasture', 'gravelly arable' and 'heathy mountain'. For each lot the following information is also given: acreage (in statute measure), rate per acre, and the valuation calculated for it. The occupiers of houses meeting a certain monetary threshold are listed at the end of the description of each townland.

Fieldwork began in County Londonderry in 1830 and by 1852 three-quarters of the island had been completed under the rules and regulations of this valuation. In 1844 a valuation based on tenements, i.e. individual holdings, within townlands was introduced. This resulted in a much more detailed investigation of land, its value and its occupiers. Two years later this new approach was given formal legal underpinning with the passing of the Tenement Valuation Act. To begin with, it applied to six counties that had yet to be covered by the Townland Valuation – Cork, Dublin, Kerry, Limerick, Tipperary and Waterford. The work of the Tenement Valuation was introduced to further counties in 1848–9 and in 1852 another Tenement Valuation Act extended the provisions of the 1846 Act to the remainder of the island.

Frances McGee has observed that 'the northern counties were both the first to be valued under the Townland Valuation and the last to be valued under the Tenement Valuation', resulting in 'two distinct sets of documents made at two well-separated periods of valuation'.[9] For County Donegal, for instance, fieldwork for the Townland Valuation was carried out between 1833 and 1840, whereas the Tenement Valuation fieldwork was conducted between 1855 and 1857. This contrasts with, for example, County Kerry, which was never subject to the Townland Valuation and where fieldwork for the Tenement

Valuation was carried out between 1847 and 1853. Such differentials have obvious consequences for the nature of the documentation generated, especially, from a genealogical perspective, with regard to comprehensiveness with which the personal names of occupiers are recorded. It should also be noted that there is an added degree of complexity during the period in which the systems overlapped.

## 6.2.2 The manuscript records of the Valuation

The two principal repositories of the documentation arising from the Valuation are the National Archives of Ireland (where the records are catalogued with the prefix OL) and the Public Record Office of Northern Ireland (prefixed VAL), each covering their respective jurisdictions. However, NAI has a significant body of material relating to Northern Ireland, though at least some of this is duplicated in PRONI. It may be observed that NAI and PRONI use different terminology in categorising the records. With regard to the manuscript books of the Valuation, NAI distinguishes between different types of manuscript books, e.g. field books, house books and quarto[10] books. However, PRONI lists all manuscript books as field books.

The manuscript books, certainly for rural areas, are organised by parish and barony (it is important to bear in mind that some parishes were divided between two or more baronies) and because of the changing nature of the Valuation there are usually multiple books of one type or another for each parish. The manuscript books were working documents and so will contain many annotations as the valuators went about their work. While these can often be of a nature that makes deciphering the various scripts difficult, much of interest can be recorded, such as a change in occupancy. Collectively, Valuation records form a vast trove of material of interest to those studying nineteenth-century Ireland. Genealogists, of course, will be most interested in records that contain personal names. What follows is based primarily on such documentation.

### Names found in the Townland Valuation

The 1833 Instructions set the threshold for the inclusion of a house (or mill or other commercial or public building) at £3 (though houses valued at £2 10s were to be noted). An Act of 1836 raised this figure to £5, though many districts in the northern counties had been completed before this change was made. Even when the minimum was £3 the majority of rural dwellings were excluded from this valuation and there were many townlands where no houses at all were recorded. Inevitably, the houses listed tended to be the homes of the better off farmers. Descriptive particulars of the houses, including the names of occupiers, were recorded separately from the data gathered on agricultural land, though both sets of information may be found bound together in a single volume. On other occasions the evidence relating to the houses in a parish can be found in a separate book, designated a house book in the NAI listings.[11]

Each house – and, as noted above, this could refer to a range of building types – was given a code to indicate its age, construction materials and general condition. The coding, as defined in the Instructions issued to valuators in 1839, was as follows:

### New or nearly new
A+ Built or ornamented with cut stone and of superior solidity and finish
A  Very substantial building and finish, without cut stone ornament
A- Ordinary building and finish or either of the above when built 20
    or 25 years

### Medium
B+ Not new, but in sound order and good repair
B  Medium age, slightly decayed but in good repair
B- Medium, deteriorated by age, and not in perfect repair

### Old
C+ Old but in repair
C  Old and out of repair
C- Old and dilapidated, scarcely habitable

### Table for Dwelling Houses
1. Includes all slated dwelling-houses, built with stone, or brick, and lime mortar
2. Thatched houses, built with stone, or brick, and lime mortar
3. Thatched houses having stone walls, with mud, or puddle mortar; dry stone walls pointed, or mud walls of the best kind
4. Basement storeys of slated houses, used as dwellings

**Table for Offices**
1. Includes all slated offices, built with stone or brick walls, with good lime mortar
2. Thatched offices, built with stone, or brick walls and lime mortar
3. Thatched offices, having good stone walls, with mud or puddle mortar, dry stone walls pointed, or good mud walls
4. Thatched offices, built with dry stone walls
5. Basement storeys or cellars used as stores

Therefore, a house with the code 2B was a medium aged dwelling, built of stone or brick, with a thatched roof, and in fairly good repair. Of course, while the valuators tried to be consistent in applying these codes, inevitably there was a degree of subjectivity. The dimensions of the house were also given – length, breadth and height to the eaves. If the house had a return or a porch, the dimensions of these would be given separately and each would have its own code. The same details were provided for any outbuildings belonging to the house. Some of these outbuildings may simply have been categorised as 'offices', though often their specific use was identified, e.g. barn, stable, piggery and byre. If the 'house' was a mill or some other industrial enterprise further details might be given, such as information on the supply of water, the millstones and how many months the mill worked each year. In addition, separate mill books exist for many counties in NAI.

## Names found in the Tenement Valuation

The Tenement Valuation was a much more ambitious initiative, recording many more personal names than the Townland Valuation. Every tenement, i.e. individual holding, however great or small, was identified along with the name of the occupier, and other details, such as the extent of the tenement and its valuation. Generally speaking, the occupier was the head of the household. The same categories of books in use under the Townland Valuation continued to be used under the Tenement Valuation along with an important addition – tenure books, also known as 'perambulation' books. The National Archives holds the tenure books for counties in the Republic of Ireland (referenced OL/6), with the exception of those for Laois/Queen's County. PRONI has the equivalent volumes for Northern Ireland, though, as noted above, these are catalogued simply as field books (reference VAL/2/B). The tenure books are the earliest manuscript volumes to record in a systematic way all tenements, occupiers and lessors. They were produced to collate the information gathered for the Tenement Valuation and were used in producing the Primary Valuation (see below).

The information recorded in the tenure books was tabulated across a double-page spread. At the top, the name of the county, barony, parish and townland were entered (later the Ordnance Survey 6-inch county sheet number was added). Originally they included the lot number, occupier, immediate lessor, description of tenement, content of farm (i.e. acreage); rent, tenure, year let and observations. The description of tenement was a succinct summary of the property, e.g. 'house, offices and land', with offices referring to outbuildings. In the later stages of the Tenement Valuation, when the work had reached the most northerly counties, the column headings were:

No. and Letters of Reference to Map (see Valuation maps below)
Townlands and Occupiers
Immediate Lessors
Description of Tenement
Area (in acres, roods and perches)
Net Annual Value (distinguishing between land and buildings)
Rent and Tenure
Reputed Area of Tenement
Measurements of Buildings
Detailed Valuation of Tenements

The final column on the right hand side (what was eventually to be titled Detailed Valuation of Tenements) was in effect a column for observations (in fact, it was titled as such in the earlier tenure books). This column can contain a broad range of information, including dimensions of buildings – houses, outbuildings, mills, etc. Information may be recorded here that does not appear in the printed Primary (Griffith's) Valuation, to be discussed below. For example, in Tobernahulla townland, Lismore and Mocollop parish, County Waterford, the manuscript book notes that John and Patrick Lomasney, the joint holders of a farm, were minors and orphans – their parents were both dead and John was the elder brother. In Kilnaheery townland, County Tyrone, a tenant of a smallholding leased from Francis Gervais had a lower rent in comparison with his neighbours. The valuator recorded in the 'Observations' column that this was because the individual had 'got hurt' in his landlord's employment.

### Online access to the manuscript books

Many of the manuscript records of the Townland Valuation and Tenement Valuation are viewable on the website of the National Archives of Ireland (go to https://genealogy.nationalarchives.ie and then select 'Valuation Office house, field, tenure and quarto books 1824–1856'. It is possible to search by the specific category of manuscript book and also by the name of the occupier and the location (down to townland level). It must be realised that what survives depends on the Valuation the county was subject to. There are of course gaps and for some counties entire runs of particular books are not available online (even though it appears that the original volumes do exist in NAI). This database contains records for every county on the island of Ireland. The volumes accessible online for counties now in Northern Ireland appear, from their neat appearance, to be the 'fair copy' books produced under the Townland Valuation. The same dataset is also available through FamilySearch.org and this does have a browse function.

### 6.2.3 Valuation maps

Among the Valuation records held by NAI and PRONI are thousands of maps. In 1824 the work of the Ordnance Survey was extended to Ireland and a mammoth exercise in mapping the entire island in great detail was carried out. These maps were produced to assist with the work of the Valuation. Separate sets of Ordnance Survey maps were produced for each county, with the number of maps depending on the extent of the county in question. The maps themselves were prepared at a scale of six inches to the mile (hence they are often called the 6-inch maps) with the individual sheets measuring approximately 100 cm by 67 cm. No country in the world was mapped to the same degree of detail as Ireland at this time. It may be useful to note here that early boundary records, including sketch maps and registers, created by the Ordnance Survey as it carried out its task of mapping

Ireland can occasionally record the names of occupiers on the edges of townlands. Some of these for parts of counties Londonderry and Tyrone, 1825–32, can be found in PRONI (OS/4).

The staff of the Valuation of Ireland used these maps in carrying out their work. Under the Townland Valuation the numbers allocated separately to the 'lots' and to the houses within each townland were plotted on the 6-inch Ordnance Survey maps. This means that it is possible to work from the manuscript books to the maps to pinpoint the location of a house recorded in the former and so, potentially, discover where one's ancestors lived (acknowledging of course that only a fraction of the homes of the rural population are recorded in the Townland Valuation). However, revisions of the numbering in the manuscript books, as well as their reuse in the Tenement Valuation, means that sometimes this is not straightforward and requires some perseverance.

With the fuller information recorded in the Tenement Valuation, the maps prepared for it include much more detail, since every holding had to be identified. Moreover, if there were two or more dwellings on a holding they had to be distinguished from each other. As noted previously, the first column in the tenure books is titled 'No. and Letters of Reference to Map' (or words to that effect depending on the date of the book). The system of numbers and letters eventually settled on was as follows. Each tenement in a townland was given a unique number. Upper case letters refer to different blocks of land held by the same individual in a single townland. While many farms were compact entities, in other instances, a farmer may have been in possession of several distinct units of land in the same townland, e.g. 4A, 4B, and 4C, together forming a tenement.

If there was more than one dwelling on a holding, lower case letters were used to distinguish between them. Where a farmer had several labourers on his farm (or perhaps other family members, such as an unmarried sister or widowed mother), each with their own dwelling, then typically his residence would be given the letter 'a', and the others 'b', 'c' and 'd', and so on. For similar reasons to the issues highlighted above, there can be difficulties with correlating the information in the manuscript books with the maps. Usually, these are not insurmountable, but researchers should be aware of them nonetheless.

## 6.2.4 The Primary (Griffith's) Valuation

The Primary Valuation, better known as Griffith's Valuation after the Commissioner of Valuation, Sir Richard Griffith, is one of the best known Irish genealogical sources, and is all the more important because of the loss of nearly all nineteenth-century census returns. It derived from the work of the Tenement Valuation and was produced in printed and easily accessible form between 1847 and 1864. A total of 251 volumes were published with the data issued initially by barony and from 1853 onwards exclusively by Poor Law Union. Within each printed volume, the information is organised by parish (or sometimes electoral division) and townland (or by street within towns and cities). Poor Law Unions often straddled county boundaries and in these instances there will usually be a separate volume for each county covered by the Union. A place-name index at the front of each volume assists researchers with identifying the page or pages on which a townland will be found.

The data is presented in tabulated format and in a consistent, succinct manner, with the columns headed as follows:

*No. and Letters of Reference to Map*
As explained above, this allows a researcher to cross-reference to the maps of the Valuation and so pinpoint the location of a house or property.

*Townlands and Occupiers*
The name of the townland is indicated along with the Ordnance Survey county sheet number(s) on which the townland is mapped. The occupier is the individual in direct possession of the tenement and in practice was usually the head of household.

*Immediate Lessors*
The immediate lessor is the individual in the landholding hierarchy directly above the occupier. In many instances this will be the name of the landowner and the information in this column can be a helpful guide to identifying the relevant collection of estate papers.

*Description of Tenement*
This is given in a very concise way. For most farms the wording will be 'House, offices [i.e. outbuildings], and land'. Tenements of farm labourers may be rendered simply 'House' or 'House & small garden'.

Many rural tenements comprised no more than 'Land', with the occupier living elsewhere.

*Area*
This is given in statute measure and in acres, roods and perches (four roods in an acre and 40 perches in a rood).

*Rateable Annual Valuation*
There follow three columns giving the rateable annual valuation of the land and of the buildings, and then the total figure. The sums are given in pounds, shillings and pence. There were 20 shillings in a pound and 12 pennies in a shilling.

For an example of the way in which the information for a townland is presented in the Primary Valuation, along with the corresponding Valuation map (redrawn), see the inside front and back covers of this book. The townland in question is Fort-town in the parish of Ballymoney, County Antrim.[12]

## Some further comments on occupiers

When two people with the same name lived in a townland the valuator often included additional information in brackets to differentiate between them. This could perhaps be physical size, occupation, or father's name. For example, in the townland of Carrickayne in the parish of Donagheady, County Tyrone, there were two occupiers named Neal O'Neill, one nicknamed 'Short' and the other 'Long', and two men named Patrick O'Neill, one 'Little' and the other 'Big'. Taking another example, Coolnasillagh is a large townland of 1,168 acres in the parish of Errigal, County Londonderry, where many of the inhabitants at the time of Griffith's Valuation were named O'Kane. The following epithets appear after the O'Kane occupiers:

| | |
|---|---|
| Bernard (Boy) | John (Ecklin) |
| Bridget (Jack) | Michael (Micky) |
| Edward (Boy) | Michael (Shaun) |
| Edward (Donald) | Patrick (Boy) |
| James (Mick) | Patrick (Brien) |

It is interesting to note that sobriquets were used even if there was only one instance of a particular forename. In addition, there were three occupiers named Patrick Mullen in this townland who were distinguished by the names Harnish, Denny and Micky. For the most part, it appears that what we are seeing here (and elsewhere) is the Irish tradition of distinguishing people using the names of their fathers.

## Online access to the Primary Valuation

Free online access to the Primary (Griffith's) Valuation is available through the Ask About Ireland website (www.askaboutireland.ie/griffith-valuation). The website includes not only digital scans of the pages from the printed Valuation books, but also Valuation maps overlaid on Google maps (unfortunately there are some gaps in coverage). Searches can be carried out by the name of the occupier and also by place-name, though there is limited flexibility in terms of spelling variations. With regard to the Valuation maps available on this website, researchers need to be aware that these are not contemporaneous with the printed Valuation, but were produced a decade or more later. Therefore, if there were changes to the arrangement of the holdings in a townland in the intervening period (e.g. the amalgamation of farms and the consequent renumbering of the tenements), it may be difficult to match up the printed Valuation with the maps on the Ask About Ireland website. Subscribers to Findmypast also have access to Griffith's Valuation, including maps that are much closer in date to the printed Valuation.

## Appeals against the Primary Valuation

Those who were dissatisfied with the valuation placed on their tenement had the right to appeal. Appeals under the provisions of the 1846 Act included hearings convened at baronial level. Records relating to appeals carried out under the 1846 Act survive in NAI for County Carlow and for parts of counties Clare, Cork, Dublin, Kerry, Kildare, Kilkenny, Laois (Queen's), Limerick, Tipperary, Waterford and Wicklow. The documentation includes sub-commissioners appeal books, appeal application books, revising surveyors' books and printed post-appeal books. The most useful of these are the sub-commissioners' appeal books, which include notes of the hearings and the arguments made by the appellants. Much fascinating information emerges concerning farming practices and rural families. To take as an example, the following details concern the farm of Luke Reilly in Coolock, County Dublin: farm taken in 1830; 60 plantation acres; lease for three lives renewable forever; £21 to be paid on the fall of each life; built house and shed, while father-in-law built stable; first taken in 1812 or 1815.[13]

A new system of appeals was introduced by the 1852 Tenement Valuation Act. Surviving records exist for parts of counties Antrim, Cavan, Cork, Donegal, Dublin City, Galway, Kildare, Kilkenny, Leitrim, Mayo, Meath, Monaghan, Sligo, Tipperary, Tyrone and Westmeath. The available documentation is mainly in the form of appeal books, containing notes by revising valuators.[14] Some books of appeals were printed, though this was eventually discontinued due to costs. There are 24 post-appeal books in NAI and a number are available via the Ask About Ireland website.[15] The latter can be searched in the same way as conducting a search for a name in Griffith's Valuation.

One of the volumes on the Ask About Ireland website is: *County of Dublin. Barony of Coolock. North Dublin and Balrothery Unions. List of Alterations made by the Sub-Commissioners of Valuation on the Hearing of the Appeals for the Above Barony. Dated the 15th day of March, 1850.* The tabulated information includes the name of the occupier and the acreage of the landholding. In addition, there are columns distinguishing between the 'Primary Valuation of the Tenements' and the 'Valuation as Altered by Sub-Commissioners' and another headed Observations. The latter explains the nature of the changes and is full of interesting information. Frequently, the amendments involved naming the correct occupier or calculating the correct acreage belonging to a tenement.

## 6.2.5 Post Griffith's Valuation manuscript books

Once the appeals, revisions and other matters had been settled, a new set of Valuation books was created. The volumes for the Republic of Ireland are known as cancelled books and these are available in the Valuation Office in Lower Abbey Street, Dublin. The corresponding books for what is now Northern Ireland are held by PRONI (VAL/12/B) and are titled valuation revision books.[16] These volumes are arranged by district electoral division within each Poor Law Union. Typically, the individual volumes cover a certain period of time, e.g. 1864–79, 1880–84, and so on, and there will usually be an index to the townlands at the beginning of the book. As well as these manuscript books there are revised Valuation maps.

These manuscript books were updated on a regular basis to record changes in occupancy and the valuation of the land and buildings. When a change of occupancy occurred, the name of the occupier was crossed out and the newcomer's name written above it, while the year was noted on the right-hand side of the page. Different-coloured ink was often used to differentiate between years. It must be remembered that the year was the one in which the change was noted by the valuator, not necessarily the year in which the change occurred. Nonetheless, the years in which changes were recorded can help to establish significant events in family history, such as dates of death or emigration. Changes in the valuation of buildings can indicate when a new house was built or when the existing one was abandoned.

On rare occasions there can even be an illuminating comment on the circumstances of a particular family. For example, with regard to my great-great-grandfather Thomas Roulston's farm in Gortavea, County Tyrone, the valuator added the following comment in 1897: Div[ision]n asked for with son Cha[rle]s, one receipt & Chas has gone to Australia. Tho[ma]s still farms upon the land.' Charles was my great-grandfather and if he did go to Australia he did not stay there very long for in 1899 the valuator crossed out Thomas's name and replaced it with his. As will be discussed in more detail in Chapter 9, by the early years of the twentieth century most farmers moved from being tenants to owners, thanks to a series of land purchase acts. This explains the initials L.A.P. (Land Act Purchase) that may be found stamped on an entry in the revision lists. The change in ownership from landlord to farmer will also be indicated by the name of the former being crossed out and replaced with the term 'In fee'.

The cancelled books in the Valuation Office in Dublin are in the process of being digitally scanned and these can be accessed onsite at present. PRONI has digitised the equivalent volumes in its custody from the early 1860s through to around 1930 and these are available for viewing via the PRONI website.[17] Searches can only be carried out by place-name (or PRONI reference), not by the name of the occupier. PRONI holds a range of records, including maps and revision lists, relating to subsequent valuations in Northern Ireland: the First General Revaluation which was introduced in 1936 (VAL/3); the Second General Revaluation which commenced in 1957 (VAL/4); and the Third General Revaluation which began in 1975 (VAL/14).[18]

## 6.2.6 Why check the manuscript books if Griffith's is available?

Many people will examine the printed Griffith's Valuation, find their ancestors and leave it at that. However, it is always worth checking the manuscript books on which the printed Valuation was based. Occasionally, some of the names of the occupiers may be different. Even in the relatively brief period between the fieldwork and the printing of the Valuation there may have been changes in occupancy – perhaps as the result of death or emigration. Errors in spelling have been known to creep into the printed Valuation, often simply a misreading of a personal name. For instance, the surname Hanton appears in Griffith's Valuation for the townland of Tullyboy in the parish of Derryloran, County Londonderry. However, upon checking the manuscript book it will be seen that the correct form of the name is Stanton.[19]

Taking the example of Rochestown, a coastal townland of 104 acres in Templetrine parish, County Cork, it is possible to show that many more names appear in the manuscript books compared with the printed Griffith's Valuation (of 1851 in this instance). According to Griffith's Valuation, there were only two farms in Rochestown, with only one resident farmer – Michael Donovan, who held 72 acres; the other landholding, extending to 31 acres, was possessed by James R. Howe. In both instances the immediate lessor was Simon D. Palmer. On Howe's farm there were five houses, four of which were occupied. In addition to his own dwelling, there were 12 houses on Donovan's farm, no fewer than nine of which were unoccupied. Comparing Griffith's with the entry in the manuscript book, dated 26 March 1849, we find 11 names that do not appear in 1851. There is an even bigger disparity when the entry in the tenure book, dated 1 February 1847 is compared, with 14 names that do not appear in Griffith's. For another example of the usefulness of the manuscript books, see Chapter 7.

# Notes

1 For a discussion of tithes in the 1700s, see Maurice Bric, 'The tithe system in eighteenth-century Ireland', *PRIA*, 86C (1986), pp 271–88.

2 The latter can be downloaded as a PDF from the Tipperary Studies website (https://tipperarystudies.ie/digitisation-project/other-genealogical-resources).

3 James S. Donnelly, *Captain Rock: the Irish Agrarian Rebellion of 1821–1824* (2009), p. 209.

4 The ratios were as follows: 1 Irish (plantation) acre equalled 1.62 statute acres; 1 Cunningham acre equalled 1.29 statute acres.

5 In some instances urban backyards and gardens were included in tithe books.

6 In the NAI database of tithe records the townlands in the parish of Drumlease can be found among those for the parishes of Drumgoon, County Cavan, and Drumhome, County Donegal; the Drumlease maps are found under Drumhome.

7 It has been pointed out that this transcription has some major flaws (e.g. Grenham, *Tracing Your Irish Ancestors* (5th edition), p. 59). Note that parishes from Drung to Duncormick were missed inadvertently in the microfilming process. The tithe applotment books are also available (in a more user-friendly format) on FamilySearch.org.

8 See the following articles by Patrick O'Donoghue, all published in *Studia Hibernica*: 'Causes of the opposition to tithes, 1830–38', 4 (1965), pp 7–28; 'Opposition to tithe payments in 1830–31', 6 (1966), pp 69–98; 'Opposition to tithe payment in 1832–3', 12 (1972), pp 76–108. See also Michael O'Hanrahan, 'The tithe war in County Kilkenny, 1830–1834' in William Nolan and Kevin Whelan (eds), *Kilkenny: History and Society* (1990), pp 481–506.

9 McGee, *Archives of the Valuation of Ireland*, p. 196.

10 Quarto books were used to record information on buildings in towns.

11 Other manuscript books include the fair copy books containing the details gathered during fieldwork in a neatly presented format; and check books, recording details gathered for a number of areas as part of a process of verification. There are also calculation books, which were produced in the Valuation office and which contained limited detail.

12 This townland is the subject of careful study by Bill Macafee in *Townlands in Ulster*, ed. W.H. Crawford and R.H. Foy (1998), pp 35–65. Much additional information on the workings of the Valuation can be found on Bill's website (www.billmacafee.com).

13 McGee, *Archives of the Valuation of Ireland*, pp 167–8.

14 McGee, *Archives of the Valuation of Ireland*, p. 179.

[15] McGee, *Archives of the Valuation of Ireland*, pp 177–8. The surviving books are mostly for counties Dublin and Kilkenny, with others for Cork, Kildare, Limerick, Tipperary and Waterford. Only one of these books is known to have been printed under the 1852 Act.

[16] PRONI has the revisions of the Valuation maps listed under VAL/12/D.

[17] Accessible at www.nidirect.gov.uk/services/searching-valuation-revision-books.

[18] Also of interest are a series of valuers' note-books in PRONI (VAL/12A). These first appeared in 1894 and record the details behind the revising valuer's decision to revise, upwards or downwards, the valuation of those premises where an addition or other alteration had been made.

[19] See introduction by Bill Macafee to *The Drapers' Company, Maps of the Estate: County of Londonderry, 1857–1858* (2014), p. xxii.

# 7

# Records of the Encumbered/
# Landed Estates Court

## 7.1 The setting up of the Court

The records of the Encumbered[1] Estates Court and its successors are of sufficient importance and extent to be dealt with in a chapter of their own. The Great Famine had a massive impact on the economic viability of many landed estates in Ireland. The sharp decline in rental income and the increase in Poor Law rates created a situation where numerous estates that were already in serious difficulties were financially ruined. Sales of such estates were problematic because the rental income was often dwarfed by the value of the encumbrances (charges upon the property, such as mortgages) on them and any purchaser would have to be prepared to take on these debts. Furthermore, in many instances family settlements limited the owner's freedom to sell his estate, while in others the legal ownership of a property had spiralled into an impenetrable degree of complexity.

In an attempt to overcome these problems two Encumbered Estates Acts were passed in 1848 and 1849. The first of these proved a failure, but under the second a new tribunal was established, the Encumbered Estates Court, to which three commissioners or judges were appointed. A large townhouse in Henrietta Street, Dublin, was taken over and the stable to its rear was converted to a courthouse. On the application of an encumbrancer (creditor), termed the petitioner, the Court had the power to force the sale of an estate where the encumbrances exceeded 50% of the net annual rental income. The money generated by the sales was used to pay the creditors and the Court granted clear title to the purchasers of the lands.

Having accepted the invitation of the commissioners of the Encumbered Estates Court to produce a printed record of the lands coming before them, Henry Allnutt began publishing *Allnutt's Irish Land Schedule and Incumbered Estates Advertiser* in May 1850 and it continued to appear until 1871. Digital access to this newspaper is provided by the British Newspaper Archive (www.britishnewspaperarchive.co.uk). Many of the purchasers of lands through the Court were from the business, manufacturing and professional classes. However, few tenant farmers were able to buy the holdings they occupied.

While established in response to dire circumstances arising from the Famine, the work of the Court and its successors continued for decades. In 1858 the Court was established on a permanent basis with enhanced powers under a new name, the Landed Estates Court, which was based in the Four Courts complex on the north side of the River Liffey, Dublin. The Landed Estates Court also had the authority to sell unencumbered estates. As a result of the Judicature (Ireland) Act of 1877 the functions of the Court were assumed by the Land Judges Court within the Chancery Division of the High Court.

The role of the Encumbered Estates Court and successor bodies has been explored in several publications. These include Mary Cecelia Lyons, *Illustrated Incumbered Estates, Ireland, 1850–1905: Lithographic and Other Illustrative Material in the Incumbered Estates Rentals* (1993). Padraig Lane has written articles on the work of the Court with a particular focus on the province of Connacht, especially County Galway.[2] See also J.A. Dowling, 'The Landed Estates Court, Ireland', *Journal of Legal History*, 26:2 (2005), pp 143–82. In 2017 Jacqueline Ann Crowley completed a PhD thesis on '"The five year experiment": the Incumbered Estates Court 1849–54' in Maynooth University.[3]

## 7.2 The Court 'rentals'

In advance of the sale of an estate a printed catalogue or prospectus, often given the general name of 'rental', was produced. Typically, the front cover provided a summary listing of the lands for sale, identified the names of the landowner and petitioner, and gave the date and time of the auction. The catalogue was divided into a number of sections, with headings including 'Descriptive particulars' and 'Conditions of sale'. (There were of course variations in the way the material was titled and presented.) The latter highlighted such things as the terms on which the land was held and any charges on the land, such as annuities to members of the landowner's family. The 'Descriptive particulars' section was often used to place the lands in their broader geographical context, such as adjoining estates and proximity to market towns. There may also be comments on the general condition of the tenant farmers.

The lands being offered for sale were usually divided into a series of separate lots (the basis of a lot was often a townland). Maps were included to indicate, first of all, the relationship of the lots to each other and then to show the farms within each lot.[4] From a genealogical perspective the most valuable information is contained in the tables listing the names of the tenants in each lot. The ways in which the relevant data is presented varies, but the following headings were commonly used:

No. (i.e. the property number on the accompanying map)
Denomination of land
Names of tenants
Quantity of land
Yearly rent
Gale days (when the rent was paid)
Tenure of the tenants
Observations

The quantity of land was expressed in acres, roods and perches and was usually in statute measure, though sometimes the extent of each holding was also given in Irish or plantation measure. Some rentals have additional columns for 'Rent charge', 'Griffith's Valuation' and 'Poor Law Valuation'. The Observations column was used to record information that could not be fitted into the other columns. This could be a comment to the effect that the original leases or their counterparts would be available to the purchaser (or, alternatively, could not now be produced).

A perusal of the rentals reveals that on many occasions details of leases issued prior to 1800 can be found, giving the names of the lessees and, if relevant, the 'lives' and status of those lives, even if 'believed to be living' was the best assessment that could be made.

There may even be a comment as to where the individuals were living, especially if in America or another part of the world. On occasions land transactions from the 1600s can be found. In February 1862 the estate of Lt-Col. Wray Palliser in the baronies of Moydow and Granard, County Longford, were offered for sale through the Landed Estates Court. In the printed rental and particulars of sale drawn up prior to the sale there are references to more than a dozen early seventeenth-century deeds, including three leases issued in 1621 by Sir James Ware to, respectively, Teigue, Patrick and Donagh O'Heriaght.

## Families in Kilcoosh, County Galway

The rentals can also reveal the names of farmers who, for whatever reason, do not appear in the printed Primary (Griffith's) Valuation. For example, according to Griffith's Valuation, dating in this instance from 1855, the immediate lessor of the townland of Kilcoosh in the parish and barony of Killian, County Galway, was named J.N. Gerrard. The townland was evidently used for grazing livestock for its entire extent of 382 acres was part of a single tenement described as 'Herd's house and land'. The herd was not named, but there were four other houses, with no land attached to them, occupied by John Gaffey, Bridget Curley, William Gordon and Catherine Monaghan. What is not apparent from Griffith's alone is the dramatic transformation of the landscape of this townland in less than two years.

In June 1853 the estate of Geoffrey Davies Esq. in the barony of Killian was offered for sale in the Encumbered Estates Court. Among the townlands included in the sale was Kilcoosh, which was alternatively known as Killahouse. The rental reveals that Kilcoosh was divided into over 30 individual holdings and names each of the occupiers of these, thereby identifying many more occupiers than appear in Griffith's Valuation. The rental further divulges that nearly all of the holdings in this townland had been let under terms set by the Court of Chancery for seven years from 1 November 1847. Rather ominously for the tenant farmers, the rental indicates that these lettings would expire on the sale of the estate and the purchaser would be entitled to immediate possession of the lands.

On taking possession of Kilcoosh, J.N. Gerrard, who lived at Gibstown, County Meath, wasted no time in setting in motion his plans to clear the tenants from it. In September 1853 the sub-sheriff of County Galway and 11 constables arrived at Kilcoosh to inform the tenants that they were going to be ejected from their farms, but would be allowed to remain as caretakers until they had harvested their crops. However, once they had done so, they were required to leave. On this occasion there was no trouble and the tenants agreed to vacate their holdings by 1 November. However, this date came and went with the tenants remaining on their farms.

On 11 November the sub-sheriff returned to Kilcoosh, this time accompanied by 36 constables. They were met by over 400 men and women determined to resist them. Following an attempt to demolish some of the houses, the threat of violence became so severe that the sub-sheriff decided it was better to withdraw. Two weeks later, he again returned to Kilcoosh, his escort at this time comprising 40 constables and 55 soldiers. On this occasion the tenants accepted their fate, and 31 houses were unroofed. Ten families were allowed to remain as caretakers, but, as Griffith's reveals, this was only a temporary measure.[5]

## The Mulvin estate, County Tyrone

Taking the example of the Mulvin estate in County Tyrone, on which one of my own ancestral lines lived, we find that this property was advertised to be sold in the Landed Estates Court on 13 May 1859 (PRONI, D1201/75). The estate was not especially large, extending to just over 979 acres in the barony of Lower Strabane. The landowner was Hugh Auchinleck who, according to the 'Conditions of sale', was in possession of the estate by virtue of a fee farm grant issued in 1678 by Sir George Hamilton to David McClenahan. The 'Conditions of sale' also indicate that the estate was subject to a jointure, or yearly rent charge, of £200 per annum, payable to Mrs Elizabeth Mary Auchinleck, the mother of the landowner, who was aged about 55.

The townlands forming the estate were Mulvin, Liscreevaghan, Claudy Halliday, Claudy Blair, Claudy Johnston, Claudy Hood and Stonewalls – an interesting use of personal names in these place-names. These lands were to be sold in eight lots. Four of the lots comprised a single townland, the rest a combination of the entirety of one townland with part of another, or, in a single case, sections of two townlands. The smallest lot, Claudy Blair, was just under 35 acres, while the largest, Mulvin, was a little over 162 acres; the other lots were in the 113–151-acre range. The 'Descriptive particulars' for the estate drew attention to the proximity of the property to the town of Strabane, less than four miles away, which was 'one of the best market towns in the north of Ireland', and noted that the city of Londonderry was 15 miles away and of easy access thanks to the Derry and Enniskillen Railway line. The land was 'of good quality' and the tenants were 'respectable and in comfortable circumstances' and paid their rents punctually.

Over the following pages in the rental, the lots were mapped and the names of the tenants and the details of their tenancies were presented. While some of the farmers were simply tenants-at-will, others held leases, though none of the leases was issued before 1850, with the exception of an 1837 lease to a member of the Auchinleck family. William John Tynan, my great-great-great-grandfather's brother, was in possession of 54 acres in Claudy Johnston, part of Lot 2. His annual rent was £55 and he was expected to pay his rent on the first days of May and November. He had been issued with a lease for three lives or 31 years (whichever was of greater duration) by Hugh Auchinleck on 25 May 1855, the lives being Tynan himself, the Prince of Wales, and the Princess Royal (Princess Victoria of Prussia). In the Observations column some of the conditions of the lease were specified, such as the rights the landowner reserved to himself (e.g. mining and game) and the requirement that a tenant should not sub-let any part of his farm without the written consent of the landowner.

## 7.3 The availability of Court 'rentals'

The official archive of the Encumbered Estates Court and its successor courts from 1849 to the 1890s was lost in the destruction of the Public Record Office of Ireland in 1922. Herbert Wood's *Guide to the Public Records* (1919) gives some idea of the scale of the loss (pp 172–9). Nonetheless, there are various surviving sets of 'rentals'. Two of these sets are in the National Archives of Ireland, including the 'O'Brien rentals', considered to be the most comprehensive set. These would appear to be the 'very valuable collection of rentals of the former Incumbered Estates and present Landed Estates Court' that were presented to the Public Record Office of Ireland in 1882 by Octavius O'Brien, prompting Sir Samuel Ferguson, the Deputy

Keeper of the Public Records to declare that they were 'by much the most valuable donation made to this office since its establishment.'[6] A few years later this set of 'rentals' was transferred to the Land Commission, hence its survival of the 1922 disaster.[7] Related documents in NAI include conveyancing registers, 1850–81, and various petitions and sale notices, etc.

There are two sets of 'rentals' in the National Library of Ireland, including the collection known as 'Burke's rentals', which was assembled by Joseph Burke and is the most complete of the sets for the period 1850–64. In his book, *Vicissitudes of Families, and Other Essays* (1859), Bernard Burke, the Ulster King of Arms, wrote:

> A valuable, and probably unique collection of THE RENTALS of the various estates sold in the Encumbered Estates' Court, has been made by Joseph Burke, Esq., of Fitzwilliam Place, Dublin, Barrister-at-Law, so long associated with the administration of the Poor Law in Ireland. These Rentals may be considered the fullest history of Irish landed property ever brought together. They contain a description of the lands under sale, the tenants' names, descriptions of the demesnes, and frequently views of the mansion houses, with maps and local statistics, much more important than the particulars of sales at Chichester House under the direction of the Court of Claims. Mr. Burke has also collected reports of the sales, the names of the purchasers, and the amount of purchase-money:— in fine, this collection is, I believe, the sole perfect series of papers connected with the Encumbered Estates' Court. The Court itself does not possess so complete a set, and I doubt if the British Museum possess any (pp 9–10).

Joseph Burke died in late 1864 and under the terms of his will bequeathed the 'rentals' to the Royal Dublin Society.[8] The collection was later transferred to the National Library.

A fifth significant set of the rentals is available in PRONI (D1201). This collection, which concerns all of Ireland, runs to 82 volumes and covers the period 1849–60. PRONI also has an index to Encumbered Estates Court sales, covering the years 1850–59, on microfilm (MIC80/2). In addition to the above major sets of 'rentals', there are numerous other smaller collections and single items in archives across Ireland. Some of these are found within solicitors' collections, others within landed estate papers.

Findmypast.ie hosts a database of the 'Landed Estates Court Rentals 1850–1885' (which includes rentals produced by the predecessor and successor bodies), as does Ancestry. These databases appear to be based on the collections held by the National Archives of Ireland. A number of archives in Ireland have digitised some of their own rentals and made these available online. For example, Armagh County Museum has digitised a number of the rentals in its custody.[9] Limerick Archives has digitised a collection titled, 'Rentals and Particulars of Sale, 1808–1923', deriving from Nash & Sons, Estate Agents and Auctioneers, which includes several Encumbered Estates Court (and successor bodies) rentals.[10]

## Notes

[1] Incumbered was the spelling in use originally.

[2] For example, 'The Encumbered Estates Court, Ireland, 1848–9', *Economic and Social Review*, 3 (1972), pp 413–53; 'The general impact of the Encumbered Estates Act', *JGAHS*, 33 (1974), pp 44–74; 'The impact of the Encumbered Estates Court upon the landlords of Galway and Mayo', *JGAHS*, 38 (1981), pp 45–58; 'Purchasers of land in counties Galway and Mayo in the encumbered estates court, 1849–58', *JGAHS*, 43 (1991), pp 95–127; 'The Encumbered Estates Court and Galway ownership' in Gerard Moran and Raymond Gillespie (eds), *Galway: History and Society* (1996), pp 395–420.

[3] Available as a downloadable PDF via the Maynooth University Research Archive Library (http://mural.maynoothuniversity.ie). See also Jacqueline Crowley, 'County Meath landed estates and the Encumbered Estates Court, 1849–1867', *Ríocht na Mídhe*, 25 (2014), pp 197–225.

[4] In 1862 the use of Ordnance Survey maps as the basis of these maps became mandatory.

[5] This episode is told in W.E. Vaughan, *Landlords and Tenants in Mid-Victorian Ireland* (1994), p. 20.

[6] *14th Report of the Deputy Keeper of the Public Records of Ireland* (1882), p. 10. Ferguson wrote: 'My acknowledgments are also due in an especial manner to Mr Octavius O'Brien, one of the Solicitors, for his liberality and public spirit in presenting to this office his very valuable collection of Rentals of the former Incumbered Estates, and present Landed Estates

Court. It extends to 91 bound folio volumes, from February, 1850 to December, 1868, and 30 unbound folio bundles, from January, 1869 to December, 1881, together with 1 volume Index, from 1850 to 1866'.

7 The *19th Report* ... (1887), p. 10 includes the following note on this transfer: 'The Land Commission, finding that they required a complete set of the Incumbered and Landed Estates Court Rentals, made application to His Honor the Master of the Rolls, for a loan of the set of Rentals presented to this Department by the late Mr Octavius O'Brien, and after some correspondence, an order dated the 20th December, 1886, was made by His Honor, directing that the Rentals in question should be handed over to the Land Commission upon certain conditions, in pursuance of which they were transferred, for a limited period, to the Land Commission.' In his catalogue of the holdings in the Public Record Office, Herbert Wood wrote, 'where the rental is not to be found, the collection called "O'Brien's Rentals" in the office of the Land Commission should be consulted' (p. 177).

8 Henry F. Berry, *A History of the Royal Dublin Society* (1915), p. 290. Burke had valued the 'rentals' at £1,000.

9 https://visitarmagh.com/places-to-explore/armagh-county-museum.

10 www.limerick.ie/discover/explore/historical-resources/limerick-archives/archive-collections/rentals-and-particulars.

# 8

# Farmers and electoral records

The 1918 general election was the first in the UK and Ireland in which all men over 21 years of age were allowed to vote, and for the first time women, though only those aged over 30, were enfranchised.[1] For centuries before this the right to vote depended on various property qualifications. Consequently rural voters tended to be farmers, though as explained below not every farmer was able to vote. Prior to the abolition of the Irish Parliament under the terms of the Act of Union of 1800, each county constituency and each borough in Ireland could return two MPs to the Irish House of Commons in Dublin.

## 8.1 The electorate

Until the mid-nineteenth century the right to vote in parliamentary elections for county constituencies was linked not simply to the possession of land, but also to the terms on which that land was held. More specifically, the franchise was restricted to adult males in possession of freehold land, that is, land owned outright in fee simple or leased for the term of at least one life. (The subject of life leases is discussed in more detail in Chapter 4.) The freehold itself had to be worth at least 40 shillings (£2) a year once the rent and other duties had been paid. The majority of tenant farmers who were qualified to vote fell under the heading of '40-shilling freeholders'. It is worth emphasising the point that the possession of a lease for years, no matter how many years, did not entitle one to vote.

Landlords in possession of the fee simple of their estates (i.e. owned their estates outright) were able to issue life leases. Those who held land for a specified term of years – and this applied to many individuals who fall into the category of middlemen – were not. In addition, certain institutional landowners were forbidden from granting life leases. For example, the bishops and archbishops of the Church of Ireland, who were in possession of huge acreages, were only permitted to let land for a maximum of 21 years. Therefore, tenants and under-tenants of church lands could not vote. Also excluded from voting were Catholics between 1728 and 1793. On the other hand, Presbyterians and other nonconformist Protestants were never specifically denied the right to vote in parliamentary elections.

The leasing policy of an individual landowner also had an impact on the numbers of voters. Even if they had the power to do so, some landlords, for economic reasons and/or political apathy, rarely issued leases for lives and so the numbers of freeholders among their tenantry were small or non-existent. However, politically ambitious landlords used their power to create freeholds to increase their electoral clout. There was no secret ballot in this era and the way an individual cast his vote was public knowledge. Inevitably, therefore, much of the impetus for the registration of freeholders came from landlords who were anxious to use the votes of their tenants to influence the outcome of elections.

As a result of the Act of Union, MPs for Irish constituencies henceforth attended the United Kingdom Parliament at Westminster. The county franchise remained the same, and each county continued to have two MPs. In 1829 the Catholic Emancipation Act was passed, which allowed Catholics to serve as MPs. However, accompanying it was the Disenfranchisement Act, which raised the minimum threshold for voting from 40 shillings to £10, reducing the Irish electorate from c. 216,000 voters to 37,000. A few years later, the Irish Reform Act of 1832 amended the franchise. Those who could vote in county elections were now: freeholders, leaseholders for life and leaseholders for 60 years or more of property worth at least £10; and leaseholders for at least 14 years of property worth £20 or more. The Franchise Act of 1850 extended the county franchise to rated occupiers of property with a minimum £12 valuation. With the passing of this act, the right to vote was no longer linked to freehold or leasehold but to occupation.

The Ballot Act of 1872 introduced the secret ballot, which prevented election officials and anyone else from finding out which way an individual had voted. Two major pieces of legislation in the mid-1880s transformed the electorate and political representation in Ireland. The Representation of the People Act of 1884 increased substantially the number of electors. The franchise now included all adult male householders; adult sons still living with their parents and servants living in the homes of their employers continued to be excluded. It is reckoned that 64% of adult males were now able to vote. As a result of the Redistribution of Seats Act of 1885 counties in Ireland were now subdivided into single member constituencies.

By this time the land issue had become paramount in electoral politics and the stance of a candidate on land reform was often one of the principal factors that distinguished him from his opponents. (See Chapter 9 for more on land reform.) Policies designed to win the support of tenant farmers were to the fore, especially in those Ulster counties with a wafer-thin majority of nationalists over unionists (or vice-versa) and where a handful of voters could decide the outcome of an election. After Partition the concerns of farmers were given electoral expression in various ways. In the 1920s there was a short-lived political movement in Northern Ireland called the Unbought Tenants' Association, which enjoyed support particularly among Presbyterian farmers in County Antrim.[2] In the Republic of Ireland the Farmers Party and later Clann na Talmhan ('Party of the Land') enjoyed significant support from sections of the farming community.[3]

## 8.2 Electoral records

Electoral records prior to the mid-1800s come in two main forms: poll books and freeholders' registers. Introduced in 1696 in an effort to curb disputes over election results, poll books record the names of voters and the candidates for whom they voted. Freeholders' registers were designed to provide evidence of the authenticity of a particular individual's claim to have the right to vote. In most of these records the information provided about the voter or prospective voter is fairly basic – his name and the location of his freehold. The latter need not necessarily have been the same as his place of residence and so some lists will also give the freeholder's abode. It became increasingly popular in the early nineteenth century for printed registers of freeholders to be produced, which usually provided fuller information. Typically, these gave the name and residence of the freeholder, specified the location of the freehold, named the freeholder's landlord, and identified the individuals named as 'lives' in the freeholder's lease.

Researchers should not discount the possibility that farmers may be listed as electors in the registers and poll books concerning what might appear to be purely urban constituencies. For instance, the Cork City constituency comprised not simply the city itself, but also its 'Liberties', which extended some 5–6 miles from the suburbs. Many tenant farmers lived in this extensive district and were able to vote if they qualified as freeholders.[4]

Additional and sometimes illuminating information can be found within many of these electoral records, often in the form of annotations or in columns headed 'Observations'. For example, a poll book concerning a by-election in County Clare in 1745 (PRONI, T3343/1) includes numerous observations on the freeholders. The following comments were made about Charles Cantrell:

> Observation: his freehold is a lease for lives made about 20th March last. Had a promise of a lease of lives before, and was two years in possession. Derives under Francis Macnamara, who demised to this voter by power of attorney from John Macnamara, the said Francis's son.
> Objection to this vote: Francis Macnamara was but tenant for life, and he being dead, that the lease dropped.
> Answer: that it is to be surrendered. Even if he were tenant for life, that he had a power to make leases for lives.

Among the objections made to certain individuals exercising their right to vote in County Armagh in 1753 was the allegation that Robert Jones had been 'seen at Mass & giving offerings to the priest' (PRONI, T808/14949). Other grounds on which objections had been made included: 'for being a minor'; 'for being married to a Papist'; 'for having a daughter aged over 14 living with him, who is a Papist'; 'for being a minor & an apprentice'; and 'for not having conformed properly'. The objections noted in a Limerick poll book of 1761 include the following entry for John Baggs of Curraghturk:

> The Voter being asked what religion his wife was of when he married answered he heard and believed she was then a Papist, but says it was before the [1697] Act, says he married about 60 years ago, does not know whether she continued a papist or not, no objection.[5]

Given the way in which county elections were dominated by the landed elite, many electoral records can be found within landed estate collections. A document of 1826 in the Foster/Oriel estate collection in PRONI is headed, 'State of my tenantry who polled or offered to poll at the Election' (D562/14698). This reveals that Lord Oriel had 270 freeholders on his estate who were registered in time for the 1826 election. Over 100 of these men did not cast a vote because of technical flaws in their registry. Correspondence within estate collections can also provide additional information on electors. The following letter of 16 June 1826 was written by William D'Arcy Irvine of Castle Irvine, County Fermanagh, to one of the Maxwells of Farnham, County Cavan:

> The bearer, a tenant of mine in this country – his name is Davis – has a farm of land for ever near Cavan and has applied to me to advise him who to vote for at the ensuing election. As he has four tenants registered, and as I am anxious for the Protestant cause, I have desired him to give them to you and also to Saunderson, provided Saunderson has pledged himself to vote against popish emancipation. He has a £20 vote himself and wishes to have it registered for another occasion (PRONI, T3422/A/4/42).

## 8.3 Available electoral records

Collections of electoral records can be found in the major repositories in Ireland, and those in NLI and PRONI can be identified using the online catalogues of those institutions. The Sources Catalogue (sources.nli.ie) can be used to identify additional material in other archives and libraries. Most of the surviving eighteenth- and early nineteenth-century electoral records for counties in Ulster have been indexed by PRONI and are available as a searchable database – the collection has been titled 'Freeholders' records' – on its website (www.nidirect.gov.uk/proni). The number of surviving records for each county varies considerably – very good for Armagh and Down, especially for the 1810–30 period, but woeful for County Tyrone, where the solitary item concerns the barony of Dungannon for a few years in the 1790s. A detailed listing of pre-1800 election records for Ulster is found in William J. Roulston, *Researching Scots-Irish Ancestors* (2nd edition, 2018); this includes some items not in the PRONI database.

The following selection of election records in the archives, as well as printed and published material, covers non-Ulster counties to around 1830. A proportion of them will be available online through various outlets.[6]

*County Carlow*
List of voters in County Carlow [*c.* 1767] – NLI, n.6305, p.7142
Rosemary Ffolliott, 'Co. Carlow freeholders in 1767', *Irish Ancestor*, 12 (1980), pp 45–7
*List of freeholders registered in the year ending 31st December, 1830* – NLI, Ms 29,778/2

*County Clare*
List of voters at the parliamentary election for County Clare, 1745 – TCD, MS 2059; PRONI, T3343/1
Lists of freeholders in County Clare, and how they voted, with observations on some of the freeholders, 1768, 1776, 1783 – NLI, MSS 14793–14795
S.C. O'Mahony and Rosemary ffolliott, 'Co. Clare voters in 1768', *Irish Ancestor*, 18 (1986), pp 14–26
Various lists of freeholders, 1820s – NLI, ILB 324
Freeholders of County Clare, 1829 – NLI, GO MS 443; NLI n.5425 p.5556; PRONI, MIC353/1

*County Cork*
An exact list of the freemen and freeholders, who voted at the election for two members to serve in Parliament for the city of Cork, 1783 – NLI, Pamphlet volume BB7473
City of Cork election ... 1826, with lists of freemen and freeholders who voted – NLI, Dix Cork [1827]

*County Dublin*
Poll book for County Dublin, with observations on many of the voters (incomplete), 1768 – NLI, MS 9362
Printed poll books concerning parliamentary elections in County Dublin, 1806, 1807, 1818, 1820 – NLI, MSS 6128–6131

*County Kerry*
List of the freeholders in the manor of Kerry, pre-1674 – National Library of Wales, Powis Castle Estate Records, 22280

*County Kilkenny*
Notes on County Kilkenny freeholders, 1775 – PRONI, T3324/6
List of County Kilkenny freeholders, 1809–19 – NLI, MS 14,181

*County Laois*
Freeholders of Queen's County, 1758–75 – NLI, GO MS 443;
   PRONI, MIC353/1, T3324/3
Queen's County poll books, *c.* 1760, 1779 – NLI, n.3446, p.3064
List of freeholders in the barony of Ballyadams, 1817
   – NLI, MS 9961
List of freeholders in Queen's County, *c.* 1827
   – NAI, CSO/OPMA/1187

*County Leitrim*
County Leitrim freeholders, 1791 – NLI, GO MS 665
List of freeholders or voters in County Leitrim arranged
   alphabetically by barony, early 1800s – NLI, MS 3830
List of freeholders of the barony of Mohill, *c.* 1807
   – NLI, MS 9628

*County Limerick*
Noel Murphy, 'List of freeholders who voted in the 1760 election in
   Limerick', *North Munster Antiquarian Journal*, 52 (2012),
   pp 115–31
List of County Limerick freeholders, 1761 – NLI, MS 14,248
County Limerick poll book, 1761 – PRONI, MIC312/1
List of freeholders in County Limerick, 1776 – NAI, M 1321–2;
   NLI, LO 159
Two registers of voters or canvassers' note-books relating to County
   Limerick, *c.* 1820 – NLI, MSS 14,118–14,119

*County Longford*
Copy of the registry book of freeholders for County Longford,
   1747–1806 – NAI, M 2745
Lists of freeholders for County Longford, *c.* 1790
   – NAI, M 2486–8
Lists of freeholders in County Longford, *c.* 1800–1835
   – NLI, GO MS 444
Collection of freeholders' certificates for County Longford,
   1828–36 – NAI, M 2781

*County Louth*

List of freeholders in the Foster/Oriel estate, 1820 – PRONI,
D562/14675

Comments on a large number of freeholders who either are or are
not to be registered in October 1824 for County Louth
– PRONI, D562/14687

'State of my tenantry [Foster/Oriel estate] who polled or offered to
poll at the Election', 1826 – PRONI, D562/14698

Printed *Lists of Registered Freeholders of the County of Louth*, 1820s
– NLI, D73 etc; PRONI, T2519/14

*County Mayo*

John Maycock, 'Voters' list prepared for election to Grattan's
Parliament in 1783 from the estate of the Earl of Altamont',
*Cathair na Mart*, 26 (2008), pp 119–22 (see also *Cathair na Mart*,
34 (2017), pp 48–9)

*County Meath*

List of freeholders for County Meath, *c.* 1775–1780 – NLI, GO
MS 442; PRONI, MIC353/1, T3324/8, T3330/3

List of freeholders in County Meath, 1781 – PRONI, T3318/3

Alphabetical list of Meath freeholders, 1794 (typescript copy)
– RIA, Upton Papers, No. 12

Volume containing listings of and notes on the County Meath
electorate prior to the 1807 general election – PRONI, T3163/2/1

List of people to be registered in County Meath with rough notes
on the back, 1823 – PRONI, D562/14686

*County Offaly*

A photostat of a memorandum book containing lists of voters in
King's County, with notes on their political affiliations, *c.* 1770
– NLI, MS 2050

*County Roscommon*

Freeholders of County Roscommon, *c.* 1780 – NLI, GO MS 442;
PRONI, MIC353/1

Poll book for County Roscommon parliamentary election, 1783
– NLI, MS 3086

Lists of freeholders in County Roscommon, *c.* 1790–1799
– NLI, MS 10,130

List of freeholders in the Strokestown area, 1815 – NLI, MS 18,765

*County Sligo*
Books recording names and addresses of County Sligo freeholders
and their dates of registration, 1783–1790 – PRONI, D4031/D/5
Alphabetical list of voters in Sligo town and county, noting dates of
registration, political leanings, addresses, names of landlords, and
other points, *c.* 1790 – NLI, MS 2169
Alphabetical list of freeholders in County Sligo, 1795–6
– NLI, MS 3136
Candidate's election book for County Sligo giving names and
addresses of freeholders or electors with other observations, 1796
– NLI, MS 2733
List of County Sligo freeholders, 1817 – NLI, MSS 9758–9759
List of freeholders in County Sligo, *c.* 1827 – NAI,
CSO/OPMA/1188

*County Tipperary*
Freeholders of County Tipperary, 1775–6 – NAI, M 1321–2; NLI,
GO MS 442; PRONI, MIC353/1, T3324/7, T3318/2, T3330/4

*County Waterford*
Lists of freeholders for different baronies in County Waterford,
1826 – NLI, EPH E423–E428

*County Westmeath*
List of voters at a poll to elect MPs for County Westmeath, 1761
(including typescript) – NLI, MSS 2296–2297
Copies of County Westmeath poll books, 1761 – NLI,
GO MS 443; PRONI, T3324/4A–B, T3330/2, MIC353/1

*County Wexford*
List of freeholders, 1790 – NLI, LO Folder 8/26
Certificates of 40-shilling freeholders on the estate of Henry Alcock
of Wilton, barony of Bantry, 1806 – NLI, n.4446, p.4117

*County Wicklow*
A list of the freeholders of the County of Wicklow who polled at an
election, 1745; a list of those who did not vote; a list of those
who have estates of inheritance in County Wicklow – NAI,
999/452; NLI, n.5481, p.5648
Poll book for County Wicklow, 1745 – PRONI, T2659/1

Annotated lists of freeholders from a County Wicklow poll book, 1745–59 – NAI, 999/630
List of freeholders of the Earl of Aldborough, *c.* 1790(?) – PRONI, D2538/E/5

# Notes

1   Women aged over 21 were given the vote in what was then the Free State in 1923 and in Northern Ireland, as was the case across the United Kingdom, in 1928.

2   In 1925 the Association's candidate, George Henderson, was returned to the Northern Ireland Parliament as one of the representatives for Antrim. Some records relating to the Association can be found in PRONI (FIN/18/4/322, FIN/30/F/A/15A–B, HA/5/1263).

3   Jason Knirck, '"A regime of squandermania": the Irish Farmers' Party, agriculture and democracy 1922–27' in Mel Farrell, Jason Knirck and Ciara Meehan (eds), *A Formative Decade: Ireland in the 1920s* (2015), pp 177–96; Tony Varley and Peter Moser, 'Clann na Talmhan : Ireland's last farmers' party', *History Ireland*, 3:2 (1995), pp 39–43; Tony Varley, 'The politics of "holding the balance": Irish farmers' parties and land redistribution in the twentieth century' in Fergus Campbell and Tony Varley (eds), *Land Questions in Modern Ireland* (2013), pp 238–65.

4   Peter J. Jupp and Stephen A. Royle, 'The social geography of Cork City elections, 1801–30', *Irish Historical Studies*, 29:113 (May 1994), pp 13–43. The authors used a bound volume of pamphlets and other electoral material titled *Cork Elections, 1812–1830* in Cork County Library.

5   Nick Reddan, 'Objections recorded in the Limerick poll book 1761', *The Irish Genealogist*, 14:4 (2017), pp 584–9.

6   For example, some excellent material for County Louth can be accessed at www.jbhall.clahs.ie/louth_freeholders.htm and for County Clare at www.clarelibrary.ie/eolas/coclare/genealogy/genealog.htm.

# 9

# Farmers and land reform

In the late nineteenth and early twentieth centuries the great majority of farmers in Ireland were transformed from tenants to proprietors as the result of parliamentary legislation. In the process the landed estate system was dismantled. This chapter outlines the impact of land reform on farmers and shows how researchers can find out more about how this affected their own farming ancestors. The exploration of records relating to land reform requires much persistence. Nonetheless, in studying them it may be possible to gain a fuller understanding of the major changes that affected farming families in Ireland during this era.

## 9.1 Land reform in Ireland

Agitation for reforming the land system in Ireland grew in strength in the course of the nineteenth century. In the mid-1800s the demand for legal recognition of the phenomenon known as Tenant Right became an electoral issue.[1] Tenant Right, also known in the north of Ireland as the Ulster Custom, meant different things at different times and in different places. One succinct description of it was given by John Hancock, the agent on Lord Lurgan's estate, when appearing before the Devon Commission in 1844:

> Tenant-right, then, I consider to be the claim of the tenant and his heirs to continue in undisturbed possession of the farm, so long as the rent is paid; and in case of an ejectment, or in the event of a change of occupancy, whether at the wish of the landlord or tenant, it is the sum of money which the new occupier must pay to the old one, for the peaceable enjoyment of his holding.[2]

The issue of Tenant Right died away after the early 1850s. However, with the election of a Liberal government headed by W.E. Gladstone in 1868 there were expectations that a programme of reform would be implemented in Ireland, including legislation concerning the land question. This led to the revival of Tenant Right as a major political issue and the passing of laws addressing the land issue. The motivations driving land reform can be found in a speech given by Andrew Elder of Ashgrove, Castlefin, County Donegal, before a 5,000-strong crowd in Ballybofey in early January 1870:

> My friends, the first act of oppression that ever fixed itself on my mind, and which occurred under my own personal observation is the following: Some years ago, when I was a boy, my father occupied a farm as tenant-at-will, and on one occasion I was sent to the Office to pay rent to the agent. While I was there, a dispute arose between two tenants respecting a mearin ditch. The agent, after hearing the circumstances, got up and said – A certain thing must be done. One of the tenants replied – I will not allow that to be done; I will not allow my land to be spoiled. The agent again rose, and addressing the tenant, said – "You have no land, sir." Up to that moment I thought my father had some land, but when I heard the words of the agent, then I began to question, in my own mind, whether he (my father) had any land at all. I came home and told my father what had occurred, and I stamped my foot on the ground, and promised never to plough a furrow of tenant-at-will land in Ireland.[3]

The impact of the land acts will be looked at presently. Before doing so, several other pieces of legislation affecting tenant farmers will be considered briefly.

## 9.1.1 Mid-nineteenth-century legislation

Chapter 4 discussed leases for lives and highlighted the difficulties for landlords in keeping track of the status of those lives, especially if they had been nominated by the tenant. In part to resolve some of the complexity associated with them, the Renewable Leasehold Conversion Act was passed in 1849. This allowed someone in possession of a lease for lives renewable forever to have it converted to a fee farm grant (i.e. a grant in perpetuity). The extent to which this was availed of by farmers is unclear – obviously it was only of relevance to a minority of tenants.

A number of deeds relating to this legislation exist in the archives. For example, dating from 1859 is a notice requiring the execution of a fee farm grant in County Antrim under the provisions of the Renewable Leasehold Conversion Act, the parties to which were William Simpson, John Johnston Kirkpatrick, both of Ballyclare, Robert Wilson Simpson of Larne and Charles Agnew of London (PRONI, D542/28).

The 1860 Landlord and Tenant Law Amendment Act – generally known as Deasy's Act from the name of the Attorney-General – was considered to favour the landlord over the tenant. However, it also introduced the 'notion of contract as the basis of relationship of landlord and tenant.'[4] In the same year the Landed Property (Ireland) Improvement Act – often called Cardwell's Act after the Chief Secretary of Ireland – was passed. This allowed tenants to claim for compensation from their landlords for improvements they had carried out, so long as they had prior permission to execute these. Some records arising from the latter act can be found in the Crown and Peace archive for County Londonderry in PRONI. These include a 'Petition and Order Book', 1861–1903 (LOND/3/1/1/1) and 'Petitions, Papers and Leases, 1872–93, 1877–91 (LOND/3/1/2/2–3).

## 9.1.2 The Irish Church Act of 1869

The first parliamentary act with major implications for land ownership was the Irish Church Act of 1869, which disestablished the Church of Ireland. Under the terms of this act the Commissioners of Church Temporalities took possession of the property of the church on 1 January 1871. This included the extensive lands of the church which were estimated to have a total annual value of over £225,000. The Commissioners were authorised to offer each of the tenants of these lands the opportunity to acquire his or her holding in fee simple. The great majority of those who availed of the terms offered to them were year-to-year tenants and those holding short leases. The purchase price was to be set by the Commissioners following a valuation of the holding. The process was a relatively straightforward one for the tenant. He was required to provide one quarter of the purchase price with the rest paid off in instalments. As a result of the 1881 Land Act the responsibilities of the Commissioners of Church Temporalities were transferred to the Irish Land Commission (see below), though by this time most of their work had been completed.

A review of the work of the Commissioners can be found in *Commissioners of Church Temporalities in Ireland Report, 1869–80* (1881). The appendix to this report includes a schedule of sales of 'Yearly and Other Tenures'. Arranged by diocese and parish, this gives the name of the purchaser, the townland, the date of the sale, the acreage of the holding, the Tenement Valuation, the annual rent and the purchase money. The surviving records of the Commissioners of Church Temporalities for Northern Ireland are available in PRONI under reference FIN/10/10. Each item in this collection has been given a unique code beginning CT. For example, CT 7440 is an instalment mortgage between Robert Hopper and the Commissioners of Church Temporalities in Ireland for £188 11s 9d for part of the lands of Drumshanbo, County Tyrone. For more on this subject, see the article by Hugh Shearman: 'State-aided land purchase under the Disestablishment Act of 1869', *Irish Historical Studies*, 4:13 (March 1944), pp 58–80. Shearman observed that 'the commissioners made a particularly conscientious and successful effort to promote the conversion of small tenant farms into peasant proprietorship.'

### 9.1.3 The 1870 Land Act

In contrast to the Irish Church Act, the 1870 Landlord and Tenant (Ireland) Act, though it may have been important as far as the relationship between farmer and landowner was concerned, did not have the same impact on changing tenants into proprietors. The Act sought to compensate tenants for improvements made by them to their holding or for any disturbance to their occupancy and provided legal recognition for Tenant Right in those areas where it was customary. The Act also provided a method by which tenants could purchase their holdings. However, in comparison with the scheme allowing tenants of church lands to purchase their holdings this one was far less successful. While there were over 6,000 purchasers across Ireland as a whole under the Irish Church Act of 1869, there were fewer than 900 purchasers under the 1870 Land Act (408 in the six counties of what became Northern Ireland).

There were various explanations for this. First of all, there was no compulsion on landlords to part with their land. Second, although tenants were provided with the facilities through the Board of Works to borrow up to two-thirds of the purchase price, which they could repay over 35 years at 5% interest, that still left them having to find the remaining third. For most farmers this was too much. Furthermore, so long as the loan remained unpaid in full the purchaser was not allowed, on penalty of forfeiture, to mortgage, assign or subdivide his farm without the permission of the Board of Works. For these and other reasons, comparatively few farmers took advantage of the provisions of this legislation to become proprietors.

## 9.1.4 The Bessborough Commission

The Bessborough Commission of 1880 investigated the impact of the 1870 Land Act and considered ways of improving the relationship between landowners and their tenants and facilitating the purchase of farms by tenants. Some 700 people gave evidence to the Commission, around 500 of whom were tenant farmers, and their testimony provides a fascinating insight into the state of agriculture and the farming community at that time. Occasionally lists of tenants in certain townlands were provided. For example, in testifying before the Commission on 28 September 1880 John Flanagan and John Taylor jun., representing the Castlefin Tenants' Defence Association, came well prepared. They provided the Commissioners with lists of tenants on a number of properties in County Donegal whose rents had been raised, including the Shanvally estate of Rev. Robert Delap and the Meenglass estate of Lord Lifford, details which made it into the printed report.[5] Among other things the Commission recommended that the '3 Fs' (fixity of tenure, fair rent and free sale) should be conceded to tenants and this was enshrined in the subsequent 1881 Land Act.

## 9.1.5 The 1881 Land Act and the Irish Land Commission

The passing of the 1881 Land Law (Ireland) Act marked another major development in land reform with, among other things, the establishment of the Irish Land Commission. Acting under the authority of the Land Commission, several dozen sub-commissioners working across Ireland were responsible for adjudicating on fair rents, initially for yearly tenancies and subsequently for leaseholders. What became known as 'first term' judicial rents were those fixed before 16 August 1896; 'second term' judicial rents were fixed between 15

August 1896 and 16 August 1911; and 'third term' judicial rents were fixed after 15 August 1911. Over the period 1881–1902 the sub-commissioners deliberated on nearly 350,000 cases, in the process helping to calm unrest among tenant farmers.

The 1881 Act also included slightly improved terms for farmers wishing to purchase their holdings. Tenants could borrow three-quarters of the purchase price and repay this at a rate of 5% over 35 years. In addition, the threat of forfeiture, should they fall behind in their repayments, was removed. However, the numbers availing of these terms were small – only 731 across the entire island, even fewer than under the 1870 Land Act. There were several reasons for this, including the fact that landlords remained under no compulsion to sell, while for many farmers raising even one quarter of the purchase price remained beyond them.

## 9.1.6 The Ashbourne and Wyndham Acts

The limited impact on land purchase of previous legislation changed with the passing of the 1885 Purchase of Land (Ireland) Act, known as the Ashbourne Act after Lord Ashbourne, the Lord Chancellor of Ireland. The Ashbourne Act allowed tenants to borrow the full amount of the purchase price from the Land Commission, which would be repaid over 49 years at 4%. While still not obliged to sell, some landlords realised that this was an opportunity to dispose of at least part of their lands to the occupying tenants. Between 1885 and 1888 more than 25,000 tenants purchased their holdings. Further land acts passed in 1891 and 1896 were designed to make land purchase more appealing. Nonetheless, while the land acts passed between 1870 and 1896 led to the sale of nearly 74,000 holdings totalling 2,500,000 acres, this was still only around 10% of the land in Ireland.[6]

The most important of the Irish land acts is generally considered to be that of 1903. Popularly known as the Wyndham Act after George Wyndham, the Chief Secretary of Ireland, it originated in a conference held in December 1902, which brought together landlord and tenant to discuss further land reform. The Wyndham Act offered the landlords a 12% bonus if they agreed to sell their entire estate (significantly for the recipient, this bonus was safe from creditors). By giving landlords a powerful inducement to sell, this act, more than any other, brought about the transfer of estates from landlord to tenant. For the purchasing farmer, the annuities he paid were significantly less than his rent. By 1921 more than 270,000 holdings on nearly 9,500 estates – just over 9,000,000 acres – had been sold.[7] Studies of the impact of land reform and especially the Wyndham Act include contributions by Patrick Cosgrove on the Leinster and Redmond estates. The former was located principally in County Kildare, while the Redmond estate in County Wexford was inherited by the Irish nationalist leader, John Redmond, following the death of an uncle in 1902.[8]

## 9.1.7 Congested Districts Board

The Land Commission was not the only body with responsibility for selling estates. The Congested Districts Board (CDB) was established by Arthur Balfour, the Chief Secretary of Ireland, under the provisions of the Land Act of 1891. It operated initially in nearly 400 electoral divisions across eight counties in the west of the island where living standards were low (Cork, Donegal, Galway, Kerry, Leitrim, Mayo, Roscommon and Sligo). The CDB was an agency for regional development, promoting local industries, facilitating the transfer of land from landlord to tenant, improving farms and agricultural practices, and expanding the rail network, among other activities. For example, in County Donegal the manufacture of carpets was promoted in Killybegs, successful lace schools were established in Ardara and Glenties, and improved harbour facilities were provided at a number of ports. By the time of its dissolution in 1923, the Congested Districts Board had purchased nearly 1.8 million acres from 874 landlords.[9]

## 9.1.8 Post Partition land acts in the Republic of Ireland

Though the land acts had transformed landholding in Ireland, in 1921 millions of acres remained in the possession of landlords and tens of thousands of farmers continued to be tenants. Many estates, even some fairly substantial properties, had been largely untouched by land purchase. In addition, the lengthy process of transferring land from landlord to tenant meant that many farmers were still waiting for the advances to allow them to buy out their farms. Continued efforts to relieve congestion were also considered to be of paramount importance. The 1923 Land Act in the Irish Free State (the forerunner of the Republic of Ireland) was intended to resolve the land issue once and for all. The Land Commission was reconstituted with powers to acquire lands by compulsion and redistribute these. The terms under which landlords were forced to sell what remained of their estates were not as advantageous as earlier land acts, but for the tenants they were a considerable improvement. As a result of the 1923 Act and subsequent legislation, most of the 114,000 landholdings that had not previously been sold were transferred into the possession of farmers by the end of the 1930s.[10]

## 9.1.9 The Land Purchase Commission, Northern Ireland

In Northern Ireland the powers and remit of the Land Commission were transferred to a new body – the Land Purchase Commission – in 1923. Two years later, the Northern Ireland Land Act altered the rate of the purchase annuity and abolished the power to fix judicial rents. Of more far-reaching significance, remaining tenanted land was automatically vested with the Land Purchase Commission. Through vesting orders the Commission was empowered to transfer the land into the ownership of the tenants. The purchase price and annuities were determined by the value of the rent for the landholding in question and the period for repaying the loan was set at 65½ years. The work of the Commission proceeded apace and around 39,000 holdings were sold under the terms of the 1925 Act. In 1935 the Northern Ireland Land Purchase (Winding Up) Act abolished the Land Purchase Commission. The Commission ceased to exist on 1 April 1937 when its jurisdiction was transferred to the High Court of Justice in Northern Ireland; its functions relating to drainage and turbary and to sporting and mineral rights passed to the Ministry of Finance.

## 9.2 The records of land reform

The records generated by the various land reform initiatives are vast in number. It must also be acknowledged that they are not easy to get to grips with and, as noted in the introductory paragraph of this chapter, much patience is needed in examining them. It may be observed that one fairly straightforward way to find out approximately when a tenant farmer purchased his holding is to check the cancelled or valuation revision books (see Chapter 6.2.5). A stamp bearing the initials L.A.P. (for Land Act Purchase) was used to indicate that a tenant had bought his holding. The date written in ink in the right-hand column of the book indicates the year *by* which (not necessarily *in* which) this had occurred.

## 9.2.1 Records in PRONI

The records arising from the operation of the land acts in the six counties of Northern Ireland are in PRONI and will be discussed under the headings of the different archival divisions in which they are found.

### *Land Registry archive*

The Land Registry archive at PRONI is a vast collection of documentation that was generated as the result of the various acts of parliament, which facilitated the transfer of land from landlord to tenant. Records created prior to 1922 were transferred from Dublin to Northern Ireland and subsequently deposited in PRONI along with material generated post-partition. The title Land Registry is slightly misleading for the records themselves relate primarily to the work of the Land Commission, not the Land Registry. (For the Land Registry, see Chapter 5.) All references to items in the collection begin LR1.

According to PRONI's catalogue, around 20% of the papers in the Land Registry archive derive from the Land Acts passed before the Wyndham Act of 1903; approximately 33% of the papers originated under the 1903–09 land acts; the rest of the papers, forming the single largest component in the archive, were created under the 1925 Act. The catalogue description may contain the phrase 'Record Number', followed by two initials and then a number. The initials LJ (Land Judges) refer to records generated by the pre-1903 land acts; the initials EC (Estates Commissioners) relate to records produced under the 1903–09 acts; and the initials NI (Northern Ireland) derive from the 1925 Land Act. The number after the initials refers to the original reference given to the estate by the Land Commission or its successor.

For the larger estates there may be more than a dozen boxes of material, while the papers of several smaller estates might be contained in a single box. When an order is placed for the Land Registry papers of an estate all of the boxes relating to it should be produced. The eCatalogue only names the county (or counties) in which the estate is found – no more specific locational information is provided. The documentation for each estate is broken down into three categories: administrative records, title deeds and testamentary papers (catalogued A, B and C, respectively). Administrative records are further subdivided:

A/1 Originating application/affidavit
A/2 Schedule of tenancies
A/3 Schedule of areas
A/4 Valuation certificate
A/5 Surveyor's report
A/6 Surveyor's affidavit
A/7 Inspector's report
A/8 Inspector's/surveyor's schedule
A/9 Estate maps
A/10 Solicitor's/agent's affidavit
A/11 Abstract of Title
A/12 Notice and requisition to Board of Public Works
A/13 Agreement for sale between vendor and tenant
A/14 Final schedule of incumbrances
A/15 Undertaking to purchase
A/16 Vesting order
A/17 Purchase Agreement
A/18 Queries and correspondence files
A/19 Miscellaneous

Some of the collections of title deeds can be quite considerable in extent. For example, the title deeds for the Verner estate in County Armagh run to more than 300 items (LR1/53L/1/B). The number of testamentary papers can also be significant. PRONI has a separate catalogue of testamentary papers in the Land Registry collection, contained in a series of typescript volumes in the Search Room. It must be acknowledged that there are many gaps in the records and very frequently the words 'Not received' will appear in the eCatalogue.

The records deriving from the work of the Land Commission provide fascinating insights into the circumstances of tenant farmers on individual estates. The role of Land Commission staff included assessing whether a farmer was likely to be in a position to afford the annual repayments of the money advanced to him to buy out his farm. The reports of the Surveyors and Inspectors employed by the Land Commission were intended to provide directions in this regard. These reports cover such matters as farm boundaries, the quality of the land, the crops grown and livestock raised, improvements that the farmer had made to his landholding, and the state of the farmhouse and outbuildings.

The 'General Report of Inspector' prepared for the Estates Commissioners included the following sections:

I    Special instructions
II   General description of estate
III  Security; verification of rental
IV  Advances exceeding £3,000; advances exceeding £500
V   Sub-tenancies and joint tenancies
VI  Advances to trustees
VII Purchase of towns and villages, etc
VIII Demesne lands
IX  Untenanted lands. Parcels
X   Valuation of other lands and rights, etc, comprised in the estate
XI  Enlargement, improvement, and consolidation of holdings
XII Evicted tenants
XIII Turbary
XIV Matters which may arise on Surveyor's report or otherwise
      concerning occupancy, ancient monuments, labourers, etc
XV  Suggested arrangements as to management of estate pending re-sale
XVI Holdings for which agreements have not been signed

Not all of these sections were completed in each Inspector's report for the simple reason that not all were relevant. Numerous interesting details on the tenants intending to buy out their farms emerge from these reports. In some instances, the Inspector had to explain why he opposed certain holdings from being sold. In the Donelong estate owned by the Duke of Abercorn he recommended that a holding in the townland of Cloghboy beside the River Foyle should not be sold to the occupier, pointing out that the individual concerned, William Young, was the caretaker or manager of the Fishery Company. Young was allowed 'to crop in rotation a certain portion of the holding, which together with the use of a house, is part payment of his wages'.

Details of evictions were also noted by the Inspectors. The following details of evicted tenants are found in an Inspector's report of an estate in County Tyrone in 1905. Joseph and Daniel O'Brien were evicted in 1885 on account of their arrears of rent – they owed four years' rent totalling £67 8s. Before this they had made an attempt to sell their holding to another farmer, but this had fallen through. The O'Briens had instigated legal proceedings against this farmer, but lost the case and ended up having to pay £33 in costs. Landlords were required to compensate evicted tenants and in this instance the agent for the estate stated that the O'Briens had received £375. By the early years of the twentieth century the O'Briens had fallen on hard times for in his report the Inspector noted:

> The O'Briens seem to be in very poor circumstances, living in a miserable hovel in a back yard in Omagh. What I saw in their house, including bed furniture and a few cooking utensils isn't worth 10/–. They live together by themselves, and both are old men, I should say considerably over 70 years of age. To propose giving these men a farm would be out of the question. Should the commissioners be in a position to give them some monetary help, I would strongly recommend that each of them get a sum of £15.

Unfortunately for the O'Briens there is marginal note stating, 'No such grant can be made'.

The reports by the Land Commission Surveyors concern such matters as boundaries, occupancy, labourers and ancient monuments. The following notes were written under the heading 'The "particulars" of occupancy of tenants, sub-tenants and joint-tenants' for the townland of Seein on the Abercorn estate in 1906:

> 2A Seein has been occupied by Mary Gillespie … & her predecessors for over three generations, at a yearly rent of 5/– payable to James Patton. The Gillespies have built a flax mill & mill pond on part of it. It is of no use to Patton who states that the Gillespies probably purchased his predecessors tenant-right a long time ago.

Other insights emerge from this report. Under the heading 'Labourers' the same Surveyor wrote: 'The majority of the labourers in this locality are hired for 3 or 6 weeks & generally are boarded in the farmers own houses'.

## Ministry of Finance files

Other Northern Ireland records relating to land reform can be found in the Ministry of Finance files (catalogued with the prefix FIN). These include: Land Judge's Estate Court records (FIN/4); Land Purchase Annuities Branch (FIN/10); Land Registry records (FIN/23); Land Law Act files and papers (FIN/40); and Land Purchase Commission (FIN/48). The PRONI eCatalogue will provide further details of what is available under each of these headings. Taking the example of documents relating to the purchase of farms under the 1870 Land Act, these are catalogued as 'Land Act Charging Orders' under reference FIN/10/1/1. There are 283 items in this collection covering the period 1871–82, and of these 123 related to the estate of the Marquess of Waterford in County Londonderry. For instance, a transaction of 14 May 1873 concerns lands in Drumneechy, part of Lord Waterford's estate (FIN/10/1/1/38). The purchaser was James Fleming, his farm was just over 26 acres in extent and his annuity to be paid over 35 years was £14.17s.

Within the Land Registry (again, this relates to the work of the Land Commission) records (FIN/23) there are Fair Rent Files, Fair Rent Registers, Evicted Tenants Files, Maps and Estates Commissioners' Files. The Evicted Tenants Files (FIN/23/4) date from the early twentieth century, though the evictions themselves occurred mainly in the latter part of the 1800s (a few pre-date 1850). In all, there are over 1,100 files covering the six counties of Northern Ireland. The PRONI eCatalogue provides for each file the names of the tenant and landlord, the year of eviction, the townland, and whether any action was taken. This subset also includes a 'List of persons in each County in Ulster who have lodged applications with the Estates Commissioners as evicted tenants, or as representatives of evicted tenants, and who have been noted as suitable for holdings', 1907 (FIN/23/4/G/1).

The forms titled 'Particulars of evicted tenants' include, among other things, the names of the tenant and landlord, the location and size of the farm, the date of eviction and the present occupier of the farm. To take an example, Hugh McGuiggan was evicted from his 19-acre farm in Eskermore, County Tyrone, in 1895. However, he continued to occupy it in a caretaker capacity. In January 1904 he submitted an appeal to the Estates Commissioners of the Land Commission (FIN/23/4/F/67). Almost exactly a year later (the reason for the time lapse is not clear) he wrote to the Commissioners explaining his situation and pointing out: 'I am an old man over eighty years of age'. He added:

> The evicting party paid me a visit some time ago for the purpose of turning me out on the roadside. As I was confined to my bed, and in the absence of a doctor's certificate, and I suppose dettered by the threat of the police sergent that should anything happen to me he would take proceedings against them. They went away without putting me out. The remnant of the property on which my holding is situated is now offered for sale. If the [1903 Land] Act is not to be a dead letter as far as I am concerned, surely it is time the Commissioners should interfere and save me from eviction and perhaps death on the roadside and my grandchildren turned adrift on the world.

There is a note that McGuiggan was 'Reinstated'. However, he did not enjoy his possession of the farm in Eskermore for much longer for he died on 8 September 1905; the age on his death certificate was given as 93.

### Crown Lands

The Crown Lands (CL) archive in PRONI has been 'artificially created' and does not correlate to a government department or ministry. Among the relevant items in this collection are the documents grouped together under the heading: Land Judges Court and Irish Land Commission Files, 1886–1913 (CL/7). These include Land Commission files and schedules, 1886–1907, running to 237 items (CL/7/1). A typical catalogue entry reads: Schedule of the sale of lands at Lower Iveagh [barony – no more precise than this], County Down, by Robert Waddell to the Irish Land Commission, 22 February 1887 (CL/7/1/12). A small collection of items can be found in the Land Judges Court files, 1895–1903 (CL/7/2), though the catalogue does not identify the lands concerned.

### Land Purchase Commission

The Land Purchase Commission archive in PRONI includes a collection of documents, ranging from testamentary papers to leases and deeds, which were used as evidence of title to property. There are some 1,430 items in this collection, of which *c.* 400 date from the seventeenth and eighteenth centuries. The PRONI eCatalogue lists these documents under reference LPC. PRONI also has copies/transcripts of original documents of the Land Purchase Commission, 1637–1903, under reference T810.

### Crown and Peace records

The Clerk of the Crown and Peace in each county played an important role in the administration of the various land acts, through keeping records of orders, applications and affidavits, etc. The Clerk (or a deputy) also attended sittings of the Land Commission or its Sub-Commission when required to do so. The records arising from these duties can be found within the Crown and Peace archive in PRONI for counties in Northern Ireland. Records relating to land reform have typically been arranged by the land act to which they relate (mainly from 1870 onwards) and range from claims for compensation to the fixing of fair rents. Surviving Crown and Peace records for the Republic of Ireland are generally found in NAI, with finding aids in the Reading Room and in county archives and libraries. (For more on Crown and Peace records, see Chapter 10.)

## 9.2.2 Land Commission records in the Republic of Ireland

Following Partition, the Land Commission was reconstituted and 'became the most important facilitator of social engineering in Ireland, as it implemented the land policy reform of successive governments'.[11] It closed finally in 1999 and its records became the responsibility of the Department of Agriculture. The Land Commission archive is vast: one estimate of the number of items in the collection is 11 million.[12] While most of the records concern the operations of the Land Commission in transferring landholdings from landlord to tenant, there are important subsets of records relating to the work of the Commissioners of Church Temporalities and the Congested Districts Board.

The archive of the Land Commission is divided into two sections: the Records Branch, comprising some 50,000 boxes, and the Administration Records, containing 70,526 items in 2,744 boxes, and an additional 7,012 bound volumes.[13] A catalogue of the records accrued by the Land Commission through the land acts of 1881–1909 was produced by Edward Keane and this is available in the Manuscripts Reading Room of the National Library of Ireland ('Records in the Irish Land Commission: Survey and Guide'). Keane's survey covered 8,447 boxes holding records deriving from 9,343 estates.[14] A searchable database of the catalogue of the Administration Records of the Land Commission can be consulted in the Reading Room of the National Archives of Ireland.[15]

Unfortunately for genealogists and historians, these records, currently stored in a facility in Portlaoise, County Laois, are not open to the public. There have been regular attempts to have these records made available to researchers, but so far without success.[16] For an exploration of the local impact of the Land Commission in independent Ireland, see Martin O'Halloran's *The Lost Gaeltacht: the Land Commission Migration – Clonbur, County Galway to Allenstown, Count Meath* (2020); the author was able to make use of the Land Commission papers through a direct connection to the properties in question. K. Buckley wrote a very interesting article on the records of the Land Commission, albeit nearly 70 years ago when the records were more accessible than they are now.[17]

Since the records of the Congested Districts Board are among those of the Land Commission, the same access issues also apply to them. However, copies of the baseline reports, which summarised living conditions in the regions overseen by the CDB, are held in the Department of Early Printed Books in Trinity College Dublin. Some of the annual reports of the CDB presented to Parliament can be read online on the Internet Archive (https://archive.org) and the Enhanced British Parliamentary Papers on Ireland resource (www.dippam.ac.uk). NLI holds the Congested Districts Board Photograph Collection.

## 9.2.3 Other records relating to land reform

While the 'official' Land Commission archive in the Republic of Ireland may be closed to researchers, there are other ways of accessing records associated with its activities. The most obvious place to look for records relating to the workings of the Land Commission is among the collections of landed estate papers. For instance, the National Library holds papers of the Medlycott estate at Rocketts Castle and Killowen, Portlaw, County Waterford, which include Land

Commission documents (MS 46,785). The records of the Westport estate, owned by the Marquess of Sligo, in NLI include papers concerning the sale of over 160,000 acres of the property to the Congested Districts Board in 1914 (MS 41,025).

It is also important to bear in mind that some estate collections in PRONI relating to properties in what is now the Republic of Ireland include papers associated with the Land Commission. These include Land Commission records for the estate of Louisa M. Graham at Ballinacragy, County Cavan, 1905–15 (D812/119/5/2); the Shirley estate in County Monaghan, c. 1880–1930 (D3531/I); and a Land Commission map showing the estate of Lady Ena Stewart-Bam in County Donegal, 1928 (D2784/19/2/6). For the Dartrey estate in County Monaghan there is a 'Register of fair rents fixed under the Land Law (Ireland) Act 1881' (D3053/8/16).

Documentation concerning land reform can also be found in county archives in the Republic of Ireland. Limerick Archives has digitised two registers of judgements of the fair rents tribunal of cases held in, first of all, Nenagh, Rathkeale, Croom, Kilmallock, Newcastlewest, Limerick and Tipperary, 1881–1916 (P20/1) and, secondly, Newcastlewest, Ennistymon, Kilmallock and Limerick, 1882–1916 (P20/2). The individuals named in each entry include, generally speaking, the landlord, landlord's agent and the tenant. Usefully each volume has an index of personal names at the start. The reason for the case being brought is noted and an 'Observations' column was used to record additional information.

Records relating to land reform can also be found among the personal papers of those who were involved in one way or another with this issue. The National Library of Ireland holds papers relating to the work of Robert Murray, a valuer with the Land Commission in the late 1800s (MSS 27,993–28,005). These include documents and correspondence concerning the valuation of particular estates, e.g. the Powerscourt estate in County Wicklow, 1887–91 (MS 27,999/4). The records of John Dillon, a prominent nationalist politician in late nineteenth- and early twentieth-century Ireland, in Trinity College Dublin include papers relating to evicted tenants, which are arranged by name and estate, as well as tenants in distress and those under threat of eviction, 1887–97 (TCD, MS 6812); the catalogue provides further details on the estates concerned.

PRONI holds some papers of those involved in the work of the Land Commission. For example, it has a volume kept by Sir Samuel Byers of Markethill, County Armagh, who was one of the Irish Land Commissioners on the circuit of hearings at the end of the nineteenth century (D3033/1). Covering the years 1892–1900, the volume includes newspaper cuttings of cases heard by Byers in counties Antrim, Armagh, Cavan, Down, Kilkenny and Monaghan. The collection also contains letters from tenants on the Gosford and Dufferin estates in, respectively, Armagh and Down.

Newspapers can be another excellent way of exploring the work of the Land Commission for the press included regular reports of the activities of that body. For example, through the *Derry Journal* I was able to learn of the process by which my forebear Andrew Elder (mentioned above in relation to his support for land reform) was able to secure a reduction in his rent for his farm in Meenahoney, near Castlefin, County Donegal in the spring of 1882. At this time he was paying £44 10s 9d in rent for this property, which was more than £10 above the rateable valuation placed on it. Andrew believed that a fairer rent would be £26 10s.

In presenting his arguments for a rent reduction, Andrew stated that the cost of labour on the farm had increased by £10, while there had been a significant decrease in the price of flax, the income from which paid the rent. In the opinion of one of the men who had been appointed to value the land on behalf of the Commissioners, 'the farming was excellent and the tenant made the best of it.'[18] On 1 June 1882 the representatives of the Land Commission visited Meenahoney and two days later ruled that the rent should be reduced to £34 10s – not as much as had been requested, but a significant reduction nonetheless.

A wealth of information on land reform survives in parliamentary papers, many of which can be accessed through the Internet Archive (https://archive.org) and the Enhanced British Parliamentary Papers on Ireland resource (www.dippam.ac.uk). Papers of interest include *Return showing all cases in which an evicted tenant (or duly appointed representative of such) has been, with the assistance of the Estates Commissioners, reinstated as a purchaser of his or his predecessor's former holding or part thereof or provided with a new parcel of land up to 31st December 1907* (1908). The information in the return is presented in tabulated format with on one side, 'Holding from which evicted', and, on the other, 'Holding with which provided'. Under the first heading the columns include the name of the estate, townland, date of eviction, rent, acreage, Poor Law valuation, and name of tenant. On the other side the columns include the name of the estate, townland and acreage, along with various financial details.[19]

An invaluable set of records are the parliamentary returns of the monetary advances to farmers to enable them to purchase their farms. For example, the *Return of the advances made under the Irish Land Purchase Acts during the month of February, 1914* [Cd 7606] (1914) includes details of tenants on the estate of Ena Dingwell Tasca Stewart-Bam in County Donegal to whom advances were made on 19 February 1914. A selection of the tenants in the townland of Carricknamanna in Donaghmore parish is given below.

| Purchaser | Area (to nearest acre) | Tenement Valuation | Rent | Purchase Price |
|---|---|---|---|---|
| James Roulston | 81 | £36 10s. | £26 | £640 |
| Andrew Rodgers | 27 | £17 10s. | £11 15s. | £289 |
| Joseph Leslie | 36 | £15 | £9 10s. | £234 |
| Joseph Temple | 38 | £15 10s. | £11 10s. | £283 |
| William J. Tynan | 71 | £48 | £32 | £788 |

Such returns make it possible to identify when a farmer began the process of buying out his farm, and the price agreed for the holding. In some instances fairly extensive lists of names of tenants can be found for a single estate and cumulatively these *Returns* contain tens of thousands of names of purchasing tenants.

# Notes

1 For a detailed study of how it impacted on the province of Ulster, see Martin Dowling, *Tenant Right and Agrarian Society in Ulster 1600–1870* (1999).

2 Quoted in James S. Donnelly, *Landlord and Tenant in Nineteenth-century Ireland* (1973), p. 21.

3 Andrew Elder was my great-great-great-grandfather. His speech was reported in the *Londonderry Standard*, 22 Jan. 1870. The *Standard* was a strongly pro-Tenant Right newspaper.

4 J.C.W. Wylie, *Irish Land Law* (1975), p. 25.

5 *Report of Her Majesty's Commissioners of Inquiry into the Working of the Landlord and Tenant (Ireland) Act, 1870 … Vol. II: Digest of Evidence. Minutes of Evidence Part I* (1881), pp 328–33.

6 Terence Dooley, *The Big Houses and Landed Estates of Ireland: a Research Guide* (2007), p. 49.

7 Dooley, *Big Houses*, p. 51.

8 Patrick J. Cosgrove, 'The sale of the Leinster estate under the Wyndham Land Act, 1903', *Journal of the County Kildare Archaeological Society*, 20:1 (2008–09), pp 9–25; and Patrick J. Cosgrove, 'The controversy and consequences of John Redmond's estate sale under the Wyndham Land Act, 1903', *Historical Journal*, 55:1 (2012), pp 128–34. See also Leonard Howard, 'Selling the Devon Estate 1907–10', *North Munster Antiquarian Journal*, 52 (2012), pp 55–70; and Conor McNamara, 'The most bitter struggle of them all: the Clanricarde estate and legislative reform in Ireland', *Journal of the Galway Archaeological and Historical Society*, 67 (2015), pp 184–201. The Clanricarde estate was over 50,000 acres. The author identified estate papers in the Harewood Archives, West Yorkshire Archives Service, though these were uncatalogued and there was virtually nothing for the period 1886–1916.

9 Dooley, *Big Houses*, p. 50. See also W.L. Micks, *History of the Congested Districts Board* (1925), Ciara Breathnach, *The Congested Districts Board, 1891–1923* (2005) Seán Beattie, *Donegal in Transition: the Impact of the Congested Districts Board* (2013); and Jonathan Bell, 'The agricultural work of the Congested Districts Board' in Ciara Breathnach (ed.), *Framing the West: Images of Rural Ireland, 1891–1920* (2007), pp 163–78.

10 Dooley, *Big Houses*, p. 62.

11 Dooley, *Big Houses*, p. 93.

12 Terence Dooley, 'Land and politics in independent Ireland, 1923–48: the case for reappraisal', *Irish Historical Studies*, 34:134 (2004), p. 176.

13 See the article by Fiona Fitzsimons, 'Records of the Irish Land Commission', *History Ireland* (Jan./Feb. 2014), available online at: www.historyireland.com/volume-22/records-irish-land-commission.

14 Dooley, *Big Houses*, p. 92. Dooley notes that the principal focus of Keane's survey was the documentation relating to title.

15 Fitzsimons, 'Records of the Irish Land Commission'.

16 See article by John Grenham in the *Irish Times*, published online on 23 Sep. 2013. See also the debate in the Dáil on 21 Feb. 2019 on the continued closure of the records. The Irish Government stated the records were considered 'working documents' and it was not possible to create a research facility due to a lack of resources. However, owners and purchasers of land and their personal or legal representatives were allowed access to copies of relevant documents. It was also stated that the National Archives had received 154,579 files concerning the termination of fair rents by the Land Commission, but these could not be made available to the public because of a lack of adequate storage facilities from which they could be retrieved for public inspection (www.oireachtas.ie/en/debates/question/2019-02-21/4).

17 K. Buckley, 'The records of the Irish Land Commission as a source of historical evidence', *Irish Historical Studies*, 8:29 (1952), pp 28–36.

18 *Derry Journal*, 31 May 1882.

19 Findmypast has a database titled, 'Estate Commissioners Offices, Applications from Evicted Tenants, 1907'. Papers of the Evicted Tenants Commission, 1891–1910, formerly in the State Paper Office, Dublin Castle, are now in NAI.

# 10

# Other places to look for farmers

## 10.1 Agricultural schools

Prior to the nineteenth century the opportunities to avail of a formal education in Ireland varied considerably. However, in the early 1800s, with a growing demand for education, the number of schools increased significantly. Among these new institutions were several schools focused on teaching – or at least incorporating within their curriculum – improved agricultural methods.[1] The value of these establishments was obvious. Appearing before the Devon Commission in 1844, Robert McCrea of Grange, near Bready, County Tyrone, was full of praise for the work of agricultural seminaries, observing, 'I think they have done more than anything else for the improvement of agriculture in this country'.

### 10.1.1 Early ventures

One of the earliest agricultural schools in Ireland was at Bannow, County Wexford. It was founded in 1821 by Rev. William Hickey, a Church of Ireland clergyman, who was a passionate advocate of agricultural improvement. He was the author and editor of a number of works, often under the pseudonym 'Martin Doyle'. An early account of the school can be found in the parliamentary report, *Agricultural School at Bannow, and the state of that district in the County of Wexford: report made to the Farming Society by their secretary* (1824).[2]

In 1827 what has been described as 'the first substantial agricultural school in the English speaking world' was established at Templemoyle near Eglinton (then called Muff) in County Londonderry.[3] Unfortunately, records created by the school are exceptionally rare, though the names and addresses of pupils receiving prizes for their examination results appeared occasionally in the press. For example, the *Londonderry Sentinel* of 3 November 1835 includes a list of the pupils awarded prizes, from which the following names and subjects have been selected:

Conduct – John Sproule, Castlederg, County Tyrone; Lindsay Clarke, Porthall, County Donegal

Arithmetic – Denis Leary, King William's Town, County Cork; John McCrea, Grange, Strabane, County Tyrone; Andrew Hunter, Castlederg

Trigonometry – John McCrea, Grange; Robert Monteith, Castlederg; James Warnock, Kilkeeragh, County Londonderry; Denis Leary, King William's Town; Samuel Hasson, Muff Glen, County Londonderry

Algebra – Alexander Moutray, Ballygawley, County Tyrone

Farming – John Sproule, Castlederg; Thomas Lendrum, County Tyrone; George Clarke, Muff, County Londonderry; Alexander Moutray, Ballygawley; Smith Davison, Moneymore, County Londonderry; George Boggs, Derry; Robert Monteith, Castlederg

Additional information on the founding of the school and the way it was conducted can be found in *Outlines of a Plan for the Establishment of an Agricultural Model School in the Province of Munster: As Recommended by the Irish Relief Committee in London of 1822* (1827) and *Account of the Templemoyle Agricultural Seminary* (1844).[4]

## 10.1.2 The National Education system and agricultural instruction

A major step forward in the provision of schooling in Ireland in general was the formation by the government of the Board of Commissioners for National Education in 1831. The Board provided state support for local initiatives, contributing money to assist with the building of schools and the salaries of teachers, as well as operating an inspectorate and publishing text books. One enterprising individual who was convinced that the National Education system should be at the forefront of teaching advanced farming methods was John Pitt Kennedy, a former army officer, who established agricultural schools at Loughash, County Tyrone, and Cloghan, County Donegal.[5] In 1837 Kennedy was appointed Inspector-General in the National Education Board with special responsibility for agricultural instruction.[6] The National Library of Ireland holds the John Pitt Kennedy Papers, which include correspondence and other materials relating to the agricultural schools founded by him, 1836–64 (MS 49,529). As noted below, there is information on the Loughash agricultural school and its pupils in the *Reports of the Commissioners of National Education in Ireland.*

In 1838, in his role with the National Education Board, Kennedy established a model farm and agricultural school at Glasnevin, Dublin, for the training of teachers. This went under a number of names including the Albert Agricultural and Dairy Training Department and later the Albert Agricultural College.[7] The records of the Albert Agricultural College are held in the University College Dublin Archives (www.ucd.ie/archives) and include journals and registers of students. The Munster Model Farm[8] near Cork was founded in the 1850s and in 1880 the Munster Dairy and Agricultural School (later the Munster Institute) was established on this site.[9] Records of the Munster Dairy School and Agricultural Institute are held by the Cork City and County Archives (U619), and include committee minutes, 1882–92, and an account book, 1902. Within the Doneraile Papers in the National Library of Ireland is the minute book of meetings of the board of commissioners responsible for the (Munster?) Model and Agricultural school and farms, 1858–9 (MS 34,130/21).

Through the National Education Board further agricultural schools were founded or supported. By 1859 there were 38 agricultural schools, of which 20 were model agricultural schools under the management of the National Education Board, with the remainder managed by local patrons.[10] In 1875 the number of farms attached to National schools totalled 228. This number declined sharply in the following years and by 1899 the number of farms associated with National schools had fallen to 38 (many of the farms were turned into school gardens). Of the model agricultural schools, only the Albert and Munster establishments remained with the Board after 1881 and in 1900 these institutions were transferred to the Department of Agriculture and Technical Instruction.[11]

## 10.1.3 Records of other agricultural schools

Other agricultural schools for which there are surviving records include Brookfield in County Antrim (near Moira). This institution was established for the children of those who attended meetings of the Society of Friends (Quakers) for worship, but were not in formal membership due to having been 'disowned' for a variety of transgressions. The records of the school are in the Friends' Historical Library, Dublin, and include accounts, annual reports and a school register, 1836–1921; a copy of this register is in PRONI (CR8/3/1).[12] Over 1,600 pupils are named in the register, which includes the dates of admission and departure, the age of the pupil on each occasion, the name of the parents of each pupil and their place of residence, and where the child moved to on leaving the school.[13]

Farm account books exist for Baleer (Balleer) agricultural school, Lisnadill, County Armagh, 1869–79 (PRONI, D2141/1) and Oldcastle agricultural school, County Meath, 1870–71 (NLI, MS 19,084). Books on individual agricultural schools include a study of Greenmount agricultural college, County Antrim, which opened in 1912: Derek W. Alexander, *Greenmount: Land of Learning. An Illustrated History* (2004). Other publications include Milo Spillane, 'Mungret agricultural school', *Old Limerick Journal*, 6 (1981), pp 26–7; Diarmaid Ó Donnabháin, 'Belvoir Model agricultural school, 1835–1866', *The Other Clare*, 11 (1987), pp 29–35; Cáit Logue, 'Kyle Park agricultural school (1843–1875)', *Tipperary Historical Journal* (1997), pp 86–91; and J.F. Collins, 'Glandore agricultural school', *Rosscarbery Past and Present*, 12 (2010), pp 184–201.

An interesting set of items in the Official Papers Miscellaneous Assorted series in the National Archives of Ireland comprises completed questionnaires sent to several agricultural National schools, giving details of numbers of scholars, outdoor and indoor instruction, lands held by each school and the rent paid for same, and the number of teachers. The schools were at Markethill, County Armagh; Loughrea, County Galway; Kyle Park, County Tipperary; Bally[ra]shane, County Londonderry; Glandore, County Cork; Loughash, County Tyrone; Larne, County Antrim; Lissan, County Tyrone; Fivemiletown, County Tyrone; Cloghan, County Donegal; Ballinakill, County Galway; Belvoir, County Clare; and the Agricultural Model Farm, Glasnevin, 1845 (NAI, CSO/OPMA/980).

## 10.1.4 Agricultural schools in parliamentary papers

The progress of agricultural schools can be followed in some detail through parliamentary papers and in particular the *Reports of the Commissioners of National Education in Ireland*. In some cases these reports also provide the names of pupils at the schools for certain periods. Taking the *Appendix to the Sixteenth Report of the Commissioners ... for the year 1849* (1850) as an example, this includes tables of pupils at several agricultural schools – Glasnevin (pp 295–6), Loughash[14] (pp 299–300), Markethill (p. 302), Larne (p. 305) – along with such details as the place of origin, name of patron, period in attendance, and subsequent employment.[15]

Looking at this report, we find that among the former students of Glasnevin Model Farm was Robert Reilly, who attended January–December 1847; he was appointed to Glandore agricultural school, but had emigrated to America by the time the listing was drawn up. Several others emigrated to America without taking up an appointment in Ireland. Robert Scott was one such student and his 'Present Occupation' was recorded as 'Botanist in Philadelphia'. For Loughash there is a list of 82 boarding pupils since its commencement in 1837. Among those who studied at the Markethill Model Agricultural School was John Lowther, who was admitted to the school in November 1845 aged 17, and who was from Cluntagh in County Down. His patron was Mr H. Ringland from County Armagh. He left the school in July 1847 and returned home, though when the return was drawn up his occupation was 'Shopman, Liverpool'.

## 10.1.5 Grant aid applications for agricultural schools

The National Archives of Ireland and Public Record Office of Northern Ireland hold extensive collections of records relating to the National Education system, including grant aid applications, correspondence registers and salary books (in both institutions these records are catalogued under the prefix ED). The grant aid application forms included a series of questions about the school, covering such matters as the date it was founded, the condition of the building in which classes were conducted, the name of the teacher and the number of pupils on the roll. The applications held by PRONI can be downloaded from its website via the archive's eCatalogue and include many concerning agricultural schools at such places as Ballycarry, Carnlough and Dundrod in County Antrim.

Taking the application made on behalf of Dundrod in 1848 as an example (PRONI, ED/1/3/46), the applicant was Rev. William Magill, Presbyterian minister of Dundrod, who was the patron of the school.

The principal of the school was Isaac Lowry, aged 23, who had studied at the Glasnevin Model Farm and possessed a certificate from the agriculturalist there. The file also includes a detailed report of the Dundrod school by a Board inspector. The farm belonging to the school was located nearby and extended to 10 acres, divided into five fields, each of two acres. The farm outbuildings consisted of a barn, stable, cow-house, piggeries and dairy. There was also a dwelling house for the teacher. The inspector observed, 'The general state of agriculture here is very backward & half a century behind some of the more favoured portions of this county', and gave his backing to the school.

## 10.2 Crown and Peace records

The Clerk of the Crown and Clerk of the Peace in each county played important roles in regional administration and in maintaining the records generated by the various bodies of local government and the judicial system. In 1877 the positions were merged as the Clerk of the Crown and Peace. As noted in Chapter 9, the Clerk of the Crown and Peace had the task of keeping records deriving from the administration of the various land acts. In Northern Ireland the surviving archives of these officials are in PRONI, while a proportion of the corresponding records for the Republic of Ireland are in NAI, though many items can be found in other repositories. Unfortunately, many early records were lost in the destruction of the Public Record Office of Ireland in 1922.

## 10.2.1 Grand jury records

Until the reorganisation of local government in Ireland at the end of the nineteenth century, the grand jury was the most important administrative body in each county, with responsibility for the construction and maintenance of roads and bridges, courthouses, hospitals and other public buildings. Grand juries had an important role in the administration of justice during the assizes. The grand jury examined bills of indictment and the evidence presented in support of them relating to criminal charges and deliberated on whether a particular bill should be rejected or considered a 'true bill', in which case it would proceed to a full trial. The Crown and Peace archive in PRONI includes the records of the grand juries in the six counties of Northern Ireland. In the Republic of Ireland grand jury records are usually available in county archives and libraries, though material is also on deposit in NAI and NLI.[16] A handsome booklet on the grand jury system, titled *People, Place and Power*, has been produced as part of the Beyond 2022 project.[17] Digitisation projects have resulted in some sets of grand jury records being made available online.[18]

The best known of the grand jury records are the presentment books, which provide a record of the sums of money that had been approved at each assize along with a brief statement of the works to be undertaken, the names of those entrusted to oversee the completion of the task in question, and the money that had been apportioned to cover the cost of this. In addition to major public works, the grand jury could raise money for a range of other activities, including the apprehension of criminals and the killing of vermin. Early presentment books were handwritten, but printed volumes began to appear in the late eighteenth century. Similar in format are the grand jury query books.[19]

From a genealogical point of view, the value of the information in the presentment and query books derives not only from the identification of the individuals responsible for overseeing the work, but also from the fact that the names of farmers were often used as a guide to the location of the sanctioned task. For example, the following entry appears in a County Louth query book of 1810 as having been approved at the spring assizes in 1806:

£26 8s. To Henry Maxwell, Esqr. Philip Markey and John Gregory to make ditches to 250 perches from Dundalk to Crossmaglen, between the south mearing of Robt. Bailie's farm in Shortstown, and west end of Bryan Donaghy's farm in same, 1s 6d per and £1 6s wages.[20]

## 10.2.2 Ejectment books

The Ejectment Act of 1816 made it easier for landlords to evict their tenants. Previously, an eviction could be a long drawn-out and expensive procedure for the landowner. Now a landlord could seek an ejectment by civil bill in a local court and if successful his legal expenses would be comparatively small.[21] The legislation stipulated that a note of the cases should be recorded in a book kept by the Clerk of the Peace in each county and surviving volumes can be found among the Crown and Peace records in NAI and PRONI. The best set of ejectment books are those for County Clare; there are 17 books for 1816–50 and 28 books for 1850–1914 (two further books are missing). A study of the

1816–50 books has been published by Nicola Jennings, who has also provided to Clare Library a summary of the 1816–35 volumes.[22] The County Clare records are exceptional for their early date with most other ejectment books, if they survive at all, available from no earlier than the late nineteenth century. As noted in Chapter 4, records relating to evictions may also be found among estate papers. To give another couple of examples here, for the Annesley estate in County Down there is a schedule of c. 200 tenants against whom it was recommended that proceedings by civil bill ejectment for non-payment of rent should be instituted (PRONI, D1503/4/8). The records of the Westport estate, County Mayo, in NLI include a sizeable collection of sessions books, ejectment decrees, civil bills and related papers from the late 1800s and early 1900s (MSS 40,977–40,980).

## 10.2.3 Registers of tree-planting

Concerns about deforestation in Ireland and the consequent shortage of timber led to a series of acts of parliament being passed from 1698 onwards to encourage tree-planting. The 1698 Act, which was to come into force on 25 March 1703, stipulated that the grand jury in each county should, in 1702, apportion the number of trees to be planted in each barony and then in each parish. Lists of the trees to be planted at parish level were to be delivered to the clergy of the Established Church and churchwardens in each parish. The final arrangements were to be made at a meeting of the parish vestry.[23] As a consequence of the procedures laid down, it is sometimes possible to find information on tree-planting in the minutes of vestry meetings. For example, there are early eighteenth-century lists of proposed tree planters in the vestry books of Raphoe, County Donegal (1703), and Seagoe, County Armagh (1709). (See Chapter 2 for more on vestry books.)

Of greater significance for the registration of tree-planting was the *Act for Encouraging the Planting of Timber Trees* of 1765. This allowed a tenant with at least 12 years still to run on his lease to retain the trees he had planted on his farm on the expiration of his lease or claim the value of them. In order to avail of these provisions, the tenant was required to lodge a certificate listing the location, number and type of trees with the Clerk of the Peace of the county within six months of the planting. The legislation required the Clerk to keep these certificates and record their details in a separate book.

Much useful background material on this subject area can be found in *A Register of Trees for Co. Londonderry, 1768–1911*, edited by Eileen M. McCracken and Donal P. McCracken and published by PRONI (1984). Other relevant publications include:

Eileen McCracken, 'A register of trees, King's County, 1793–1913', *Journal of the County Kildare Archaeological Society*, 15 (1973–4), pp 310–18
Eileen McCracken, 'A register of trees, Co. Kildare, 1769–1909', *Journal of the Kildare Archaeological Society*, 16 (1977–8), pp 41–60
Donal P. McCracken and Eileen McCracken, 'A register of trees, Co. Cork, 1790–1860', *Journal of the Cork Historical and Archaeological Society*, 81 (1976), pp 39–60
Eileen McCracken, 'Tree planting by tenants in Meath, 1800–1850', *Ríocht na Mídhe*, 8:2 (1988–9), pp 3–20
Eileen McCracken, 'Tenant planting in nineteenth century Ireland'. *Quarterly Journal of Forestry*, 67 (1973), pp 221–6
R.W. Tomlinson, 'Tree planting by tenants in County Down during the eighteenth and nineteenth centuries', *Irish Geography*, 29:2 (1996), pp 83–95
William J. Smyth, 'The greening of Ireland – tenant tree-planting in the eighteenth and nineteenth centuries', *Irish Forestry*, 54:1 (1997), pp 55–72
Rachael Byrne, *Cracow Landscape Monographs 2: Clothing the Irish landscape. A case study of tenant tree planting in Co. Mayo 1765 to 1910* (2016)

## Tree-planting registers in PRONI

The following registers can be found in the Crown and Peace archive.

County Antrim, 1841–1901 – ANT/7/6/1 (separate register for Carrickfergus, 1838 – ANT/7/6/2)
County Armagh, 1916 – ARM/7/6/1
County Down, 1769–1860 – DOW/7/3/2/1–3
County Londonderry, 1773–1894 – LOND/7/7/1
County Tyrone, 1831–1916 – TYR/7/3/1–2

## Tree-planting registers in NAI

The following county registers were listed in the McCrackens' *Register of Trees for Co. Londonderry* as being available in what was then the Public Record Office of Ireland (now the National Archives of Ireland).

County Cavan, 1779–1911
County Cork, 1790–1859 (3 vols)
County Kildare, 1765–1894 (2 vols)
County Kilkenny, 1765–1894 (2 vols)
County Limerick, 1803–1906
County Longford, 1831–1910
County Louth, 1829–1906
County Mayo, 1775–1819
County Monaghan, 1807–1909
County Offaly (King's County), 1793–1913
County Sligo, 1804–92
County Tipperary, 1772–1900 (2 vols)
County Waterford, 1803–1917

In his abovementioned paper, Smyth makes the following comments on these registers:

> ... those for Longford, Louth and Monaghan are so incomplete as to be not very useful for research purposes. The better ledgers relate to Cavan, Cork, Kildare, Kilkenny, Limerick, Londonderry, Offaly, Sligo, Tipperary and Waterford. The information entered in these ledgers vary. Some, like that for Co. Cork, are very detailed and include entries in chronological order which state the names of the tenant and the landlord, the location of the plantation by parish and barony, the date of plantation and the number of each types of trees planted. Some county records do not detail the number or type of trees but simply provide a record of the number of tenants registering per annum (p. 60).

The registers themselves can vary in the way the relevant data is presented. A typical entry in the register of tree-planting in County Down reads as follows:

Drumbo. Thomas Hunter planted 40 Scotch Elm, 43 English Elm, 30 Lime, 25 Sycamore, 17 Ash, 35 Ash, 1 Sycamore, 9 Lime, 2 Beech, 6 Round Tree, 1 Horse Chestnut & 57 Ash. Certified 9 April 1782.

An Act of 1784–5 concerning tree-planting required tenants to place a notice in the *Dublin Gazette* announcing their intention to register trees, though only, it seems, if they were unable to notify the head landlord.[24] These advertisements make up, at least in part, for gaps in the survival of the county registers. The following example is from the *Dublin Gazette* of 3–5 March 1789:

NOTICE is hereby given, pursuant to Act of Parliament, that I intend to register 470 Scotch Fir, 500 Ash, 20 Oak and 10 Elm Trees, all planted by me on that Part of the Lands of Ballynemona, in the Parish of Ballicanow and County of Wexford, held by me from the Right Honorable Arthur Lord Viscount Valentia. Dated this 4th Day of March, 1780. HUMPHREY HARTLEY.

The National Library of Ireland holds the most complete set of issues of the *Dublin Gazette*, while online access is available for certain periods through a number of providers, including, for free, the website of the Oireachtas Library & Research Service.[25]

## 10.3 The flaxseed premiums of 1796

In 1796, as part of a government initiative to encourage the linen industry in Ireland, free spinning wheels or looms were granted to farmers who planted a certain acreage of their holdings with flax. The names of over 56,000 recipients of these awards have survived in printed form, arranged by county and parish (by barony in County Longford), but unfortunately not by townland. Two copies of this book are known to exist, one in the Linen Hall Library in Belfast and the other in the Irish Linen Centre and Lisburn Museum in Lisburn, County Antrim. The Ulster Historical Foundation has indexed this source and made it available as a free searchable database (www.ancestryireland.com/scotsinulster).

There are names from every county in Ireland, with the exception of Dublin and Wicklow. Nonetheless, it is clear that there was considerable variation between counties as to the number of premiums claimed, reflecting in part the quantity of flax grown in each. Nearly 60% of the recipients were from the province of Ulster, with the major flax-producing counties of Donegal and Tyrone heading the list with over 7,000 claimants each. On the other hand, the numbers of recipients in some of the more southerly counties are much smaller, in a few cases in single figures.

## 10.4 Agricultural census returns

The most important and extensive of the government-commissioned agricultural censuses dates from 1803 and will be looked at presently. However, it would be remiss not to mention an earlier agricultural census for County Louth, which was found in the records of the State Paper Office in Dublin Castle (now in the National Archives of Ireland). This has been transcribed by Dermot MacIvor in his article, 'An eighteenth century corn census of County Louth', *Journal of the County Louth Archaeological Society*, 11:4 (1948), pp 254–86, and an index to the names can also be accessed online.[26] It is undated, but is believed to have been compiled around 1740. The census covers the baronies of Upper Dundalk, Ardee, Louth and Ferrard, and includes the names of nearly 1,700 farmers by townland.

## 10.4.1 The agricultural census of 1803

The threat of an invasion of Great Britain and Ireland by France recurred periodically during the late 1790s and the early years of the nineteenth century. The government in London made plans in 1797 and 1798 to abandon coastal areas and introduced new legislation for defending the kingdom. This legislation required the lord lieutenant in each county to compile returns, especially from maritime parishes, enumerating livestock and the wagons and horses available for transport, and giving the quantity of 'dead stock' (crops stored). During a scare in 1803 about an invasion of Ireland, resulting from the planned but abortive insurrection of that year, similar returns were made under the same legislation, which now, following the Act of Union, applied to Ireland. The surviving returns relate to many parishes in County Down and the northern parishes of County Antrim.

The surviving returns for County Antrim are in the National Archives of Ireland (Official Papers, 153/103/1–16) and a microfilm copy is available in PRONI (MIC678/1). The returns for County Down were made to the Marquess of Londonderry, the governor of the county, and are in the Londonderry Papers in PRONI (D654/A2). A detailed analysis of the returns for County Down is provided by Duncan Scarlett in Ian Maxwell *et al.*, *Researching Down Ancestors*, published by the Ulster Historical Foundation in 2004. This is essential reading for it notes gaps in the coverage and also highlights instances where the returns for some townlands have been placed incorrectly with those of another parish. In all, there are around 11,300 names for County Down.

Some of the returns include remarks and observations that provide additional information on those named. For example, Robert Hamill of Dunnyverny (Dunaverney), Ballymoney parish, was in Carrickfergus Gaol. Alexander Neilly of the same townland was 'sickly'. Other comments specify that the individual listed was a labourer, old, a Quaker, a widow, or a priest. Three men were identified as 'carpenters and working abroad'. One thing that comes through is the small number of livestock that the farmers were in possession of. Taking the townland of Moninacloygh (Monanclogh) in the parish of Armoy as an example, no-one was in possession of oxen or bulls, while the largest number of cows possessed by any one farmer was six. Most farmers owned at least one horse, but no-one owned more than three. One farmer owned 18 sheep, but no-one else had more than seven.

## 10.5 Chief Secretary's Office Registered Papers

The voluminous Chief Secretary's Office Registered Papers (CSORP) in the National Archives of Ireland cover the period 1818–1924. They include letters, petitions and reports submitted to the Chief Secretary, the most senior official in the Irish administration after the Lord Lieutenant. A project to catalogue these papers for the years 1818–52 is ongoing and the results to date can be accessed on a sub-section of NAI website (www.csorp.nationalarchives.ie). Numerous items relate to farmers and agriculture. By way of example, in 1822 the farmers of the townlands of Castledooey, Woodhill and Doorable in County Donegal petitioned the Lord Lieutenant for a reconsideration of court fine of £40 imposed upon them for the burning of a house belonging to Henry McMenamy in Castledooey (CSO/RP/1822/453). They claimed that the judgment had been 'procured by unjust swearing' and were unable to pay the fine. However, another letter in this file argued that the accused had the opportunity to appear before the assizes, but had failed to do so and therefore 'they ought now abide the consequences of their own neglect'.

Many files in the CSORP concern the issue of tithes (see Chapter 6 for more on tithes). For instance, in September 1825 eight farmers in County Cavan – Andrew Carolan, Philip McConnon, Philip Rock, William Rock, Michael Rock, John Carolan, Owen Lecky and Charles Lynch – petitioned the Lord Lieutenant asking him to intervene with the Church of Ireland incumbent of Mullagh, Rev. Spencer Meara (McMara in the petition) to set the rates of tithe payable on their crops (CSO/RP/1825/1196). The petitioners complained that their crops had been harvested for ten days, but they had not been told how much was due. In the meantime, their harvested crops remained in the fields and were vulnerable to deterioration. Furthermore, the collector of the tithes, Rev. Edward Mahaffy, lived six miles away. Other files relate to the regulation of markets and the sale of agricultural produce. Dating from 1825 is a petition of the dairymen and principal farmers in the neighbourhood of Wexford town to the House of Commons (CSO/RP/1826/941). The memorialists, 53 in number, were anxious that new laws regulating the butter trade would continue to act against fraud committed by 'petty venders'.

An additional set of documentation within the records of the Chief Secretary's Office has been termed 'Official Papers Miscellaneous Assorted'. A partial catalogue of the OPMA series is available on the Archives Portal Europe website (www.archivesportaleurope.net). This online catalogue includes c. 1,500 descriptions, representing c. 30% of the series. According to the introduction to the series on this website, the documentation in this collection extends to some 50 linear feet of material of a highly varied nature dating from around 1750 to the 1880s. A finding aid to the complete series is available in the Reading Room of the National Archives. Documents in this series include a list of persons ejected from the estate of Thomas Rothwell in Aughnamullen, near Ballybay, County Monaghan, 1844 (NAI, CSO/OPMA/969). This provides the names of the tenants (c. 60 in all), notes that most of their houses have been demolished, and indicates where each of them was currently living.

## 10.6 Testamentary records

Prior to 1858 the Church of Ireland was responsible for administering all testamentary affairs. Ecclesiastical or Consistorial Courts in each diocese were responsible for granting probate and conferring on the executors the power to administer the estate. When the estate included property worth more than £5 in another diocese, responsibility for the will or administration passed to the Prerogative Court under the authority of the Archbishop of Armagh. It must not be thought that just because the Church of Ireland was responsible for administering wills, only persons who belonged to that particular denomination left wills. Unfortunately, nearly all original wills probated before 1858 were destroyed in Dublin in 1922. However, indexes to these wills do exist and are available on the website of the National Archives of Ireland. In addition, the principal repositories in Ireland all have substantial collections of duplicate wills and will abstracts.

The testamentary authority of the Church of Ireland was abolished by the Probate Act of 1857. Testamentary matters were brought under civil jurisdiction and exercised through district probate registries and a Principal Registry in Dublin. Bound annual indexes of testamentary papers called 'calendars' were produced and sets of these are available in PRONI and NAI. The district registries retained transcripts of the wills that they proved. Thus, while the original wills were destroyed in Dublin in 1922, the transcript copies in will books survived. Both PRONI and NAI have digitised the will books of the district registries (the pre-1904 will transcripts for the Principal Registry do not survive) in their custody for the period 1858–*c.* 1900 and these can be searched through the websites of these institutions. Original wills from 1900 onwards are in PRONI or NAI (1904 for Principal Registry wills).

### 10.6.1 Wills and farmers

Testamentary papers can illuminate the lives of our farming ancestors. In his will of 23 December 1781 William McVittie of Aghalisabea in County Monaghan left detailed instructions on the disposal of his livestock to family members (PRONI, T581). For example, his eldest grand-daughter Mary was bequeathed a branded cow called Shernagerragh, while another grand-daughter, Elinor, received a cow called Picky. Even the unborn child of his daughter-in-law was left the 'yellow Rigid Cow'. It is important not to discount the possibility that farmers may appear incidentally in the wills of landowners. For example, in 1727 William Weldon of Dublin included instructions in his will that his wife and son were to allow Thomas Clerke to enjoy his holding in Lishianstowne, County Meath, at the present rent until his death.[27]

Wills can provide clues to broader family relationships. Michael O'Kane of Drumaweir, near Greencastle in the Inishowen peninsula of County Donegal, died in 1857. In his will he bequeathed £20 per annum to his wife Ann McLaughlin (usefully giving her maiden name) for the rest of her life. Two of his residuary legatees were Patrick O'Kane, farmer, and Mary Anne O'Kane, spinster, both of Ballymoney (near Dungiven), County Londonderry. It would appear that these were the testator's father and sister and that he was from Ballymoney originally. Wills may also help with tracing family members who went overseas. For instance, in 1863 Robert Stewart of Upper Binnelly, County Tyrone, left £100 to his daughter Catherine in Australia and £50 to his son Daniel in America.

## The will of Robert Rolleston of Gortavea, County Tyrone

In April 2004 the will of my great-great-great-grandfather, Robert Rolleston, was discovered in a solicitor's office in Strabane, County Tyrone. It is dated 16 July 1847 and is a rare example of an *original* will of an Irish farmer surviving from before 1900. It does not appear to have been probated officially – there is no record of it in the index to wills probated in the diocese of Derry – which explains, at least in part, its survival. The will provided new information on the family history, as well as an insight into the testator's circumstances and his values.

Robert Rolleston lived in the townland of Gortavea (he spelled it Gortavey) in the parish of Donagheady, County Tyrone. He began his will by appointing three men to act as trustees and executors of his estate: his brother Rev. Thomas Rolleston of Killea, County Donegal, his neighbour Thomas Ramsey of Gortmesson, County Tyrone, and Alexander Sinclair Humphreys of Killea, County Donegal, Esquire. One of the most important pieces of new information from the will was the identification of Robert's brother Thomas. Having established this connection, we were able to go back one further generation, since the records of Trinity College Dublin, which Thomas attended in the early 1800s, indicate that his father was named James. The trustees were authorised to pay Robert's debts and funeral expenses and to carry out the instructions in his will.

To his son Hugh Love (Love was the maiden name of Robert's wife Mary) he left £100. Interestingly, he was at this time residing on the island of Antigua in the West Indies, though what he was doing there is unclear. The sums of £150 and £50 were left, respectively, to his sons Thomas and William. There were conditions attached to these bequests and the trustees were empowered to withhold the sums of money if 'the conduct of my said sons or any of them be such as they may disapprove of … It is my hope that the conduct of all my sons may be such as to give satisfaction to the trustees and to all their friends'. The farm in Gortavea was left to his son James, though again this was dependent on his satisfactory behaviour.

Robert does not refer to his wife by name, but he notes that she had £125 in her own possession which she was intending to leave to their youngest son William. He also made provision for her during her widowhood, specifying that if James married he should live in the 'Lower Dwelling House', leaving the other house for his mother and brothers. In addition, James was to 'provide and keep for their use a Cow in full milk with five hundred weight of good Oatmeal and three tons of Coal or Turf of equal value & pay to and for their use the sum of Fifteen pounds in money yearly'. Further obligations placed on James included the 'education & maintenance of his brothers and his mother as at present'.

Over six years later, on 18 November 1853, not long before he died, Robert added a codicil to his will. The bequest to Hugh Love was reduced to £50 as he had already been given some of his father's money, while the bequest to William was increased to £150. The farm in Gortavea was not to go solely to James, but was to be divided equally between him and Thomas. Robert also directed that if either James or Thomas wished to sell their portion of the farm, it should go to the other. If Thomas married he had to set apart part of the house for his mother's exclusive use. Finally, as two of the original trustees had died – Rev. Thomas Rolleston and Thomas Ramsey – he appointed his neighbours, George Love of Gortavea and Samuel McClements of Tamnaclare, both farmers, as their replacements.

# Notes

1   Austin O'Sullivan and Richard A. Jarrell, 'Agricultural education in Ireland' in Norman McMillan (ed.), *Prometheus's Fire: a History of Scientific and Technological Education in Ireland* (2000), pp 376–404; Richard A. Jarrell, 'Some aspects of the evolution of agricultural and technical education in nineteenth-century Ireland' in Peter J. Bowler and Nicholas Whyte (eds), *Science and Society in Ireland: the Social Context of Science and Technology in Ireland, 1800–1950* (1997), pp 101–17.

2   See also, P.A. Doyle, 'Bannow School (1821–1826)', *The Past: The Organ of the Uí Cinsealaigh Historical Society*, 1 (Nov. 1920), pp 122–8; and Bernard Browne, 'Rev. William Hickey. The Bannow model farm and school', *Bannow Historical Society Journal*, 2 (2010), pp 109–17.

3   David Kennedy, 'Templemoyle Agricultural Seminary 1827–1866', *Studies: An Irish Quarterly Review*, 29:113 (March 1940), pp 119–26.

4   Both of these publications are available on Google Books.

5   The Edgeworth Papers in NLI include material relating to the education of John Conry at the agricultural schools at Loughash and Cloghan (MS 22,821).

6   Kennedy quickly became frustrated with his job at the National Education Department as his proposals for improving educational provision were ignored and in March 1839 he resigned his post. In the 1840s he was the secretary to the Devon Commission on the state of agriculture in Ireland and also served as secretary to the Famine Relief Commission. He later spent some time in India, before settling in England. He died in London in 1879. He was described in the *Dictionary of National Biography* as 'a man of great ability and great simplicity, thoroughly unworldy and disinterested'.

7   *Albert Agricultural College Centenary Souvenir 1838–1938* (1938). Dermot J. Ruane and Mary Forrest, 'Agricultural education at the Albert College, the Royal College of Science and University College Dublin' in *Farming and Country Life 1916: history talks presented at Teagasc Athenry, 10 & 11 June 2016* (2016).

8   Various documents relating to the establishment of the Munster Model Farm are in the Cork City and County Archives (U140/J/03/01).

9   Anna Day, *More than One Egg in the Basket: the Munster Institute in History* (1990).

10  Susan Parkes, *A Guide to Sources for the History of Irish Education, 1780–1922* (2010), p. 59 n.65.

11  D.H. Akenson, *The Irish Education Experiment: the National System of Education in the Nineteenth Century* (1970), p. 343.

12  PRONI also holds an annual report of the Brookfield Agricultural School, 1846 (D3300/192/1).

13 *Brookfield Agricultural School, Moira, Ireland: Its Origin and History* (1890), a copy of which is in the Linen Hall Library, Belfast, and G.R. Chapman, 'Friends Agricultural School Brookfield near Moira, 1836–1922', *Review: Journal of Craigavon Historical Society*, 5:2 (1985), pp 5–10 (this can be accessed online: www.craigavonhistoricalsociety.org.uk/rev/chapmanfriends.html).

14 Loughash is particularly well documented in parliamentary papers. See the *Report from the select committee of the House of Lords appointed to inquire into the practical working of the system of National Education in Ireland* (1854), pp 1529–30, for a listing of pupils at the agricultural school.

15 There are also shorter lists of names for Dunmanway Model Farm, County Cork, and Rahan Model Farm, King's County (Offaly).

16 An interim listing of grand jury records can be found at: https://beyond2022.ie/wp-content/uploads/2021/05/Grand-Jury-Sources-Interim-listing.pdf.

17 The publication can be downloaded here: https://beyond2022.ie/the-grand-jury-system-in-ireland.

18 See, for example, the extensive collection of County Donegal grand jury records at www.donegalcoco.ie//culture/archives/donegalgrandjurydigitised.

19 The purpose of query books varies somewhat, ranging from books recording preliminary enquiries into the proposed works prior to the presentment being made to volumes itemising the expenditure on completed tasks. In other instances query books seem to be synonymous with presentment books.

20 The books for County Louth have been made available at www.louthcoco.ie/en/services/archives/online-digital-archives/louth-grand-jury-query-books.

21 W.A. Maguire, *The Downshire Estates in Ireland, 1801–45* (1972), pp 53, 60; James S. Donnelly, *Captain Rock: the Irish Agrarian Rebellion of 1821–1824* (2009), p. 228

22 Nicola Jennings, 'A troubled landscape: the ejectment books of County Clare', *The Other Clare*, 36 (2012), pp 60–62. Extracts available at www.clarelibrary.ie/eolas/coclare/genealogy/don_tran/court_rpts/ejectments_1816_1835/ejectments1816_1835.htm.

23 M.L. Anderson, 'Items of forestry interest from the Irish Statutes prior to 1800 AD', *Irish Forestry*, 1:2 (1944), p. 9.

24 Anderson, 'Items of forestry interest from the Irish statutes', p. 20.

25 www.oireachtas.ie/parliament/about/libraryresearchservice.

26 www.jbhall.clahs.ie/1740_corn_census_of_county_louth.htm.

27 This example is from Edward MacLysaght (ed.), *The Kenmare Manuscripts* (1970), published by the Irish Manuscripts Commission.

# 11

# Farming organisations

Over the centuries farmers in Ireland have banded together for various purposes. These include the defence and protection of their livelihoods and the desire to encourage agricultural improvement. Some of these organisations were focused on local issues. For example, PRONI has the minutes of a 'Toll Fund' subscribed to by farmers in the Holywood, Dundonald and Castlereagh areas of County Down to protect themselves against the exaction of illegal market tolls in Belfast, 1813–51 (D795). Other organisations, however, have been countrywide and concerned with matters of national interest, often with far-reaching consequences. This chapter reviews the records of a number of farming organisations.[1]

## 11.1 Farming societies and similar bodies

Since the first half of the eighteenth century different organisations have promoted improved farming practices and represented the interests of farmers. One of the aims of the Dublin Society (from 1820 the Royal Dublin Society (RDS)), founded by members of the landed gentry in 1731, was agricultural improvement. Its ideas were disseminated among farmers of different classes and not just the gentleman farmer. Among the works published by the Society was a volume by John Hood, *Tables of Difference of Latitude and Departure for Navigators, Land Surveyors, &c.* (1772), which became a standard work on the subject area.[2] In the opening decades of the nineteenth century the Society was responsible for the publication of statistical surveys of most counties in Ireland (see Chapter 1 for more on these surveys).

The Royal Dublin Society maintains a library and archive at its headquarters in Ballsbridge, Dublin (www.rds.ie/library-archives). The Agricultural Archive comprises a range of material including:

minutes of the RDS Committee of Agriculture (1830s–1930); minutes of the Royal Agricultural (Improvement) Society of Ireland (1841–80); catalogues of Irish and UK Farming Societies (1800s–1950s); and catalogues of the RDS Spring and Bull Shows (1831–1992). The online digital collections include the printed volumes of the Society's *Proceedings*, 1764–1973, and listings of prizes, premiums and awards for various activities, including agriculture, 1778–1900.[3] Other farming organisations at a national level include the Farming Society of Ireland, founded in 1800 and dissolved in 1828.[4]

In addition to countrywide organisations, other farming societies were established from the 1700s onwards. One early document is a set of minutes of a meeting in 1757 of the Farmers' Society of the County of Donegal concerning premiums for ditching and flax-growing, which is available in the National Records of Scotland (GD10/953).[5] The records of a number of other farming societies can be found in PRONI. These include: Kennaught Farming Society, County Londonderry: lists of premiums, exhibitors, etc, 1854–65 (D1550/163/8A–D); Moneymore Farming Society, County Londonderry: cash book, 1871–5 (D3632/Y/25; MIC617/194); Newry Union Farming Society, counties Armagh and Down: catalogue of livestock, butter, etc, entered for competition at the show to be held in Newry on 28 June 1873 (D1152/3/30); and Portaferry Farming Society, County Down: reports on ploughing competitions and cattle shows organised including prize winners, 1845 (D3334/5). The Royal Ulster Agricultural Society (RUAS) originated as the North-East Agricultural Society of Ireland, founded in 1854. It acquired its present name in 1901. PRONI has extensive records relating to the RUAS, including minute books and cash books beginning in 1854, letter books from 1897 onwards and records relating to members from 1894 onwards (D3489).

Records of farming societies in the National Library of Ireland include: volume of accounts of the Inistioge Farming Society, County Kilkenny, 1837–44 (MS 42,115); minute book, finance accounts and lists of subscribers of the Lismore Farming Society, County Waterford, 1863–81 (MS 7207); accounts and subscriptions received by Mark Deering of the Rathvilly Agricultural Society, County Carlow, 1841–6 (n.4659, p.4647); and minute book of Ballineen Agricultural

Society, County Cork, 1845–7 (n.1194, p.1394). A discussion of the latter volume is found in T. Shea, 'The minute-book of the Ballineen Agricultural Society', *JCHAS*, 51 (1946), pp 52–60; the article includes an appendix listing the names and addresses of those present at a number of the meetings.[6] The Cork City and County Archives has a history of the Munster Agricultural Society, founded in 1857 (U619/8).

Other publications on the activities of farming societies include Cathal Smith, 'Apostles of agricultural reform: the Ballinasloe Agricultural Improvement Society in an era of high farming and high famine, 1840–1850', *JGAHS*, 64 (2012), pp 128–45; Cait Logue, 'The Nenagh Union Agricultural Society', *Tipperary Historical Journal* (2018), pp 146–54; and Denis G. Marnane, '"Positively afraid of their own landlord": Landlords and tenants, farming societies and agricultural shows in County Tipperary in the nineteenth century. Part 1', *Tipperary Historical Journal* (2019). The printed *Report of the Tuam Agricultural Society for the Year Ending December 1843* is in the National Archives of Ireland (CSO/OPMA/956).

The Irish Farmers' Union (IFU) was formed in 1911 as a Dublin-based association, and in 1919 it was established as a countrywide organisation. There are several individual items as well as collections of records relating to the IFU in the National Library of Ireland. These include the minute book of council meetings of the Irish Farmers' Union, 1912–19 (MS 19,027). There are also financial records of the Irish Farmers' Union, 1919–1933, including share certificates and bonds, 1922–8 (MS 43,565), and a smaller set of IFU papers, 1920–27 (MS 43,567). NLI also holds an account book, 1924–8 (MS 19,076) and a receipt book for subscriptions to the County Dublin Farmers' Association, 1925–7 (MS 43,565/20). In addition, it has the minute book of the Tallaght branch, 1922; with lists of members of other County Dublin branches (MS 19,028). The main body for farmers today is the Irish Farmers' Association, founded (as the National Farmers' Association) in 1955.[7]

Following a public meeting in December 1917, the Ulster Farmers' Union (UFU) was formed officially in January 1918 and records from 1919 are available in PRONI (D1050/13). These include minute books of the Executive Committee from 1919 onwards and minutes of a number of branches, including Belfast, Dundonald and

Dundrod. Early records of the North-west branch of the UFU, 1917–21, are also in PRONI (D1583/48). With regard to individual branches, PRONI has a membership/subscription book for the Derrygonnelly branch of the UFU, 1944–6 (D4580/4/5). The *Ulster Farmers' Journal* was the organ of the UFU and PRONI has the minute books and trading accounts of the Directors of the Ulster Farmers' Journal Ltd, 1920–68 (D1050/13/A/J/1–3). See Alastair MacLurg, *Ulster Farmers' Union: the History of its First Seventy Years 1917–1987*, a copy of which is in PRONI (D1050/13/F/5).

## Killyleagh, Killinchy, Kilmood and Tullynakill Farming Society

Looking more closely at one farming organisation, PRONI has records of the Killyleagh, Killinchy, Kilmood and Tullynakill Farming Society in County Down, including treasurer's accounts and reports, 1858–63 (T1981) and a minute book, 1906–21, containing many newspaper cuttings (D3550/3). Also available in PRONI is a bound volume titled *Reprints of Reports of Proceedings of the Killyleagh, Killinchy, Kilmood and Tullynakill Branch of the North-East Farming Society*, published in 1912 and covering the years 1828–35 (D3550/1) and a printed report of the proceedings of the society for 1852 (D3550/2). Much of the information in these reports relates to the award of premiums to farmers for excellence in their farming practices. For example, in the report for 1828 we find the following entry for the best cultivated farms:

> We award the First Premium to Mr James Johnston of Ballywillen, whose farm contains sixty-six acres, and appears to be judiciously sub-divided into eighteen fields, with white-thorn hedges, very properly cut and cleaned out. There are two stone and lime piers, with a gate into the greater number of his fields: the fields appear well drained and divided into ridges, from ten to eighteen feet wide, according to the moisture of the ground. ... has of stock four horses and two draught bullocks, eight milch cows, five two-year-old cattle, four one-year-old [cattle], six sheep and eight pigs; feeds the horses always in the house, and the milch cows during the night, and by this means and the general arrangement of the farm-yard and offices, has much convenience for the collection of manure, of which he seems to take advantage. ...

Other premiums awarded in this year included the best agricultural produce and the best livestock. The premiums for the cleanest and neatest labourers' cottages went to: 1st John McKenny; 2nd George Lowry; 3rd Patrick Flannigan (all of Ballywillen); 4th Hugh Gribben (Drumreagh); and 5th David Duncan (Ballydrain). In the report for 1829 we find that first place in the category for the ploughman who ploughed his ground within the set time 'in the best and neatest manner' was awarded to George McConnell of Ringdufferin – his son Steele McConnell was the ploughman. Lists of subscribers for a number of years are also found in these reports – in short, they contain a wealth of information about farming in those parishes on the western shore of Strangford Lough.

Within the burial ground adjoining Killyleagh Presbyterian Church there is a very tall pillar monument, commemorating the abovementioned James Johnston of 'Ballywoolen' (Ballywillen), 'who lost his life by a deplorable accident on the 11th day of January 1844 in the 46th year of his age, whilst returning from the discharge of his duty as an officer of the Farming Society of this district'. The inscription further records that the memorial had been 'erected by the Killyleagh, Killinchy, Kilmood and Tullynakill Farming Society and other friends in grateful acknowledgment of his usefulness as a member of the society and to testify how greatly he was respected in life and in death lamented'. Newspapers provide further detail on the circumstances of his death. On the evening in question Johnston and another man named Patterson had been returning from a ploughing match when:

> passing over a hill at Balloo, which is being cut down near the bridge, the night being dark and no paling having been erected for the protection of passengers, the horse and gig were precipitated a depth of eleven or twelve feet, and Mr Johnston killed on the spot (*Belfast Commercial Chronicle*, 15 Jan. 1844).

The other man was seriously injured, but survived. Subsequently, the road contractor, John Reid, was tried at the Down assizes for negligence and found guilty of manslaughter (*Belfast Commercial Chronicle*, 13 March 1844). He was acquitted of any malicious intent and fined £10 (reduced to £5). This is not the only monument in this churchyard to a member of the local farming society. The memorial to

William Farrell of Rathcunningham (d. 1856) was erected by 'the officers of the farming society and a few personal friends'.

## 11.2 Associations for rural women and young people

Contained in over 200 archival boxes, the records of the Irish Countrywomen's Association (ICA), *c.* 1930–1991, are held by the National Library of Ireland (MSS 39,284/1–39,890). The ICA grew out of the United Irishwomen, which had been founded in 1910 with the aim of encouraging 'better living' for women in rural areas. The collection includes many records relating to local guilds and federations. A detailed catalogue – Collection List No. 76 – is available on the NLI website. See also Sarah McNamara, *Those Intrepid United Irishwomen* (1995) and Aileen Heverin, *The Irish Countrywomen's Association, a History 1910–2000* (2000).[8]

The Young Farmers' Clubs of Ulster was founded by W.S. Armour, for a short time the editor of the *Northern Whig* newspaper, who had observed similar clubs in different parts of the world. The first club was Limavady, established in 1930, and many others were founded in the following decades in Northern Ireland. Today there are over 50 clubs (https://yfcu.org). See S. Alexander Blair, 'William S. Armour: founder of the Young Farmers' Clubs of Ulster', *The Glynns*, 33 (2005), pp 10–14; and by the same author, *Ulster's Country Youth: the First Fifty Years of the Young Farmers Clubs of Ulster* (1978). A number of works on individual clubs have been published.

In the Republic of Ireland, Macra na Feirme ('Stalwarts of the Land') was established in 1944 for young people in rural areas. Originally it was called the National Young Farmers' Association and the present title was adopted officially in December 1946. The key figure in its founding and early development was Stephen Cullinan, a rural science teacher, who served as the first honorary secretary and treasurer of the movement. In 1948 the *Young Farmers' Journal* was started in 1948 with the support of Macra na Feirme, and with Cullinan as its editor; it was renamed the *Irish Farmers' Journal* in 1950. Today there are some 170 clubs (https://macra.ie). Various books and articles have been published including Alexander Henry, *Macra – A Way of Life* (2005), produced by the Wicklow Macra na Feirme; and Joe Coffey, *Macra na Feirme, 1944–2019: a history in pictures* (2019).

## 11.3 Records of farmers and land reform campaigns

The issue of land reform is looked at in much more detail in Chapter 6. Records of the various tenant associations campaigning for better conditions for farmers are comparatively rare.[9] An account of efforts in north County Antrim to secure land reform is S.C. McElroy, *The Route Land Crusade: Being an Authentic Account of the Efforts made to Advance Land Reform by the Route Tenants' Defence Association* (n.d.). The National Library of Ireland has some important collections of documents relating to the activities of the Irish National Land League, better known simply as the Land League. The Land League was founded in Dublin in the autumn of 1879 and was the most important campaigning organisation during the Land War which targeted landlordism. Many farmers across Ireland joined local branches of the Land League, though it also included a significant number of townsmen who provided vital leadership. Nonetheless, it was primarily a farmers' organisation, which drew large numbers of farmers into political activity for the first time.[10]

The Land League papers in NLI include returns from over 150 different branches. There are many documents concerning the relief of evicted tenants, numerous items of correspondence and various lists of expenses in connection with the work of the Land League. The following is a selection of the material held by NLI:

Letters from various sources in the United States of America, containing subscriptions to the League, an account of moneys received and a list of subscribers, memoranda from branches in various counties including membership and expenses forms in connection with evictions, etc (MS 8291)

34 letters to Thomas Brennan, Secretary of the Land League, from officers of local branches in Connaught; mainly re expenses or relief of evicted tenants, 1880–81 (MS 17,693)

Memoranda for Land League on *c.* 100 cases of rack-renting in the Templederry area of County Tipperary; with particulars of landlords, tenants, holdings and leases, *c.* 1880 (MS 17,712)

Area files of the Land League for counties Antrim, Carlow, Clare, Cork, Fermanagh, Galway, Longford, Mayo, Meath, Sligo, Tipperary (mainly incomplete), 1880–81 (MS 17,709)

Bills for expenses of Land League branches, mainly Naas and Cork, and
two subscription lists including one of Thurles subscribers to the
Prisoners' Fund, 1881 (MS 17,715)

58 monthly branch reports of the Land League, mainly for branches in
counties Mayo, Roscommon, Tipperary, and concerning
proceedings, subscriptions, evictions, etc, 1880–81 (MS 17,706)

Other records in NLI relating to individual branches include the
minute book of the Raheen, County Laois, branch, 1880–81, with
some accounts (MS 9219); the minute book of the Rathvilly, County
Carlow, branch, 1880–81 (MS 842); accounts of the Kildare branch
containing mainly lists of fees paid for membership, 1880, and a roll
of membership and other papers, c. 1880 (MSS 9281–9282); and the
minute book of the Kildare branch, 1881 (MS 21,909). There is also
a set of 22 returns listing leases, rents and fines by members of the
Land League, mainly in branches in counties Roscommon and
Tipperary; with particulars on the pressure by landlords on tenants to
accept leases; the leases date from the period 1850–80 (MS 17,711).

Collections with material of relevance in the National Archives of
Ireland include the Irish National League Papers, which include some
material relating to the Land League. Within the collection of
business records in NAI is a register of members of the
Manorhamilton, County Leitrim, branch of the Land League, 1881
(LEITRIM 2003/91). Documents in PRONI include a list of
members of the Land League on a portion of the Downshire estate,
County Down, including details of the annual rents, Poor Law
valuations and subscriptions, 1881 (D1481/5/F); and a register of
members of the Ballinascreen, County Londonderry, branch of the
Land League, 1881–6, giving the date of admission, townland and
landlord (D3318/1).[11]

The Ladies' Land League was formed in 1881 to continue the
campaign in the event of the men leading the Land League being
arrested.[12] A range of records are in NLI. For the Maryborough (now
Portlaoise), County Laois, branch there is a minute book, 1881–2
(MS 2070), and a list of members and subscribers, 1882 (NLI, MS
9221). The surviving records of the Roundwood, County Wicklow,
branch include correspondence, a list of members, receipts for grants
paid, and some completed imprisonment, prosecution and eviction

forms, 1880–83 (MS 17,794). There is also a collection of 121 letters to Virginia Lynch, joint secretary of the Ladies' Land League, mainly concerning expenses and relief of evicted tenants, 1881 (MS 17,699). Other valuable records are the 100 eviction forms completed for the Ladies' Land League, from counties Cavan, Clare, Kildare, Longford, Mayo, Monaghan, Roscommon, Tyrone and Westmeath; these include particulars of tenant's families, rents, landlords etc, mainly 1881 (MS 17,714).

## 11.4 The co-operative movement

The agricultural co-operative movement in Ireland began in the late nineteenth century and was pioneered by Sir Horace Plunkett.[13] He was concerned at the threat to the marketing of Irish agricultural produce in Great Britain from foreign producers, and believed that Irish farmers needed to work together to meet this challenge. The Irish Agricultural Organisation Society was founded in 1894 with Plunkett as President. One of its main successes was the establishment of a network of co-operative creameries across Ireland, which resulted in considerable improvements to the dairy industry and the viability of milk production for small farmers. A weekly publication, the *Irish Homestead*, ran from 1895 to 1923 when it amalgamated with the *Irish Statesman*. The Society was later renamed the Irish Co-operative Organisation Society, and continues to play a vital role in the Irish dairy industry today. Following Partition, the Ulster Agricultural Organisation Society was established in Northern Ireland.

The co-operative movement in Ireland has been explored in a number of studies. These include: Patrick Bolger, *The Irish Co-operative Movement, its History and Development* (1977), George Chambers (with Ian McDougall), *The Origins of the Dairy Industry in Ulster* (2017), and Patrick Doyle, *Civilising Rural Ireland: The Co-operative Movement, Development and the Nation State, 1889–1939* (2019).[14] Studies of individual co-operatives, often produced to coincide with a notable anniversary, include Noreen McDonnell, *Callan Co-operative Agricultural and Dairy Society Ltd, 1899–1999* (1999); John O'Donnell, *A Border Co-op: the Town of Monaghan Centenary, 1901–2001* (2001); Teddy Fennelly, *A Triumph of Co-operation over Adversity: The History of Donaghmore Co-operative Creamery Ltd* (2003); and John Hough, *Mitchelstown Co-operative*

*Agricultural Society, Ltd: a History, 1919–1990* (2019). For further works, see the Irish History Online database.

An extensive collection of files of the Irish Agricultural Organisation Society are held in the National Archives of Ireland; written permission from the Irish Co-operative Organisation Society is required before these records can be consulted. A catalogue containing an alphabetical listing of local co-operatives for which files are available is in the NAI reading room. These are catalogued under ICOS 1088, with general reference files under ICOS 1089. The records of individual co-operatives may also be found in the Business Records archive in NAI, e.g. the papers of Ballaghaderreen Co-operative Agricultural and Dairy Society, County Roscommon (BR ROS 12), and of Hollyford Co-operative Agricultural and Dairy Society, County Tipperary (BR TIPP 2).

PRONI has an extensive collection of records relating to co-operatives in Northern Ireland, as well as a selection for the Republic of Ireland. These include minute books, share ledgers, cash books, wage books and records of customers. By way of example, for Deerpark Co-operative, near Glenarm, County Antrim, the following items are on deposit in PRONI: share ledgers, 1908–1970; minute book, 1908–55; correspondence, 1939–71; purchase journals and ledgers, 1908–67; milk records, 1930–58; butter sales book and ledger, 1909–55; accounts, including cash books, ledgers, statements, etc, 1908–68 (D3076).

Records relating to co-operatives may also be found in collections of estate papers. For example, among the Lissadell Papers in PRONI are boxes of material relating to Sir Josslyn Gore-Booth's involvement in the co-operative movement in County Sligo, comprising account books, loose letters and papers, printed matter, etc, concerning the Drumcliff dairy and mills, and the Ballinphull and Ballintrillick creameries, 1895–1939 (D4131/M/11A–B). There are also separate boxes relating to Sir Josslyn's involvement with the Irish Agricultural Organisation Society, the Department of Agriculture and Technical Instruction and County Sligo Agricultural Committee, 1902–06 (D4131/M/14–15).

Linked with the broader co-operative movement was the formation of co-operative credit societies. A photocopy of the minute book of the Valentia Island Agricultural Bank, 1904–14, is available in NLI

(MS 33,704). The printed *Rules of the Valentia Island Agricultural Bank* are available in NAI (RFS/SA/374/A). These declared: 'The objects of an Agricultural Bank are to assist its members with capital, to educate them in the true uses of credit, and to foster the spirit of mutual help or co-operation.'

## 11.5 Government departments and county committees

The Department of Agriculture and Technical Instruction (DATI) was established in 1899 thanks in large part to the work of Sir Horace Plunkett, the indefatigable promoter of agricultural improvement and the co-operative movement. DATI was responsible for agricultural and technical (vocational) education. The records of DATI are held by the National Archives of Ireland. Following Partition, DATI was absorbed into the Department of Lands and Agriculture in the new Free State (records in NAI), while in Northern Ireland a Ministry of Agriculture was established (records in PRONI). Among other documentation relating to the work of DATI are the letters and papers of T.P. Gill, Secretary, Department of Agriculture and Technical Instruction, 1900–23, which are in NLI (MSS 13,478–13,526). The work of DATI can also be followed through the printed parliamentary reports.

Under the terms of the Agriculture and Technical Instruction (Ireland) Act of 1899 county councils were authorised to appoint an advisory committee. These Agricultural Advisory Committees made proposals and recommendations on a range of matters: improvements to agricultural practices, the award of premiums to farmers, and grants towards agricultural and horticultural shows. Records relating to these committees in what is now the Republic of Ireland may be held by county archives. For example, Donegal County Archives has 23 bound volumes of letters addressed to the County Committee of Agriculture, 1901–13 (DON/CDCA). The correspondence covers such matters as livestock breeding, prizes for agricultural improvement, training in a range of farming procedures, and matters relating to veterinary hygiene. Cork City and County Archives has records relating to the work of the County Committee of Agriculture, 1901–80 (CCCA/CC/CM/AG). Likewise Louth County Archives holds the minute books of the County Committee of Agriculture, 1901–85. Annual reports of the different county committees may have been published and some of these can be found in the National Library of Ireland and in county libraries. PRONI has records of the Agricultural Advisory Committees in counties Antrim, Armagh, Londonderry and Tyrone (AG/2).

## Notes

1 For twentieth-century organisations, see Louis P.F. Smith, 'The role of farmers' organizations', *Studies: An Irish Quarterly Review*, 44:173 (Spring, 1955), pp 49–56; Louis P.F. Smith and Sean Healy, *Farm Organisations in Ireland: a Century of Progress* (1996).

2 One of my distant forebears, John Hood lived at Moyle, near Newtowncunningham, County Donegal.

3 For more information on the RDS, see Henry F. Berry, *A History of the Royal Dublin Society* (1915), and Kevin Bright, *The Royal Dublin Society, 1815–45* (2004).

4 PRONI has a printed list of the members of the Farming Society of Ireland, 1803 (D562/7886).

5 Eileen McCracken, 'Premiums offered by the Donegal Farmers' Society (1757)', *Donegal Annual*, 7 (1967), pp 225–8. See also James MacCarte, 'County Louth medals. With an account of the Louth Farming Society, established 3rd Feb. 1830 and the Louth Horticultural Society, established 1856', *Journal of the County Louth Archaeological Society*, 3:1 (1912), pp 29–30; and 'County of Monaghan Farming Society, 1801', *Clogher Record*, 2:3 (1959), p. 468.

6 Copy available online at www.corkhist.ie/wp-content/uploads/jfiles/1946/b1946-006.pdf.

7 *The Path to Power: 60 Years of the Irish Farmers' Association* (2015).

8 Some records are held in local archives, e.g. Longford County Archives Service has seven boxes of ICA papers for 1945–2007.

9 NLI has a list of subscribers for the New Ross Tenant League, County Wexford, including expenses and members' addresses, 1852–63 (MS 42,606).

10 Sam Clark, 'The social composition of the Land League', *Irish Historical Studies*, 17:68 (1971), pp 447–69.

11 Copy also in NLI (MS 50,183).

12 Marie O'Neill, 'The Ladies' Land League', *Dublin Historical Record*, 35:4 (1982), pp 122–33.

13 Since the 1860s a number of co-operative stores had been founded, though progress was slow. The Belfast Co-operative Society serviced the retailing needs of urban workers.

14 Published essays include: Frank Brennan, 'The co-operative creameries and their role in the social and economic development of County Cavan' in Jonathan Cherry and Brendan Scott (eds), *Cavan: History and Society* (2014); Proinnsias Breathnach, 'Agricultural change and the growth of the creamery system in Monaghan, 1855–1920' in P.J. Duffy and Éamonn Ó Ciardha (eds), *Monaghan: History and Society* (2017), pp 617–41; and Ingrid Henriksen, Eoin McLaughlin and Paul Sharp, 'Contracts and cooperation: the relative failure of the Irish dairy industry in the late nineteenth century reconsidered', *European Review of Economic History*, 19:4 (2015), pp 412–31.

# 12

# Records generated by farmers

While not commonly found, records generated by farmers themselves offer opportunities to delve more deeply into the personal side of family history. Meticulously-kept account books can record in a systematic way the farmer's income and expenditure. There may be information on his attendance at fairs and markets and the purchase and sale of livestock and crops. An account book may reveal whether a farmer supplemented his income through his involvement in, for example, spinning or weaving linen. Diaries can also include a similar range of information, along with observations on the weather, farming activities through the year, local occurrences and broader historical events, and perhaps even details concerning the farmer's own family.

Aside from the farmer and his family, the names that appear in these records may include those from whom he was buying, or to whom he was selling, and the labourers who worked for him. Events associated with neighbouring families might be recorded, such as births, marriages and deaths, as well as comments on emigration. It must be acknowledged that the individuals who kept such records tended to be in possession of large farms and were those who felt the need to maintain good record-keeping. Far fewer small farmers kept account books or diaries. The survival of records by individual farmers is very much hit and miss. Some of these volumes, or occasionally just loose sheets of paper, are on deposit in archives, though many remain in private custody as treasured heirlooms.

## 12.1 Examples of records produced by farmers
A superb set of diaries kept by an Irish farmer are of those James Harshaw (1797–1867), who operated a substantial farm in the parish of Donaghmore, County Down. The diaries mainly cover the period

from *c.* 1840 to 1867. Through the efforts of Marjorie Harshaw Robie, an American descendant of the family, six of the original diaries were placed in PRONI in 1996 and given the reference D4149. These had been sent to America and were in the possession of one of Harshaw's sons before disappearing for the better part of a century until they were rediscovered in a bank. Many years ago PRONI had microfilmed the seventh and final diary of James Harshaw (MIC39). There are also transcriptions of all seven diaries by Robie, while digitised copies of the diaries are available for consultation in Newry and Mourne Museum.

The diaries include accounts and copies of documents, among them letters and wills. Together they provide an exceptionally detailed insight into local farming practices, including the sowing and harvesting of a range of crops, livestock reared, the impact of the weather on agriculture, labourers' activities and wages, and market prices, etc. More broadly, the diaries include much information on James Harshaw's involvement in his local Presbyterian congregation, politics and land reform, poor relief initiatives and other public roles. There are numerous references to the emigration of local families, as well as local baptisms, marriages and deaths. The PRONI eCatalogue includes summary information on the contents of the diaries as well as excerpts from them. It is obvious from even a casual perusal of these that the value of these diaries goes far beyond the Harshaw family. For instance, we find recorded on 11 April 1857: 'William and Jo Neill and Molly and William Marshall emigrating to America'. There are also minutes and other documents relating to the work of the Donaghmore dispensary.[1]

Another invaluable set of diaries is even more extensive. Covering the period 1848–91, the diaries were kept by William Fee McKinney of Sentry Hill in the parish of Carnmoney, County Antrim. The original diaries, along with a substantial collection of documents, photographs and artefacts, remain at Sentry Hill.[2] Extracts from the diaries of 1848–61 are included in PRONI's eCatalogue under reference T3234 and, like the Harshaw diaries, range from the everyday to the extraordinary as the following excerpts indicate:

> 14 Feb. 1850: Samuel McGladdery and William J. Keers commenced to set potatoes for my father.
> 26 Jan. 1852: Mrs Wilson had a young son this morning which is considered very remarkable as her husband is nearly 3 years dead and she has had 13 children before this one.

12 March 1853: Joseph McGaw, Tom Mullen and I went to Larne for
seed oats from Robert Tweed of Islandmagee.

14 Dec. 1858: Drove 6 loads of John Launder's oats to Uncle John's
barn to get thrashed.

11 Nov. 1859: A woman died in Sally McClintock's house yesterday
and her husband who called himself William Murphy from
Ahoghill got 9s. 0d. from my father and Miss Smith for the purpose
of buying a coffin. He also collected some from other persons and
then went away about 1 o'clock leaving his wife unshrouded and
uncoffined and no person knows where he went.

PRONI has a microfilm copy of the diary of William Fee McKinney
for March 1860 to May 1861, which includes his account of a voyage
from Cork to New York and from there to Ottawa where he worked
as a farm hand and store clerk (MIC486/1). A superb study of the
McKinney family is Brian M. Walker, *Sentry Hill: an Ulster Farm and
Family* (1981).

An excellent set of farm accounts for the years 1839–48 survive for
a property at Burren, near Dunleer in County Louth, possessed by the
McGrane family. These were discussed in an article in the *Journal of
the County Louth Archaeological & Historical Society* in 1996 (see below
for full details). At over 400 acres the farm was of considerable extent
and a steward, James McEvoy, was employed to assist with the
management of it. There was also a herd – initially Patrick Fay, then
Thomas McGeogh and after him Owen Monaghan. The accounts
include the names of individuals who bought items from the farm,
e.g. Joseph McLaughlin, who purchased 'Pinks' (potatoes), and
Michael Gannon, a miller in Dunleer, who bought oats. Information
is also recorded on household expenditure on such things as clothing
and footwear. The accounts reveal that well over 100 families and
individuals had dealings of one form or another with the farm in this
period. Most of them were cottiers and labourers renting small plots
of land for growing potatoes in return for labour, though cash
payments became increasingly common.

## 12.2 Publications on farmers' records

The records of some farmers have been the subject of a publication,
either as a stand-alone book or an article in a periodical. A selection
of these is presented below.

*Anon, Montiaghs, County Armagh*
Florence Gracey, 'A farming diary for 1885', *Review: Journal of the Craigavon Historical Society*, 8:2 (2002–03);[3] the diary was kept by an unidentified farmer in the townland of Derryadd in Montiaghs in north County Armagh.

*Brennan, Duleek, County Meath*
C.C. Ellison, 'Brennan farm accounts, 1840–1880', *Annala Dhamhliag: the Annals of Duleek*, 5 (1976), pp 20–26.

*Cleland, Drumaghlis, near Crossgar, County Down*
A more unusual subject of study is John Moulden's exploration of the book collection (now on deposit in the Ulster Museum) of a farming family from Drumaghlis, near Crossgar, County Down: '"James Cleland his book": the library of a small farming family in early nineteenth-century County Down' in Marc Caball, Andrew Carpenter (eds), *Oral and Print Cultures in Ireland, 1600–1900* (2010).

*Coulter, Dundalk, County Louth*
E. Charles Nelson, 'A Dundalk farmer's library in 1803', *The Linen Hall Review*, 4:3 (Autumn, 1987), pp 14–16; the library was maintained by Samuel Coulter of Carnbeg, near Dundalk.

*Delany, Woodtown, Dunshaughlin, County Meath*
W.E. Vaughan, 'Farmer, grazier and gentleman: Edward Delany of Woodtown 1851–1899', *Irish Economic and Social History*, 11 (1982), pp 53–72; based on two volumes of stock purchases and sales accounts for the farm of the Delany family (NLI, MSS 19,347–19,348).

*Filgate, Balbriggan, County Dublin*
*Extracts from the Farm Diary of Lowther Lodge, Balbriggan, 1803–1822*, transcribed and edited by Elizabeth Balcombe (2008); the diary was kept by a gentleman farmer, Townley Patten Filgate.

*McGrane, Burren, Dunleer, County Louth*
Pádraig Faulkner, 'A County Louth farm on the eve of and during the Famine: Burren farm accounts book, 1839 to 1848', *Journal of the County Louth Archaeological & Historical Society*, 23:4 (1996), pp 438–51.

*McKeag, Macosquin, County Londonderry*
Michael McKeag, 'An account of produce sold: Alexander McKeag's farm
book', *North Irish Roots*, 13:1 (2002): looks at a volume kept by a farmer
in Macosquin.

*Morrison: Crookedstone, County Antrim*
Annette McKee, 'William Morrison's eighteenth-century pocket book',
*DIFHR*, 43 (2020), pp 28–36; transcription of a book kept by a farmer
in Crookedstone, Killead parish, recording day to day events, 1700s
(PRONI, D3300/109).

*Nevin, Ballywarren, County Down*
Extracts from the diary of James Nevin, Ballywarren, Down parish, County
Down, 1767–97, *Lecale Review*, 14 (2016), pp 24–7 (reproduced from
*Down Recorder*, 3 April 1920).

*Peacock, Adare, County Limerick*
Marie-Louise Legg, *The Diary of Nicholas Peacock 1740–1751: the Worlds of
a County Limerick Farmer and Agent* (2005), based on a manuscript
volume  in NLI, provides an insight into the life of a mid-eighteenth-
century farmer near Adare in comparatively good circumstances. Peacock,
who lived at Kilmoreen, also acted as a land agent for his relatives, the
Hartsonges.

*Prendergast, Leighlinbridge, County Carlow*
Edward Moran, 'The Prendergast account book', *Carloviana*, 56 (2007),
pp 35–44;[4] the article is concerned with the accounts kept between 1863
and 1880 when Patrick Prendergast farmed at Closutton, near
Leighlinbridge.

*Taylor, Taughboyne, County Donegal*
Sean Beatty, 'Laggan farm accounts', *Donegal Annual*, 49 (1997), pp 77–85
(also published in Jim Mac Laughlin (ed.), *Donegal: the Making of a
Northern County* (2007), pp 235–41); discusses a farm records book kept
by Andrew Taylor of Craigadoos in the parish of Taughboyne from 1869
onwards.

## 12.3 Records in archives and libraries

The records listed below are mainly to be found in the National
Library of Ireland and the Public Record Office of Northern Ireland,
with others in the National Archives of Ireland and elsewhere. Items

are listed alphabetically under the name of the farming family, while those that cannot be assigned to a particular family are listed separately at the end. This listing is not meant to be exhaustive and further records may be found through a search of the respective institutions' catalogues. Although the principal focus was on identifying records relating to tenant farmers, some of the items listed below relate to the home farms of minor estates.

*Adams, Chequer Hall, Ballyweaney, County Antrim*
Bundle of linen and household accounts of John Adams, *c.* 1780–*c.* 1810 – PRONI, D1518/2/2
Cash book of John Adams, Chequer Hall, Ballyweaney, linen merchant (bought yarn to give out to weavers in their cottages), 1782–6 – PRONI, D1518/2/3
Cash account book, John Adams, Ballyweaney, 1789–1803 – PRONI, D1518/2/4

*Alexander, Moneymore, County Londonderry*
Farm account book of David J. Alexander, Larrycormick, Moneymore, 1906–24 – PRONI, D2983/1

*Bell, Crossgar, County Down*
Ledgers of poultry sales kept by John Bell, Crossgar, 1890–1946 – PRONI, D2357/2–3

*Betty, Irvinestown, County Fermanagh*
Farm account book of William Betty, Coolaness House, Irvinestown, 1759–1863 – PRONI, D2347

*Blackwell, Newtown North, County Limerick*
Farm account book relating to lands of the Blackwell family at Newtown North, Macha, etc, late 1800s – NLI, n.5557, p.5717

*Boylan, Carbury, County Kildare*
Farm account books of the Boylan family of Coonough, Carbury, *c.* 1824–1883, *c.* 1853–1916; also a farm wages book, *c.* 1853–1871 – NLI, n.6322, p.7214

*Brady, Omagh, County Tyrone*
Farm and household account book of John Brady, Omagh area, 1757–66 – PRONI, T2748/1

*Brakinridge, Ballykeel, County Down*
Rent and farm account book of the Brakinridge family, Ballykeel
[Dromore parish?], *c.* 1779 – PRONI, T1344/2

*Buchanan, Crevenagh, County Tyrone*
Account book of Crevenagh and Edenfell farms of the Buchanan family,
1862–84 – PRONI, T1644/1

*Byrne, Upper Aughrim, County Wicklow*
Papers relating to the farm of James Byrne, Upper Aughrim, 1888–1964
– NLI, MS 51,148

*Campbell, Templepatrick, County Antrim*
Volume containing a range of material relating to Templepatrick Presbyterian
Church, including farm accounts, 1799–1812, during the ministry of
Rev. Robert Campbell – PRONI, CR4/12/A/1 (use MIC1B/11/1)

*Canavan, Dunsilly, County Antrim*
Cash account book of the Canavan family, Dunsilly, 1765–1832
– PRONI, T2188/1

*Carey, Fermoy, County Cork*
Farm accounts of Mr Carey, Strawhall, near Fermoy, County Cork,
1760–1830 – University College Cork Library Archives, MS U/41

*Carey, Fermoy, County Cork*
Wages account book titled 'John Carey's Acct Book … Labourers' (includes
the names of workmen, hours worked, wages paid, tasks undertaken), for
an estate or landholding near Fermoy, County Cork (the property seems
to be near Ballyknock (Ballynoe parish) and Ballymacoy (Monanig
parish), 1792–7 – Cork City and County Archives, U050

*Carlisle, Knockbracken, County Down*
Diary of Samuel Carlisle, farmer, Knockbracken, 1840–45 – PRONI,
D1952/2

*Casement, Sheepland Beg, County Down*
Farm account book/diary recording the management of a farm owned by
Robert and William Casement in the townland of Sheepland Beg,
Dunsfort parish, 1799–1833: it is mainly concerned with recording the
names, wages and terms of employment of a series of labourers, both
regular and occasional – PRONI, D3034/1

*Chambers, Tullynaskeagh, County Down*
Farm account book of the Chambers family, Tullynaskeagh, 1884
– PRONI, T1443

*Courtenay, Benburb, County Tyrone*
Domestic, farm and rent account book of the Courtenay family, Benburb
area, 1776–1806 – PRONI, D1179/1

*Crea, Ringawaddy, County Down*
Farm accounts, Crea family, Ringawaddy, 1857–93 – PRONI, D884/2

*Denniston, Drumnacross, County Longford*
Family papers and farm account books, of the Denniston family,
Drumnacross, 1792–1923 – NAI, BR LON 11

*Drennan, Limavady, County Londonderry*
Over 100 documents relating to the Drennan family of Carse Hall,
Limavady, including land reclamation correspondence, estimates and
accounts concerning Ballykelly, Myroe and Lough Foyle and Lough
Swilly, 1838–1908; specifications, plans, receipts and accounts of James
Drennan concerning improvements to and maintenance of buildings and
machinery, *c.* 1896; farm diaries, account books, etc, relating to the
Drennan farm at Carse Hall, 1924–59 – PRONI, D1513

*Erskine, Dunaverney, County Antrim*
Account book of William Askin (Erskine) Dunaverney, Ballymoney:
includes genealogical notes on the Erskine family as well as accounts of
the selling and purchase of yarn, livestock, potatoes and payments to
hired servants etc, *c.* 1800 – PRONI, T2082/1

*Fagin, Moatefarrell, County Longford*
Copy of a cattle sales book relating to James Fagin, Moatefarrell, 1861–77
– NAI, BR LON 12

*Fahy, Deerpark, County Clare*
Papers of Jerome A. Fahy, farmer and accountant, Deerpark, near Quin,
including diary entries 1902–52 – NLI, MS 49,802/1–15

*Ferguson, Grange, Cookstown, County Tyrone*
Farm and domestic workers' wages book and farm account book,
1878–1905 – PRONI, D392/2

*Filgate, Ardee, County Louth*
Farm accounts of the Filgate family, Ardee, 1834–5, 1844–74; 1845–56
– NLI, MSS 11,944–11,945

*Filgate, Lissrenny, County Louth*
Stock returns and farm accounts of William Filgate, Lissrenny, 1839,
1845–9 – NLI, MSS 23,435–23,437

*Finlay, Tullyrap, County Donegal*
Various documents of John Finlay of Tullyrap, County Donegal, including
payment/order book for wheat, meal, etc, 1906–07, and day book for
same 1879–1906 – PRONI, D2609/3/1

*Gibbons, Ballynegall, County Westmeath*
General cash books of James Gibbons, farmer, of Ballynegall, 1804–09,
1816–21, 1825–40 – NLI, MSS 5329–5337

*Gilfillen, Lismacarol, County Londonderry*
Farm diaries and accounts of the Gilfillen family of Lismacarol, 1868–81,
1882–92, 1897–1908, 1909–18 – PRONI, MIC93/1–2

*Gollock, Coachford, County Cork*
Farming diary and account book, possibly kept by Thomas Gollock, Forest,
Coachford, 1824–6 – NLI, n.5810, p.6016

*Gourley, Derryboy, County Down*
Manuscript farm note book of James Gourley, Derryboy, with notes
concerning Killyleagh, Killinchy, Kilmood and Tullynakill Farming
Society, 1883–90 – PRONI, D2293/1
Memoranda book containing agricultural and genealogical jottings,
*c.* 1880–1900; diary extracts re farm management, 1883–1902; cash
book re farm management, 1885–1903 – PRONI, D1065/3

*Hanly, Carrowerin, County Roscommon*
Wages book of Patrick Hanly of Carrowerin, with notes on farming
operations, 1838–41 – NLI, n.4918, p.4950

*Hardman, Drogheda, County Louth*
Farm and personal account book of members of the Hardman family of
Drogheda, 1788–1849 – NLI, MS 16,212

*Harshaw, Donaghmore, County Down*
Diaries of James Harshaw of Donaghmore, 1830s–1860s – PRONI,
D4149 (see above)

*Hayes, Cahir, County Limerick*
Records of cows served, calves born and other farm accounts, *c.* 1837–1861,
compiled by Nicholas Hayes, Cahir, Bruff, County Limerick(?)
– NLI, n.5812, p.6018

*Henning, Waringstown, County Down*
Farm account book mainly concerned with cows, 1854–5; wages and
miscellaneous farm account book, 1855–7; account book re lime and
including short farm account, 1856–75; all kept by John Henning of
Waringstown – PRONI, D2321/6–8

*Hogg, Rathmullan, County Down*
Farm account book for Tallygowan [sic] Rathmullan, Ballylucas area,
1845–66 – PRONI, D2235/1

*Holmes, Benburb, County Tyrone*
Farm account and stock book, possibly kept by a Holmes family: includes
details of wages paid and money lent to various people, etc, Benburb
area, *c.* 1780–*c.* 1821 – PRONI, D1782/3

*Holt, Coolavacoose, County Kildare*
Diary of John Holt of Coolavacoose, Carbury, mainly relating to farming,
*c.* 1861–1869; farm diary and notebook of Samuel Holt of same,
*c.* 1898–1901 – NLI, n.6322, p.7214

*Hutchinson, Beechy Park County Carlow*
Account-book recording wages, domestic and farm expenses, cattle
dealings, etc, maintained by John Corrigan and others, for J.F.
Hutchinson, Beechy Park, near Rathvilly, *c.* 1830–50 – NLI, MS 14,336

*Johnston, Glynn, County Antrim*
Household and farm account books of George B. Johnston, Glynn,
1875–8, 1897–1904 – PRONI, D1783/9–10

*Kearns, Ballygannon, County Wicklow*
Diary of James Kearns, farmer, of Ballygannon, Kilcoole, County Wicklow,
1845–54 – MS 36,186

*Kelly, Buneallagh, County Offaly*
Farm account books of Kelly family, Buneallagh, parish of Croghan,
1855–95 – Offaly Archives, OCL P25

*Keoghan, Navan, County Meath*
Farm account book of Keoghan family, Navan, 1855–84
– NAI, BR MEATH 6

*Kerr, Duff's Hill, County Antrim*
Diary of Samuel Kerr, farmer of Duff's Hill, Carrickfergus, 1880–81
– PRONI, T2931/1–2

*Kinsella, Rathrush, County Carlow and Derrykearn, County Laois*
Photocopy of wages book and farm account book of the family of Kinsella
of Rathrush, Tullow, and Derrykearn, *c.* 1867–1901
– NLI, MS 21,186

*Knox, Seacon, County Antrim*
Farm account book, Knox family, Se[a]con, Ballymoney, 1894–1900
– PRONI, T2992/2

*Lambert, Ballycushlane, County Wexford*
Farm diary and account book of the Lambert family, Ballycushlane, near
Broadway, 1800–67 – NAI, BR WEX 2

*Leonard, Balloy, County Meath*
Farm records of the Leonard family of Balloy House, Stamullin, including
financial records and farm diaries, 1928–2000 – TCD, MS 11573

*Lucas, Ruan, County Clare*
Diary of a member of the Lucas family farming in the parish of Ruan,
1739–41 – NLI, MS 14,101

*Maguire, Garryspillane, County Limerick*
Farm account books of Bryan Maguire, Garryspillane, 1887–1923
– NAI, BR LIM 1

*Mahon, Castlegar, County Galway*
Account book of Ross Mahon, Castlegar, relating to cattle and sheep, and
also servants' wages and notes on agriculture, *c.* 1724–1738
– NLI, MS 19,965

*Martin, Ballooly, County Down*
James Martin's farm workers' wages book, Ballooly, 1779–1817
– PRONI, D2722/1

*McDonnell, Mount Talbot, County Roscommon*
Farm accounts, diaries of the McDonnell family, Mount Talbot,
1898–1972 – NAI, BR ROS 1

*McHendry, Sixtowns, County Londonderry*
Account book of the McHendry family, particularly Thomas, relating
to their tanyard business in Sixtowns, Draperstown, 1797–1883
– PRONI, T3232/1

*Meyler, Harristown, County Wexford*
Farming ledger of Thomas Meyler, Harristown, 1837–45 – NLI, MS 5355
Workmen's accounts for Meyler family, Harristown, 1846, 1848, 1851–2
– NLI, MSS 7396–7399

*Mill, Ballywillan, counties Antrim and Londonderry*
Account book of the Rev. William Mill, Anglican incumbent of Ballywillan
parish, including farm accounts, 1827–31 – PRONI, CR1/34/F/1A–1B

*Moore, Carndonagh, County Donegal*
Records possibly created by Robert Moore of Carndonagh, including a
farmer's record book, concerning livestock breeding, sowing seed, plan of
corn stacks, etc, 1856–83, and account book for a grain market, 1881–7
– PRONI, T2799/2/4–5

*Moore, Killyleagh, County Down*
Farm account book, probably belonging to James Moore, Lisinaw and Clay
etc, Killyleagh, 1830–33 – PRONI, T3011/1

*O'Donoghue, Rineanna, County Clare*
Farm accounts of Timothy O'Donoghue, Rineanna, *c.* 1806–1819
– NLI, n.5985, p.6539

*Ogle, Delvin, County Westmeath*
Records of house and farm, Ogle family, Delvin, 1846–1932
– NAI, BR WM 9

*Orr, Glasdrumman, County Down*
Farm and household account book of the Orr family Glasdrumman,
Annalong: includes details of the hire of domestic and farm labour
and household accounts, 1731–1861 – PRONI, T3301/1

*Pike, Dungannon, County Tyrone*
Farming book (probably kept by W.J. Pike) containing accounts of
workmen's wages, potatoes sold, cost of building a corn kiln, acreage
of fields, etc for a farm at Derryvale, Dungannon, 1808–17
– PRONI, D3039/2

*Pratt, Agher, County Meath*
Farming accounts of Benjamin Pratt, Agher, 1726–42, 1734–43
– NLI, MSS 5248, 5250

*Reynolds, Drumafevy, Ballymoney, County Antrim*
Flyleaf pages from a farm account book of the Reynolds family of
Drumafevy [Drumnafivey?], Ballymoney, County Antrim, *c.* 1800
– PRONI, D1013/2/1

*Richardson, Kilruddan, County Tyrone*
Farm account book of the Richardson family, Kilruddan, mid-1800s
– PRONI, T1579

*Robinson, Mealough, County Down*
Small, leather-bound notebook, used as a diary or commonplace book by
William Robinson, farmer, Mealough, and including details of work on
the farm, 1841–60 – PRONI, D4062/1

*Rollins, Clough, County Longford*
Notebook of Mrs James Rollins, Clough, Kenagh, with accounts of farm
receipts and expenditure, 1917–22 – NLI, MS 18,251

*Rothwell, Rockfield, County Meath*
Farm account book of Thomas and Richard Rothwell of Rockfield, Kells,
1816–18 – NLI, MS 16,835

*Scully, Kilfeakle, County Tipperary*
Diary kept by James Scully,[5] Kilfeakle, near Tipperary town, mainly
concerning his extensive farming activities, 1773–1814 – NLI,
MS 27,479 (A summary of a talk on the diary by J.F. McCarthy appears
in the *Irish Book Lover*, 30:5 (1948), pp 110–11.)

*Snoddy, Tureagh, County Antrim*
Accounts, 1859–68, that appear to concern the Snoddy family, Tureagh,
Raloo (earlier accounts, 1821–2, seem to relate to a beer and spirits
business run by a member of the family); other accounts relating to
Snoddy property in Tureagh, Ballytober and Ballyrickard,
*c.* 1860–*c.* 1880 – PRONI, D2985/2/1–2

*Stewart, Ballymorran, County Down*
Farm and account book of James Stewart, Ballymorran, Killinchy, 1838–81
– PRONI, T1342

*Sullivan, Liscarroll, County Cork*
Miscellaneous memoranda of farm and household expenses, and of
domestic occurrences, by Sullivan, Liscarroll, 1750–60, with nineteenth-
century additions – NLI, MS 1501

*Ussher, Cappagh, County Waterford*
Account book of Ussher farm at Cappagh, 1869–73 – NLI, MS 3979

*Walmsley, Kilkeel, County Down*
Mill wages book of Andrew Walmsley of The Green Mills, Kilkeel, at the
back of which are farm accounts, 1884–1906 – PRONI, D2254/3/1

*Winter, Agher, County Meath*
Farming accounts of Samuel Winter, Agher, 1778–82 – NLI, MS 5251

UNIDENTIFIED

*Ballinasloe, County Galway*
Herd book, 1734–72, and farm accounts, 1740–85, Ballinasloe area
– NLI, MS 498

*Ballyclare, County Antrim*
Notebook containing inventory of goods to be sold at various farms
in the Ballyclare area, 1845 – PRONI, T2387/1

*Cork and Imokilly, County Cork*
Farm wages book relating to property in the baronies of Cork and Imokilly,
1798–1802 – NLI, MS 5695

*Ennis, County Clare*
Accounts of a farmer probably in the vicinity of Ennis, 1857–67
  – NLI, MS 19,476

*Glenbaun, County Tipperary*
Copy farm account book, Glenbaun, near Clonmel, 1826–44
  – NAI, BR TIPP 11

*Lough Swilly, County Donegal*
Account book relating to the farming of the Lough Swilly intakes at
  Blanket Nook, Inch, Black Brae and Burt, 1872–6 – PRONI, D3243/1

*Rutland, County Carlow*
Farm account book and diary, Rutland, 1870–94 – NLI, MS 19,455


## 12.4 Correspondence

The correspondence generated by members of farming families can be immensely helpful, not just for the individuals concerned, but also for their neighbours and the wider family circle. Often these letters were sent back and forth between emigrants and family back home and sometimes were passed around neighbours. The Public Record Office of Northern Ireland has an outstanding collection of letters written by or to Irish emigrants, which was built up over many decades. Researchers should consult PRONI's eCatalogue to identify material of potential relevance. The Irish Emigration Database, created and maintained by the Mellon Centre for Migration Studies (MCMS) at the Ulster American Folk Park, Omagh, County Tyrone, is also worth checking for it includes transcriptions of many emigrants' letters; it can be accessed for free via the DIPPAM website (www.dippam.ac.uk). Other archives have collections of such letters, while further correspondence remains in private possession.[6]

The following excerpt is from a letter that was shown to me by a neighbouring farming family. It was written by Mrs Lowry of Cullion, County Tyrone, to her daughter Hannah in Canada on 30 July 1893 and reveals contemporary ideas of what it meant to live comfortably, albeit a world removed from twenty-first-century notions of comfort:

I can now live very comfortable; all I require is health; we have 6 milk cows, 6 year olds and 6 calves, and two good horses, and we keep a breeding sow and she still has 2 litters in the year and we still keep a good stock to ourselves, so you see we can live very comfortable.

As much as anything Mrs Lowry wished to reassure her daughter that life was not as tough at home as Hannah may have feared from the other side of the Atlantic.

## Notes

[1] James Harshaw is the subject of a biography by Marjorie Harshaw Robie in the *Dictionary of Irish Biography*. See also the article by Tim Ferriss, 'The Harshaw Diaries' in the magazine of the Poyntzpass and District Local History Society, *"Before I forget…"* (available online at: www.poyntzpass.co.uk).

[2] Sentry Hill is cared for by Antrim and Newtownabbey Borough Council and the house and grounds are open to the public (https://visitantrimandnewtownabbey.com/things-to-do/heritage-attractions/sentry-hill).

[3] Available online at: www.craigavonhistoricalsociety.org.uk/rev/graceyfarmingdiary.html.

[4] Available online at: http://carlowhistorical.com/wp-content/uploads/2016/02/Carloviana-No-56-2007.pdf.

[5] There is a biography of Scully in the *Dictionary of Irish Biography*.

[6] A remarkable volume of 800+ pages is Kerby A. Miller, Arnold Schrier, Bruce D. Boling, David N. Doyle, *Irish Immigrants in the Land of Canaan: Letters and Memoirs from Colonial and Revolutionary America, 1675–1815* (2003). Professor Miller's huge collection of emigrants' letters has been donated to NUI Galway and there are plans to digitise this correspondence.

# 13

# Labourers, cottiers and farm workers

On the eve of the Great Famine of the 1840s, the majority of those employed in the agricultural sector were not farmers, but labourers. The 1841 census recorded 471,062 farmers in Ireland and 1,105,258 'male labourers and farm servants'. The latter total did not distinguish between farm servants – often boys and young men who 'lived in' and were provided with sustenance and shelter by the farmer – and the cottiers and labourers who lived separately, but worked for the farmers. It has been estimated that farm servants made up around a third of the total in this category. Already barely subsisting, the Famine hit the cottiers and labourers very hard and thereafter there was a significant decline in their numbers. According to the 1881 census, there were 441,928 farmers in Ireland and 215,008 agricultural labourers (198,579 males and 16,429 females). The disappearance from the landscape of the settlement marked 'Cotterstown' on an 1817 barony map of County Kilkenny is emblematic of the changing fortunes of this group.[1]

## 13.1 Difficulties with definition

One of the difficulties with defining this class is the variation in the meaning of terms such as cottier in different parts of Ireland. The following discussion of terminology appears in the printed report of the parliamentary investigation of the mid-1830s into the condition of the poor in Ireland:

> The term "cottier" is so variously applied and understood in Ireland that it may be useful to state from the evidence the meaning attached to it in different districts.
> In some parts of the country a "cottier" is merely another name for a small occupier of land under ten acres. This seems to be the case in

the counties of Clare, Kerry, Limerick, Tipperary, Waterford, and in some districts of King's. They are sometimes denominated cottier-tenants, a name we shall adopt. They pay a money-rent, which is often derived from wages earned in the better parts of Ireland, and in England.

The most prevalent meaning of the term "cottier" is that of a labourer holding a cabin, either with or without land, as it may happen (but commonly from a quarter to three acres are attached), from a farmer or other occupier, for whom he is bound to work, either constantly at a certain fixed price (usually a very low one), or whenever called upon, or so many days in the week at certain busy seasons, according to the custom of the neighbourhood, the convenience of the landlord, or other local or personal circumstances. This is done in the counties of Tyrone, Fermanagh, Monaghan, Wicklow, Queen's County, part of King's County, Kilkenny, and other places. In Leinster he has frequently nothing found him beyond his cabin, and perhaps work for three-fourths of the year. This class, in order to distinguish them from the former, we shall denominate cottier-labourers. They make their contract with the farmer for the cabin and land they hold in a money value, and the work they perform is set off against the rent at a price agreed upon, universally under the wages paid to other workmen. The system is undergoing dissolution in several counties; as the farmers, it is said, through economy, prefer to have their work done by occasional labourers.

In other places the term "cottier" is synonymous with that of "cottager" in England, and merely means the occupier of a cabin, without any reference to his occupation of land, if any, which may be attached. The word is thus applied in the counties of Dublin, Louth, Meath, Armagh, Down, and Cavan.[2]

Given what the above paragraphs reveal about the challenges of devising straightforward and all-encompassing definitions, it is best to adopt a broad approach when exploring the lives of cottiers, farm servants and agricultural labourers. Several studies are very helpful, including David Fitzpatrick, 'The disappearance of the Irish agricultural labourer, 1841–1912', *Irish Economic and Social History*, 7 (1980), pp 66–92; and Caoimhín Ó Danachair, 'Cottier and landlord in pre-Famine Ireland', *Béaloideas*, 48/49 (1980/1981), pp 154–65.[3] Pádraig Lane has studied agricultural labourers, notably their involvement in politics, in numerous publications (see the Irish History Online website: https://catalogues.ria.ie).

## 13.2 Records of agricultural labourers, etc

Formal written records setting out the relationship of an agricultural labourer with the tenant farmer for whom he or she worked are rare. Nonetheless, some of the farm account books highlighted in Chapter 12 will include references to labourers. For example, a diary (1799–1833) relating to the running of a farm by members of the Casement family in the townland of Sheepland Beg, Dunsfort parish, County Down, includes records concerning the hiring of labourers (PRONI, D3034/1). The labourers, who were both regular and occasional employees, are named and their wages and terms of employment are given. Mention is also made of expenses arising from the provision of necessities to them, such as shoes and tobacco. The following is an entry in this document: 'John Burns hired for May 1817 [for the half-year to November 1817] at 4 pounds wages he is paid all his old wages the day his father was buried'.

### Estate papers

Labourers can also be found in estate records.[4] First of all, there were labourers who worked directly for the landowner, perhaps on the demesne farm or in some other capacity, such as herding cattle. Estate accounts might include information on particular tasks assigned to the workers and their rates of pay. The household book of the Marquess of Kildare includes the following entry from 19 August 1766: 'I desire that the present Pig Boy John Peppard be discharged and no more employed upon any account as a Day Labourer till my further orders, and that for the future no Pig Boy to have more than 6d per day.'[5] In a few instances there will be formal wage books for estate workers. Relevant items can be found by searching the various catalogues discussed in Chapter 3. For example, the Inchiquin Papers include a significant number of items relating to employees, among them estate accounts for Dromoland, County Clare, which are primarily concerned with the wages paid to workers, 1827–31 (NLI, MS 14,812).

Estate records can also reveal something of the lives of the labourers and cottiers who lived under the tenant farmers. In general, landowners were concerned at the prospect of too many people holding small plots of land from farmers. They feared that their presence exhausted resources, such as turf, contributed to poor agricultural practices, and resulted in disorder. In 1799 the agent on the Downshire estate wrote to Lord Downshire complaining that his attempts to direct a stretch of road had been 'opposed by a nest of cottiers belonging to one Todd, who does not reside on any part of the land' (PRONI, D607/G/200). In 1817 Sir John James Burgoyne lamented to the Marquess of Abercorn that, 'A great cause of distress to the tenants is the running away of their cottiers who have got into the habit of abandoning their houses and taking away their goods in the night' (PRONI, D623/A/130/25). Landlords frequently tried to limit the number of cottiers through clauses contained in the leases issued to tenants. (See Chapter 4 for more on this.)

While the issues relating to labourers and cottiers recur in estate correspondence on a regular basis, the individuals themselves often remain anonymous. Occasionally, however, they are mentioned by name. In 1758 the Earl of Abercorn wrote to his agent about one particular cottier:

> Jos[eph] Brown has writ to me to know what right I gave Shane Loage to his tenement. As far as I recollect, two or three cottiers there applied to me long before Jos[eph] Brown thought of taking the land, of whom only oLoage [sic] was sufficiently settled, to make me take notice of him. And I accordingly promised it him at 15s rent. Afterwards when Brown took the land, I turned oLoage over to him, to be his cottier at that rent, lest Brown should otherwise not have a good bargain (PRONI, D623/A/15/111).

On other occasions, there are listings of at least some of the cottiers on an estate. For the O'Hara estate in County Sligo there are rent rolls of Coolany 'tenants and cottiers', 1761 (NLI, MS 36,318/13). The papers of the Gosford estate include a small folio volume of 1847 containing a 'Return of cotters and tenants' on a subdivision of the property in County Armagh known as the Graham estate (PRONI, D1606/3/48/10). The Inchiquin papers include a return of the state of agriculture on the estate of Sir Lucius O'Brien in County Clare, 1849 (NLI, MS 45,212/4). This runs to 39 pages and is organised by townland under the headings, 'Names of tenants, undertenants or labourers, stock, cultivation, grass, buildings and observations'.

The records of the Brownlow estate in north County Armagh include a letter book of 1839–47 within which is 'A List of Tenants at

Will who have Cotters on the Estate of the Right Hon. Lord Lurgan', dating from 1839 (PRONI, D1928/J/5). A note appended to the list states that it was taken from the 'Bailiff's book of 1838'. The details are presented in three columns, headed townland, tenant and cottiers. Often it is only the surname of the cottier that is given. It would seem that in some instances the cottiers were members of the tenant farmer's family. For example, on the farm of Eugene McCann in Ballynemoney the cottiers were James, Hugh and Mat McCann.

The records of the Shirley estate in south County Monaghan include some excellent documentation on cottiers. Covering the years 1840–47 is a set of particulars of cottiers (PRONI, D3531/M/5), while dating from 1875 are two lists of cottiers on parts of the estate, one compiled by Owen MacConnon and the other by Thomas Finnegan (D3531/S/91–2). Looking more closely at the records of the 1840s, the names of the cottiers are listed by townland and then by tenant farmer. The details given for the cottiers include a description of their tenements (e.g. 'house' or 'house, garden, bog'), the yearly rent paid by the cottiers, and the number of members of the household (distinguishing between males and females). An 'Observations' column provides additional information.

### Valuation records

Valuation records, the subject of Chapter 6, can also be used to trace cottiers and labourers. As noted in that chapter, the occupants of very small holdings were included in at least some tithe applotment books. The printed Primary (Griffith's) Valuation ought to include the overwhelming majority of households in this class. Having said that, the transient way of life of many agricultural labourers means that sometimes they can slip from view. This is where searching the manuscript books of the Tenement Valuation can be so helpful. The example of Rochestown, County Cork, was discussed, where it was shown that the manuscript books contained many more names than the printed Valuation.

Another demonstration of the value of the manuscript books can be found in the example of Drumadreen in the parish of Bovevagh, County Londonderry. The Primary Valuation, issued in 1858, indicates that property 7 in that townland was in the possession of Joseph Hunter and comprised offices (i.e. outbuildings) and 24 acres of land. No dwellings were listed for this holding. However, when the field book for the parish was produced a couple of years earlier, the property was in the possession of Samuel Long and living on the holding were two labourers, Arthur Begley and John Brolly, the former occupying a house and small garden, the other simply a house (PRONI, VAL/2/B/5/17B). If only the printed Valuation had been consulted, the presence of these two households in Drumadreen would never have been known.

## 13.3 Labourers' cottages

In the 1880s local authorities were allowed to construct houses which could be rented to labourers. As a result, the housing of the labouring class improved significantly.[6] The Labourers' (Ireland) Act in 1883 (to be followed by further acts in the following years) authorised Boards of Guardians to instigate schemes for constructing dwellings for labourers, with an accompanying half acre. Government loans were provided, but local expenses were to be covered by the rates levied by the Guardians in their respective Poor Law Unions. The initiative proved unpopular with both farmers and rate-payers. In 1886 one farmer expressed his views on the subject to a Land Commission inspector, arguing that 'the farmers think it is a great hardship that they (the labourers) should have splendid houses built for them, while they (the farmers) who have to pay the rates for building these houses have to live in miserable cottages.'[7]

There was considerable variation in the numbers of cottages built across Ireland. In the province of Munster 5,492 cottages had been built by 1892, with another 3,235 cottages in Leinster. However, by the same date a mere 63 cottages had been built in Connacht and only 43 in the province of Ulster. Despite the slow progress in many areas, the benefits of the scheme were obvious. In 1892 it was noted that the labourer 'now rendered independent, seeks employment wherever he pleases, instead of being ... more or less dependent upon the particular farmer by whom he was usually employed and housed.' The Local Government Act of 1898 transferred responsibility for the operation of the various Labourers' Acts to the newly created rural district councils. Under a subsequent Act of 1906 £4.5 million was made available to the scheme and the number of cottages constructed more than doubled in the next decade.

Records relating to the collection of rents paid by labourers for their cottages can be found in a number of archival collections. A few survive in the records of the Boards of Guardians. For example, PRONI has a labourers' rent account book of 1896 for the Poor Law Union of Omagh (BG/26/CQ/1). Most surviving records are to be found within the collections of the rural district councils. Those for Northern Ireland are in PRONI, while for the Republic of Ireland these records are generally held locally and may be found within county archives and libraries. Tipperary Studies (https://tipperarystudies.ie) has digitised a Labourers' Cottage Rent Book 1887–1890 for the Poor Law Union of Cashel and made this available online.[8] This is broken down by electoral division and records the townland, tenant, date of agreement, monthly rent, and arrears, etc. There is also an 'Observations' column containing various comments such as 'must reduce arrear', as well as notes reflecting the laxity of the rent collector.

## Notes

[1] F.H.A. Aalen, Kevin Whelan and Matthew Stout (eds), *Atlas of the Irish Rural Landscape* (1997), p. 75.

[2] *Poor Inquiry (Ireland): Appendix (H)–Pt. 2. Remarks on the evidence taken in the poor inquiry (Ireland), contained in the appendices (D.) (E.) (F.) by one of the Commissioners* (1836), p. 4.

[3] Others include: Michael Beames, 'Cottiers and conacre in pre-Famine Ireland', *Journal of Peasant Studies*, 2 (1975), pp 352–4; Anne O'Dowd, *The Irish Migrant Farm Worker, 1830–1920* (1990); George Robinson, 'The early tied worker: cottiers hiring, apprenticeship, both articled and indentured', *Review: Journal of the Craigavon Historical Society*, 7:1 (1995–6), 48–9; Dominic Haugh, 'The Agri labourer in Irish society', *The Other Clare*, 32 (2008), pp 67–72; Pat Feeley, 'The agricultural labourer in County Limerick', *The Old Limerick Journal* (available online at www.limerickcity.ie/media/agricultural%20labourer.pdf).

[4] Adrian Grant, 'Landed estate records as a resource for the study of the rural worker', *Saothar*, 38 (2013), pp 169–73; Paddy Ryan, 'Cottiers on an 18th century Tipperary estate', *Tipperary Historical Journal* (2014), pp 28–39.

5  Terence Dooley, 'Copy of the marquis of Kildare's household book, 1758', *Archivium Hibernicum*, 62 (2009), p. 206.
6  F.H.A. Aalen, 'The rehousing of rural labourers in Ireland under the Labourers (Ireland) Acts, 1883–1919', *Journal of Historical Geography*, 12:3 (July 1986), pp 287–306; Enda McKay, 'The housing of the rural labourer, 1883–1916', *Saothar*, 17 (1992), pp 27–38.
7  McKay, 'Housing of the rural labourer', p. 27.
8  https://tipperarystudies.ie/wp-content/uploads/2018/12/Cashel%20Labourers%20Cottage%20Rent%20Book%201887-1890..pdf.

# 14

# Conclusion

In bringing this book to a conclusion one is left feeling that there is still so much more to say and so many other record collections that could be mentioned. For example, destitute farmers ended up in workhouses and can be found in the registers kept by these institutions from c. 1840 onwards. Farmers can also appear in the minute books of the Boards of Guardians that managed the workhouse in each Poor Law Union as suppliers of a range of agricultural produce.[1] Farmers availed of loan funds and an excellent set of records is available for the Irish Reproductive Loan Fund for the period leading up to and including the Great Famine. Some fascinating material on farming families is available for counties Clare, Cork, Galway, Limerick, Mayo, Roscommon, Sligo and Tipperary.[2]

Numerous other records could be referenced. Someone researching a farming ancestor in the vicinity of Tullow, County Carlow, at the turn of the twentieth century should consider the account books of a veterinary surgeon named William A. Young as potentially helpful (NAI, CAR 17). Likewise, the ledger for the years 1923–8 of Hugh John Gibson, a blacksmith of 'The Cross', Carrickmannan, could be helpful for those pursuing a farmer in this part of County Down in the early 1900s (PRONI, MIC466/1). The records of the Great Munster Fair Commissioners, 1852–1912, which are held by Limerick Archives (ref. LK/GMF), may well reveal some new details of someone's farming forebear in this part of Ireland.[3]

It goes without saying that the internet has revolutionised genealogy over the last two decades.[4] Not only are the well-known genealogical sources (civil, church and census records, Griffith's Valuation, etc) so much more easily accessed, the digitisation of many other collections has allowed family historians greater insights into their ancestors' lives.

Taking my great-great-great-grandfather Andrew Elder, who farmed at Ashgrove, Castlefin, County Donegal, as an example, church and civil records searched the 'traditional' way revealed when he married and died and where he was buried, and the dates of the birth/baptism of his children. However, much new information was brought to light through online newspaper databases, such as his involvement in the 1852 general election and his campaigns for Tenant Right in the 1870s – now I know what he actually said at some of meetings he attended and participated in.

Through newspapers, I also learned that 58 of Andrew's friends and neighbours turned up to plough his farm on 22 January 1857 and afterwards all sat down to an enjoyable dinner and spent the evening singing, and that in 1877 he gave 10 shillings towards a fund to build a new home for the evicted parish priest of Glencolumbcille. Online petty sessions court records and minutes books of the Boards of Guardians for County Donegal reveal that on 28 May 1870 he was fined one shilling for erecting a fence on a road and on 28 March 1881 it was proposed that he should be elected to the Killygordon dispensary committee. I even know that in 1884 he owned a dark grey terrier – a decade ago how many people would have considered dog licence registers as a source worth checking? It is unlikely that I would have discovered very many of these stories and details had the records not been so easily accessible.[5]

Even so, 'brick walls' remain and many gaps in our knowledge of our ancestors may never be filled. A gaping hole in my own family tree concerns the fate of my great-great-grandfather Thomas Roulston of Gortavea, County Tyrone. We know that he was alive in July 1897 when the farm was transferred to his son Charles. However, he does not appear in the 1901 census. No civil record of his death has been found; no newspaper notice reported his passing; he does not appear in the burial register of the church to which he belonged; and in the family Bible, while his date of birth has been entered, his date of death remains a blank. He simply vanishes. Perhaps some day I will resolve this mystery. But maybe not. Nonetheless, the search goes on.

# Notes

1  The records of the Boards of Guardians can be found in PRONI for
   Northern Ireland and in various repositories in the Republic of Ireland –
   often they are available at local level. Increasingly these records are being
   made available online (e.g. through Findmypast). An account of the
   development of the workhouse system by Raymond Gillespie can be read
   at: www.askaboutireland.ie/learning-zone/secondary-students/history/
   social-change-the-workhou.

2  The original records are in The National Archives, Kew, and can be accessed
   online through Findmypast ('Poverty Relief Loans') and Ancestry
   (Sustainability Loan Fund').

3  www.limerick.ie/discover/explore/historical-resources/limerick-
   archives/archive-collections/great-munster-fair.

4  For a broader look at what is available online, see Chris Paton, *Tracing Your
   Irish Family History on the Internet* (2nd edition, 2019).

5  I explore his life more fully in 'Andrew Elder (1821–86) of Ashgrove,
   Castlefin: campaigner for land reform', *Donegal Annual*, 72 (2020),
   pp 87–95. The British Newspaper Archive
   (www.britishnewspaperarchive.co.uk) was the principal source for press
   items. Findmypast hosts the databases of petty sessions records, dog
   licence registers and Boards of Guardians minutes for County Donegal;
   the first two are also on Ancestry.

# Archives and libraries

Many archives and libraries holding material of interest for those researching farming ancestors have been referred to in this book. Addresses and websites for the most important of these institutions are given below. The Archives and Records Association, Ireland, maintains an Archives Directory providing links to repositories across the island (www.araireland.ie/archives-directory). See also Seamus Helferty and Raymond Refaussé, *Directory of Irish Archives* (2003), and Robert K. O'Neill, *Guide to Irish Libraries, Archives, Museums & Genealogical Centres* (2013).

## NATIONAL ARCHIVES OF IRELAND
Bishop Street
Dublin 8
Ireland
Website: www.nationalarchives.ie

## NATIONAL LIBRARY OF IRELAND
Kildare Street
Dublin 2
Ireland
Website: www.nli.ie

## PUBLIC RECORD OFFICE OF NORTHERN IRELAND
2 Titanic Boulevard
Belfast, BT3 9HQ
Northern Ireland
Website: www.nidirect.gov.uk/proni

## REGISTRY OF DEEDS
Henrietta Street
Dublin 1
Ireland
Website: www.prai.ie

# Index